MW00811271

Two NATO Allies at the Threshold of War

Two NATO Allies at the Threshold of War

Cyprus: A Firsthand Account of Crisis Management, 1965–1968

Parker T. Hart Foreword by Lucius D. Battle

An Institute for the Study of Diplomacy Book
Duke University Press   Duke Press Policy Studies
Durham and London, 1990

Printed in the United States of America
on acid-free paper ∞

Library of Congress Cataloging-in-Publication Data
Hart, Parker T.
Two NATO allies at the threshold of war: Cyprus, a firsthand
account of crisis management, 1965–1968/Parker T. Hart: foreword
by Lucius D. Battle.
p. cm.—(Duke Press policy studies)
"An Institute for the Study of Diplomacy book."
Includes bibliographical references.
ISBN 0-8223-0977-7 (alk. paper)
1. Cyprus—Politics and government—1960– 2. Turkey—Foreign
relations—Greece. 3. Greece—Foreign relations—Turkey.
I. Title. II. Series.
DS54.9.H38 1989
956.4504—dc20 89-16941

To Jane, Meg, and Judy

Contents

Maps

Foreword

Lucius D. Battle

In November 1967 I was assistant secretary of state for Near East and South Asian affairs (NEA). It was a troubled period, not only in the Middle East but for the world in general. The Viet Nam war was at its height; there were minor crises around the world. In the NEA area, we had just gone through the six-day Arab-Israeli war, as well as a crisis in Yemen where a couple of Americans were falsely arrested, charged with blowing up an ammunition dump.

Everyone in the upper echelon of the State Department and at the White House was obsessed with Viet Nam. It was difficult to shift their focus to the island of Cyprus. There was little concern even for a situation that might lead to a war between two NATO allies, Greece and Turkey. But all the signs were there! These signs led me to urge that a special presidential envoy be sent to the area in an effort to forestall the impending crisis.

There was no response initially. But in a few days we had clear intelligence that the Turks, weather permitting, would move the following day to invade the island of Cyprus. With this evidence I told Secretary Dean Rusk and Under Secretary Nicholas Katzenbach, and in turn we told President Johnson, that there was a choice: either send an envoy to try to mediate the situation or recognize that there would be a war the following day.

The president did not oppose the plan and had no problem with our first choice, Cyrus Vance, so Katzenbach promptly telephoned Vance. Vance had had a back problem and had been in the hospital. He had also just left government, where he had been deputy secretary of defense, and was trying to make money and get a little rest. Our plans for him would interfere with both pursuits.

He did agree, good soldier and public servant that he is, to take on the mission, but said, "I don't know anything about Cyprus." Katzenbach replied, "Luke will come up and brief you in New York." It was essential that Vance leave that same day. Given our past difficulties with the Turks, who properly resented some of the language of our last strongly worded message to them—over an impending crisis in 1964—it was agreed that we not ask them, but *tell* them, very gently, that the envoy was coming, and that we have him in the air before the Turks were informed, or the world learned, of the U.S. action.

The plan was that I would fly up on a military plane to meet Cy Vance in the New York airport and give him a general briefing. He would then take off before the White House announcement made public the fact that such a mission was under way.

We sat in the plane, Vance with his back brace behind him. John P. Walsh, who was to go as a member of the Executive Secretariat with all the basic documents, was well informed on all these matters. But the documents would be heavy going. When I talked with Vance, he had had no chance to read any of the material and asked, "What are my instructions?"

"It's very simple," I said, "you're supposed to stop a war!"

"How do I do that?" he asked, to which I replied that we in NEA had put down some thoughts as to where there could be bargaining and where there might be an opportunity to advance the cause of peace. We talked for a few minutes, until we heard on the radio the announcement that the President was sending the Honorable Cyrus Vance on a special mission of peace.

I said to Vance, "I've got to get off this plane immediately and you have to get in the air. If we wait very long, we'll get a message of rejection, but if you're in the air, they will not turn you back." At least that was my reading, and it proved to be accurate.

From then on it was one of the strangest and, in many respects, one of the most interesting, projects that I was ever engaged in during my many years in the Department of State. There were very few written telegrams back and forth from the department to any of the three posts involved (Ankara, Athens, and Nicosia), but there were innumerable telephone calls between Vance and others of his group and Joseph J. Sisco, who was assistant secretary for international organizations, Arthur J. Goldberg, our ambassador to the United Nations in New York, and me.

The result of all this was that very little was written down, and it was some years before a record of the crisis was prepared. A group of us, some years later, got together at Airlie House. We had virtually all the major participants—Vance, the ambassadors to Greece and Turkey (the one to Cyprus having been transferred to Peru), Arthur Goldberg, Joseph Sisco, John Walsh, and myself. Together we reconstructed the events as best we could, using such written records as existed of telegrams and other instructions that went out. But it was not an analysis—as this book is—of a major foreign policy crisis.

The handling of that crisis was an amazing series of events. It can be truly said that a war was avoided, or at least postponed for a number of years. The hero of the whole project was Cyrus Vance, who behaved in an unbelievably professional way. It was, I think, his first venture into diplomacy, and very good training it was for the burdens that later came his way as secretary of state. All the participants had been extremely effective: the U.S. ambassador to Turkey—the author of this book—Parker T. Hart, the U.S. ambassador to Greece, Phillips Talbot, and the U.S. ambassador to Cyprus, Taylor G. Belcher, showed exemplary skill in the highest traditions of the career foreign service.

In 1973, several of the participants in this affair gathered in Rome to meet with the leaders of the two contending forces on Cyprus—Rauf Denktaş representing the Turkish Cypriots, and Glafcos Clerides for the Greek Cypriots.[1] We sat for several days at Thanksgiving 1973 hearing the two of them debate the issues that separated their two factions. Each of us who was non-Greek or non-Turk had a topic assigned. Mine covered external forces affecting solutions to the Cyprus problem. In my opening presentation, I said that I had one piece of advice: "Don't count on anybody else. Solve your own problem." There had been great difficulty in persuading the U.S. government to involve itself in 1967; there would be even more difficulty the next time there was a crisis—and there would be a crisis.

After each of us had made his presentation, a debate would start, largely between Denktaş and Clerides. The debate went on through most of the day, culminating around 5:00 P.M. with Clerides and Denktaş going arm in arm to the bar together. They had been friends for years, had saved each other's lives, and recognized that each had a role to play, but did not quite know what to do about it.

The group adjourned with a small degree of optimism that these two leaders might get together and solve this age-old problem of Cyprus. It did not work. In 1974 the new crisis we all had feared came. That time the Americans were unable to involve themselves, being still bogged down with Viet Nam and other problems that took precedence.

We know the tragedy that ensued. Among the great losses was the assassination of former Deputy Assistant Secretary of State Rodger P. Davies, who was ambassador to Cyprus at that time. He was one of the finest men I have ever worked with in any field of human endeavor, and I was particularly sad that his life was lost in the absence of a settlement for which he, along with others in the NEA bureau, had long pressed.

The entire story is a sad one, but the story of the 1967 events is not. They look even now as a rather shining example of what diplomacy in action can do. All of us who had a role, particularly Cyrus Vance, can look with pride on our achievements at that time.

It was important that this book be written and that there now be a clear analysis of the events that, for a time at least, eased one of the classic conflicts of our time.

Preface

The purpose of this case study, sponsored by the Georgetown University Institute for the Study of Diplomacy, is not to trace the entire history of the Cyprus problem, or of Greek-Turkish tensions, or even of all United States interventions to prevent a war between these two NATO allies. Rather it is a firsthand account of one particularly crucial period in an ongoing dilemma in Western and American security. The episode is viewed from the vantage point of the American Embassy at Ankara, where I served as ambassador from 1965 to 1968, and it includes as a centerpiece the emergency shuttle mission of Cyrus R. Vance, President Lyndon B. Johnson's special emissary, who negotiated, between November 24 and December 3, 1967, an alternative to Greek-Turkish hostilities.

The book is intended equally for all persons interested in acquiring a better grasp of the diplomatic process and for those concerned with Cyprus as an intercommunal tragedy and with the integrity of the North Atlantic Treaty Organization. Still-classified government archives which cannot be quoted have been consulted in detail to refresh my own memory of events, but the interpretation of this voluminous material is mine alone. I have also drawn upon published United Nations documents, especially reports by the secretary-general to the Security Council; upon firsthand accounts of colleagues and those of the Chief of Staff of the United Nations Forces in Cyprus; and upon the archives and oral histories of the Lyndon Baines Johnson Library, among other sources, to provide factual clarity in a complex and confusing picture. In the absence of parallel accounts by my erstwhile colleagues in Athens, Nicosia, Washington, and New York, I have done my best to present their diplomatic moves objectively and, where feasible, have consulted them directly.

My special thanks for valuable critiques and inputs go to these friends and colleagues, in particular to U.S. ambassadors Taylor G. Belcher (Cyprus, 1964–69) and Phillips Talbot (Greece, 1965–69), for their patience in reading the full text and their invaluable detailed assistance; to the Honorable Raymond A. Hare, my predecessor in Ankara (1961–65) and friend for over forty years, and the Honorable George C. McGhee, another predecessor in Ankara and friend, for their review and encouragement; to the late Fraser Wilkins, first U.S. ambassador to Cyprus (1960–

64), who, just before his death, provided a very useful input; to Brigadier Michael Harbottle, chief of staff, United Nations Forces in Cyprus, during the period covered by this book, for his careful review in Washington, October 6–8, 1986, of chapters 4 and 5, recounting events in which he played a central role; and to Dr. Philip H. Stoddard of Washington, D.C., and Professor Bruce R. Kuniholm of Duke University for their detailed analyses and constructive suggestions.

I am most obliged to the Honorable Lucius D. Battle, former assistant secretary of state for Near Eastern and South Asian affairs (1967–68), for taking time from his demanding schedule as president of the Middle East Institute to write a most informative foreword.

I am indebted to the Honorable Cyrus R. Vance for his review of the entire manuscript and for his encouragement. This country and NATO owe him much more than can be expressed here for his mission of peace.

My thanks go also to my old friend and deputy in Ankara, William C. Burdett, later U.S. ambassador to Malawi, who was also good enough to read the entire manuscript and make valuable suggestions; to Dr. Elaine D. Smith, eminent Turkologist of the U.S. Foreign Service and retired consul general in Izmir; to William A. Helseth, retired FSO with deep experience in Turkey, whose help was of crucial importance; and to William R. Crawford, Jr., sixth U.S. ambassador to Cyprus (1974–78), for his very useful comments.

My warm appreciation also goes to Margery Boichel Thompson, the editor of the Institute for the Study of Diplomacy, for her expert guidance through a succession of drafts; to Charles Dolgas, Jeffry Robelen, and others at the Institute for their patient word processing of these drafts; to Richard W. Van Wagenen, distinguished scholar, and Ellen Laipson of the Congressional Research Service for their valuable assistance in locating published materials.

I am indebted also to David C. Humphrey, archivist of the Lyndon B. Johnson Library of Austin, Texas, for providing declassified records from the archives of the National Security Council; and to the J. Howard Pew Freedom Trust for making possible the publication of this book.

Last of all, I owe more than can be stated to my wife Jane, for her expert editing and encouragement and far more for her devoted support and understanding during the events here described.

—P.T.H.

Dramatis Personae

Acheson, Dean Gooderham. Lawyer, author, government official. U.S. secretary of state, 1949–53. Special presidential envoy on Cyprus situation, 1964.

Alexandrakis, Menelaos. Greek ambassador to Cyprus, 1967.

Allen, Sir Roger. British ambassador to Turkey, 1967.

Averoff-Tossizza, Evangelos. Economist, journalist, politician. Fought in Greek resistance, 1939–45. Minister of foreign affairs, 1956–63, and minister of defense, 1974–80.

Ball, George Wildman. Lawyer, author, government official. U.S. under secretary of state, 1961–66, and permanent representative to the United Nations, 1968.

Belcher, Taylor Garrison. Career diplomat. U.S. consul, then consul general, Cyprus, 1957–60. Ambassador to Cyprus, 1964–69.

Brosio, Manlio. Italian lawyer and diplomat. Secretary general of the North Atlantic Treaty Organization (NATO), 1964–71.

Bulak, Adnan. Career diplomat. Director general for Cyprus affairs, Turkish foreign ministry, 1967–68.

Burdett, William Carter. Career diplomat. Deputy chief of mission, U.S. Embassy, Ankara, 1967–70. Ambassador to Malawi, 1970–74.

Çağlayangil, İhsan Sabri. Government official and politician. Foreign minister of Turkey, 1965–71.

Clerides, Glafcos John (also spelled Glavkos). Greek Cypriot lawyer and politician. Head of Greek Cypriot delegation, Constitutional Committee, 1959–60. President, House of Representatives of Republic of Cyprus in 1968.

Constantine, King of the Hellenes. Ascended to the throne 1964. Left Greece December 13, 1967.

Davies, Rodger Paul. Career diplomat, 1946–74. U.S. Ambassador to Cyprus, 1974 (assassinated at post).

Delivanis, Miltiades. Career diplomat. Greek Ambassador to Turkey, 1966–69.

Demirel, Süleyman. Engineer and politician. Prime Minister of Turkey, 1965–71; 1975–77; 1979–80. Head of Justice Party, 1964–80. Head of True Path Party since 1987.

Denktaş, Rauf (also spelled Denktash). Turkish Cypriot lawyer and politician. President of the Turkish Cypriot Communal Chamber, 1960–73. President of the Turkish Republic of Northern Cyprus since 1983.

Ecevit, Bülent. Journalist, writer, politician. Prime Minister of Turkey, 1974. Head of Republican Peoples Party, 1972–80.

Economou-Gouras, Paul. Career diplomat. Minister of foreign affairs of Greece, September–November 1963, 1966–67.

Eralp, Orhan. Career diplomat. Permanent Representative (ambassador) of Turkey to the United Nations, 1964–69.

Erkin, Feridun Cemal. Career diplomat. Foreign minister of Turkey, 1962–65.

Fénaux, Robert. Career diplomat. Ambassador of Belgium to Turkey, 1961–68, and dean of the diplomatic corps in Ankara in 1967–68.

Georgkhadjis, Polykarpos (also spelled Georkajis). Greek Cypriot politician. Minister of the interior of the Republic of Cyprus, 1960–69. Prominent in EOKA guerrilla leadership (assassinated 1970).

Goldberg, Arthur Joseph. Lawyer, U.S. Supreme Court Justice, and government official. Permanent representative (ambassador) of the United States to the United Nations, 1965–68.

Goldschlag, Klaus. Canadian Ambassador to Turkey, 1967.

Grivas, Lt. General George. Cypriot-born Greek army officer. Founded and led underground organization in Athens during German occupation in Second World War. Founding leader of EOKA, militant force to unite Cyprus to Greece, 1955–58, operating under *nom de guerre* "Digeinis." Commander-in-chief, Greek mainland forces in Cyprus and Greek Cypriot forces, 1963–67.

Harbottle, Brigadier Michael Neale. British army officer. Chief of staff to the commander of the United Nations Forces in Cyprus (UNFICYP), 1966–68.

Hare, Raymond Arthur. Named Career Ambassador of the United States, 1960. U.S. ambassador to Turkey, 1961–65. Assistant secretary of state for Near East and South Asian affairs, 1965–66. President, Middle East Institute, 1966–69.

Hart, Parker Thompson. Career diplomat. U.S. Ambassador to Turkey, 1965–68. Assistant secretary of state for Near East and South Asian affairs, 1968–69. President, Middle East Institute, 1969–73.

Hollyfield, Edward. Captain, U.S. Navy, Bureau of International Security Affairs, U.S. Department of Defense, 1967.

Howison, John McCoul. Career diplomat. Country director for Turkish affairs, U.S. Department of State, 1966–68.

Huxtable, Major Charles. British army officer. UNFICYP escort commander, 1967.

İnönü, İsmet. First prime minister of Turkey, 1923–37, and again in 1961–65. President, 1938–50.

Ioannides, General Dimitrios. Head of Military Government of Greece, 1973–74.

Işik, Hasan Esat. Diplomat and politician. Foreign Minister of Turkey, 1965.

Johnson, Ellen. Secretary, U.S. Department of State, and member of Cyrus Vance mission to Turkey, 1967.

Johnson, Lyndon Baines. President of the United States of America, 1963–69.

Karamanlis, Constantine G. Lawyer and politician. Prime Minister of Greece, 1955–58; 1958–61; 1961–63; 1974–81.

Kollias, Constantine. Jurist and politician. Prime Minister of Greece, 1967. Attorney General of Greece, 1968.

Küçük, Fazil (also spelled Küchük). Turkish Cypriot journalist and politician. Vice president of the Republic of Cyprus, 1960–73 (titular), but unable to exercise duties of vice president, from 1963, due to civil disturbances. Leader of Turkish Cypriot Community, 1959–73. President, "Provisional Turkish Cypriot Administration," 1967–75.

Kuneralp, Zeki. Career diplomat. Secretary general of the Foreign Ministry of Turkey, 1966–69. Turkish ambassador to the United Kingdom, 1964–66 and 1969–72.

Kyprianou, Spyros. Lawyer and politician. Foreign Minister of Cyprus, 1960–72. President of Republic of Cyprus, 1977–88.

Makarios III. Archbishop of Cyprus and Ethnarch, 1950–77 (born Michael Christodoulos Mouskos). Greek Cypriot religious and political leader. President of Cyprus 1960–77. Leader of movement for *enosis* (union with Greece) from 1950.

Martola, Lt. General Armas Eino Iimari. Finnish army officer. Commander, UN Forces in Cyprus, 1966–70.

McNamara, Robert Strange. Corporate and government official. U.S. Secretary of Defense, 1961–68. President, World Bank, 1968–81.

Menderes, Adnan. Prime minister of Turkey, 1950–60.

Osorio-Tafall, Bibiano F. Mexican educator and UN official. Special representative of the secretary-general of the United Nations in Cyprus, 1967.

Papadopoulos, Colonel George. Career army officer. Prime Minister and Minister of Defense of Greece, 1967–73. Minister of foreign affairs, 1970–73. Regent of Greece, 1972–73.

Papandreou, Andreas George. Educator and politician. Prime Minister of Greece, 1981–89, and founder of the Pan-Hellenic Socialist Movement.

Papandreou, George. Prime Minister of Greece 1944, 1963–65. Father of Andreas Papandreou.

Paraskevopoulos, John. Economist, banker, and politician. Prime minister of Greece, 1966–67.

Pérez de Cuéllar, Javier. Peruvian diplomat. Permanent representative to the United Nations, 1971–81. Secretary-general of the United Nations since 1982.

Pipinelis, Panayiotis. Career diplomat. Prime minister of Greece, 1963. Minister of foreign affairs, 1967–70.

Plaza Lasso, Galo (best known as Galo Plaza). Ecuadorean politician and United Nations official. President of Republic of Ecuador, 1948–52. United Nations mediator in Cyprus 1964–65.

Rolz-Bennett, José. Guatemalan educator, government official, and United Nations official. Personal representative of UN Secretary-General U Thant for Cyprus discussions, 1964. Under Secretary of the United Nations for Special Political Affairs, 1965–67.

Rossides, Zenon George. Greek Cypriot lawyer and government official. Ambassador of the Republic of Cyprus to the United States and permanent representative of Cyprus to the United Nations, 1960–79.

Rusk, Dean. Educator, foundation executive, government official. U.S. secretary of state, 1961–69.

Sampson, Nicos. Greek Cypriot EOKA gunman who seized power briefly, overthrowing Makarios, 1974.

Sgourdeos, Alexander. Ambassador of Greece to Turkey, 1965–66.

Sisco, Joseph John. Career diplomat. U.S. assistant secretary of state for international organization affairs, 1965–69. Under secretary of state for political affairs, 1974–76.

Spandidakis, Lt. General Gregory. Career army officer. Defense Minister of Greece, 1967.

Stephanopoulos, Stephanos. Lawyer and politician. Prime Minister of Greece, 1965–66.

Sunay, General Cevdet. Career army officer. President of the Turkish Republic, 1966–73.

Talbot, Phillips. Foundation executive, government official, and diplomat. U.S. ambassador to Greece, 1965–69.

Theodoropoulos, Byron. Career diplomat. Assistant secretary general, Foreign Ministry of Greece, 1968.

Topaloğlu, Ahmet. Minister of defense of Turkey, 1967.

Toumbas, Vice Admiral John. Career naval officer and politician. Foreign minister of Greece, 1966.

Triandafylides, Michael. Judge of the (Greek) Cypriot Supreme Court, 1967.

Türkmen, İlter. Career diplomat. Assistant secretary general, Ministry of Foreign Affairs of Turkey, 1967–68. Ambassador to Greece, 1968–72, the Soviet Union, 1972–75, and France, 1989–. Foreign minister, 1980–84. Permanent representative of Turkey to the United Nations, 1975–80 and 1985–88.

Ürgüplü, Ali Suat Hayri. Lawyer, jurist, government official, and politician. Prime minister of Turkey, January–October 1965.

U Thant. Burmese politician and statesman. Secretary-General of the United Nations, 1962–71.

Vance, Cyrus Roberts. Lawyer and government official. President Lyndon Johnson's special envoy on the Cyprus situation, 1967. U.S. Secretary of State, 1977–80.

Varnava, Antoinetta. Cypriot employee of the U.S. Embassy, Nicosia, who lost her own life trying to save U.S. Ambassador Rodger P. Davies on August 19, 1974.

Veniamin, Khristodoulos (also spelled Christodoulos). Greek Cypriot government official and politician. District commissioner, Limassol, 1967.

Waldheim, Kurt. Austrian diplomat and United Nations official. Secretary-General of the United Nations, 1971–81. President of Austria, 1986–present.

Walsh, John Patrick. Career diplomat. Acting executive secretary for U.S. Secretary of State Dean Rusk, 1967. U.S. ambassador to Kuwait, 1969–72.

Yavuzalp, Ercüment. Career diplomat. Chargé d'affaires of Turkey in Cyprus, 1967.

Yost, Charles Woodruff. U.S. career diplomat, 1930–71. Career Ambassador of the United States.

Brief Turkish Pronunciation Guide

a	as in *father*
c	like the *j* in *joy*
ç	like the *ch* in *choice*
e	as in *get*
g	as in *get*
ğ	unpronounced; lengthens the immediately preceeding vowel—thus *Çağlayangil*, a name recurring in this text, is pronounced: CHAH-LIE-YAN-GIL
ı	undotted *ı* pronounced like the *i* in *first*
	like the *i* in *pick*
j	like the *s* in *measure*
ö	like the *ö* in the German *schön*, vaguely like *u* in *purple*
ş	*sh*, as in *sheet*
ü	as in the German *fünf*, vaguely like *ew* in *hew*
u	like the *oo* in *look*
y	as in *yes*; but as a dipthong with a preceding *a—ay—* pronounced like *die* or *buy*
ˆ	this sign over a vowel lengthens the vowel sound

Abbreviations and Acronyms

AKEL: *Anorthotikon Komma Ergazomenou Laou* (Progressive Party of the Working People), i.e., the communist party, established 1941

CYPOL: Cypriot Police (entirely Greek Cypriot at the period described in this book)

EOKA: *Ethniki Organosis Kyprion Agoniston* (National Organization of Cypriot Fighters)

Justice Party (Turkey)

NSC: National Security Council (Turkey)

PASOK: *Panhellinion Socialistiko Kinima* (Panhellenic Socialist Movement)

RPP: Republican People's Party (Turkey)

TMT: *Türk Mukavemet Teşkilâtı* (Turkish Fighters Organization)

UNFICYP: United Nations Forces in Cyprus

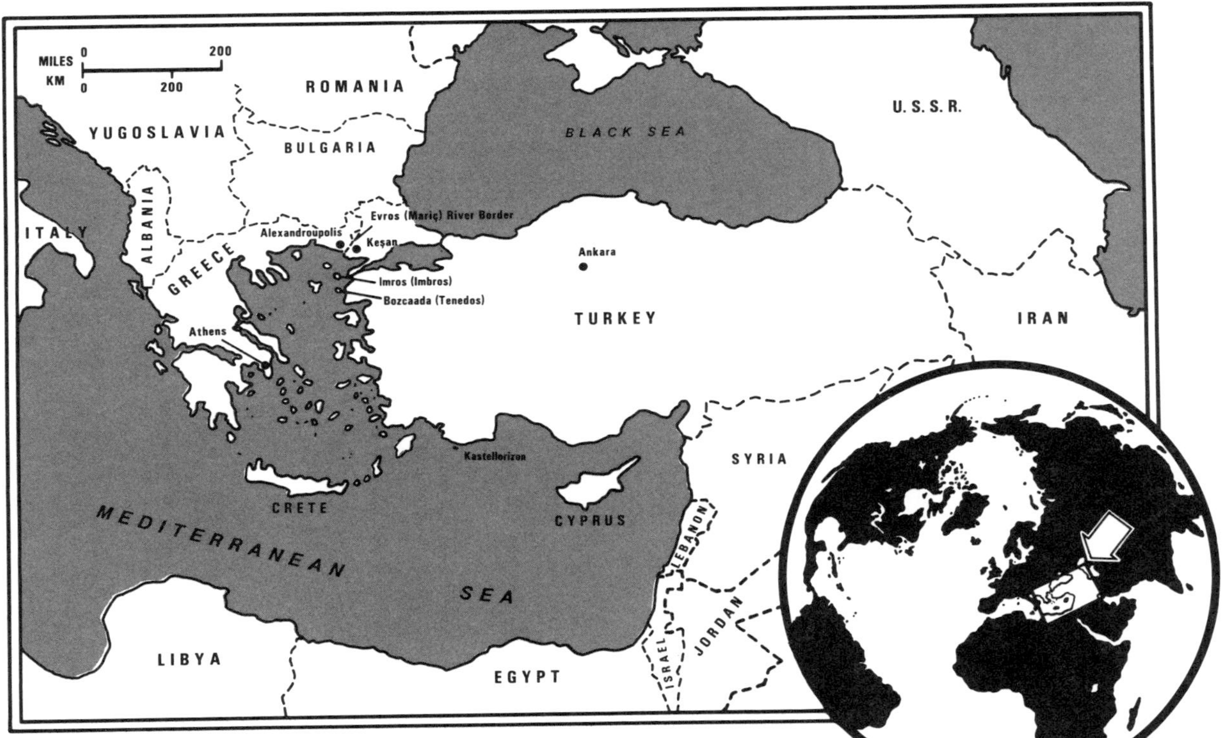

Map 1 Eastern Mediterranean region, showing strategic position of Cyprus in relation to NATO's southeastern wing (Greece and Turkey) and the surrounding nations of the Warsaw Pact and the Middle East. (Map by David Hagen)

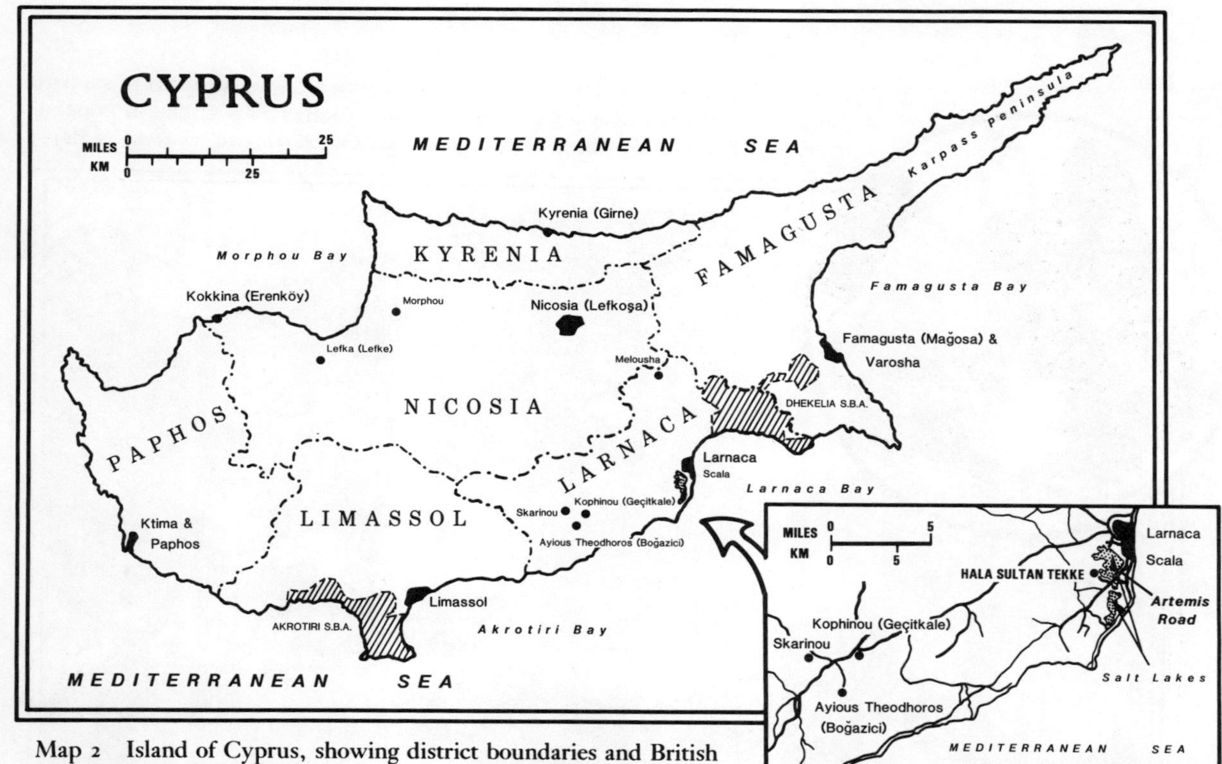

Map 2 Island of Cyprus, showing district boundaries and British Sovereign Base Areas. Inset: Portion of Larnaca District, showing major roads. (Map by David Hagen)

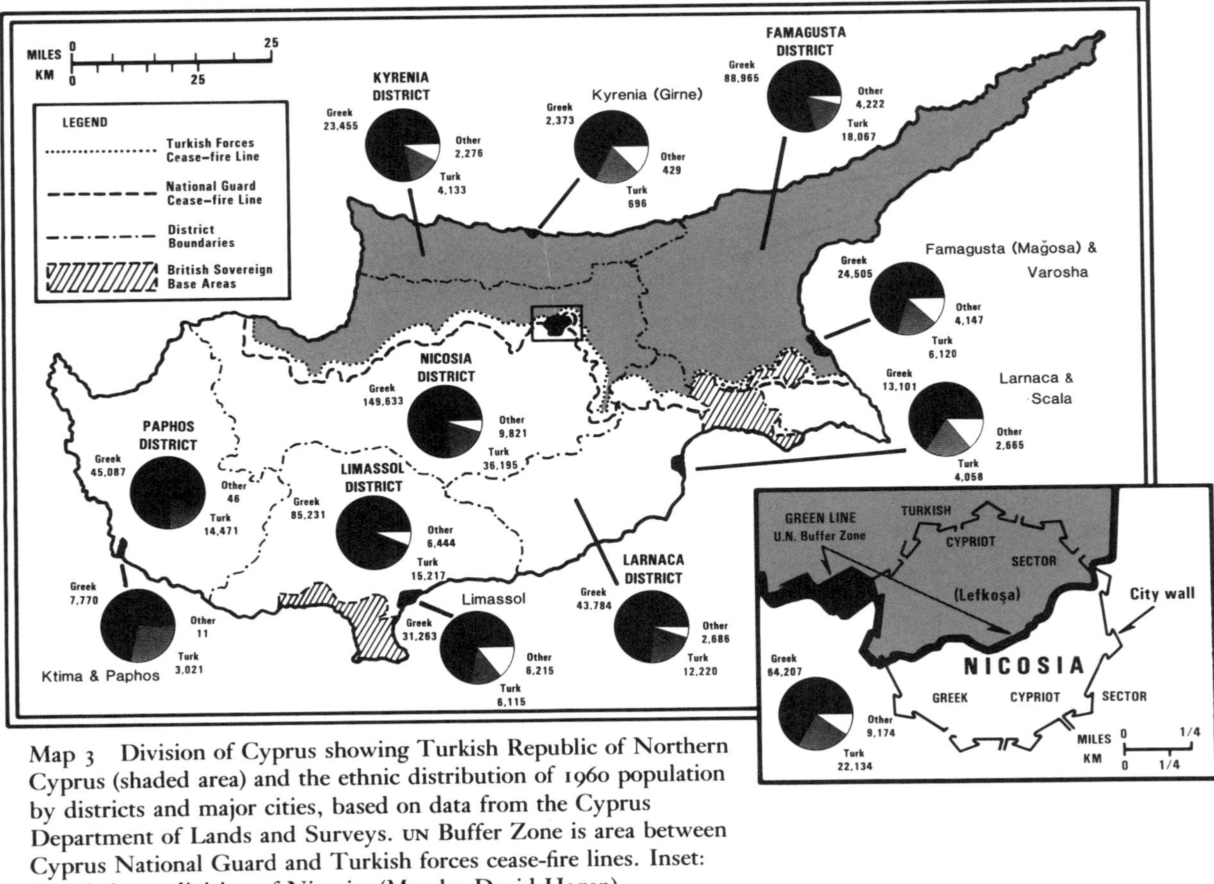

Map 3 Division of Cyprus showing Turkish Republic of Northern Cyprus (shaded area) and the ethnic distribution of 1960 population by districts and major cities, based on data from the Cyprus Department of Lands and Surveys. UN Buffer Zone is area between Cyprus National Guard and Turkish forces cease-fire lines. Inset: Detail shows division of Nicosia. (Map by David Hagen)

Part 1
Background and Build-up to Crisis

1
Introduction

The crisis of 1967 which brought Greece and Turkey to the edge of war was an extension of intercommunal strife unleashed in late 1963. My own involvement, however, began in late 1965 when I had just begun my service as U.S. ambassador in Ankara. The events recounted here in considerable detail provide an on-site account of diplomatic moves between Greece and Turkey, combining efforts to support their respective ethnic brothers on Cyprus in their rights and aspirations with moves to avoid deterioration that would lead to a military confrontation.

Neither Greece nor Turkey wanted to endanger the integrity of the southeast wing of the North Atlantic Treaty Organization, which ensured them strategic support against the Warsaw Pact. For both, however, violence and popular emotions eventually overtook long-range considerations. Greece and most Greek Cypriots had desired *enosis*—union with Greece—since the early nineteenth century, while Turkey and Turkish Cypriots were ready to go to war, if necessary, to prevent this, particularly after the massacre of Turkish Cypriot villagers in November 1967 by a preponderance of mainland Greek forces led by General George Grivas. Intense diplomatic efforts by the United States, Great Britain, and Canada preceded the mediation by Cyrus Vance on behalf of President Lyndon Johnson. Vance's mission came at the last moment, when the future of NATO and peace in the eastern Mediterranean hung by a thread.

Diplomatic experience teaches that devising alternatives to warfare in compressed and explosive situations beyond the immediate control of external parties cannot be charted or modeled in advance. Decision making in Athens and Ankara by the "motherland" governments lagged behind shifting and rapidly escalating clashes on Cyprus itself. These clashes heightened suspicions and tensions in both capitals, repeatedly torpedoing diplomatic moves toward conciliation at the very moments when they offered hope of some success.

The reader will see the importance of accurate assessments of motivations and events, as well as the importance of instantaneous communications. Diplomats on the spot and special emissaries sent out by Washington, the United Nations, and NATO were heavily dependent initially on independent, objective information garnered by their embassies or representatives, but from that point relied upon their own seasoned experience and the intuition derived from it. As the crisis reached its zenith, coolness, flexibility, patience, and, above all, stamina counted decisively in the success of the mediator, as in the efforts of all who supported his labors.

In this case it is clear also that, in such a kaleidoscopic scenario, second-guessing of the mediator by Washington would have been disastrous. The White House left Vance virtually alone. Johnson's only instructions to him, made at the start of his trip, were to do everything in his power to stop a war from starting and to count on Washington to provide everything he required in the way of help. Help was indeed given, especially by Secretary of State Dean Rusk; by the Bureau of Near Eastern and South Asian Affairs, headed by Assistant Secretary of State Lucius D. Battle, who coordinated interagency and international support; by Joseph J. Sisco, assistant secretary for international organization affairs, who coordinated activity involving the U.S. permanent representative to the United Nations, Arthur J. Goldberg; and, notably, by Ambassador Goldberg himself.

It must be added that in this, as in other cases, luck is always essential, especially in the personalities of the leaders of the disputant states and in the timing. The disputant parties must have arrived at a frame of mind, underneath the tough talk, that prefers compromise to warfare, compromise that appears to achieve on each side the most basic national objective or, at the very least, to preserve national dignity. And how fortunate if the personalities involved are statesmen who never lose sight of the fact that resorting to war is usually the abandonment of rationality and who refuse to be stampeded by public or private pressures! The reader will see who these personalities were on the Turkish and Greek sides.

It will also become clear that mediating diplomats must steer away from any semblance of humiliation or "victory" by one party over the other. Especially must they avoid the appearance of a "triumph" of American pressure over the will of a lesser power, no matter how great the temptation to win plaudits for "toughness" in the American press. The weight of such leverage over small nation-states carries with it the poison of aggravated sensitivity, of festering resentment by the populace of the country on which it is applied. What is certain is that the ultimate backlash, and the damage to future U.S. relations, can be heavy.

Few are the young and upwardly mobile politicians on Capitol Hill or the White House staff who are so self-denying as to seek anonymity in such a mission. But such an emissary was Cyrus Vance. He achieved his objectives not only because of his exceptional abilities but also because of his humility. He came, he accomplished, and he returned to his privacy.

Prologue

With these considerations in mind we now look at the split personality of an island about the size of the state of Connecticut with a population of 685,000, approximately equal in number to that of the District of Columbia. Seventy-seven percent of that population are ethnic Greeks; 18 percent are ethnic Turks. (The latter figure does not include additional settlers from mainland Turkey after 1974.)

Why are these two communities unable to live commingled?

The reasons are essentially psychological, founded upon ethnic, religious, and cultural differences and a history of bloodletting and extremism. They include an inward orientation, reluctance to cross the language barrier, abiding mutual distrust, economic disparity, and frustrated self-determination. Antagonism comes to children not only via the family; it is aggravated by textbooks in school.[2]

One may ask how Greek Cypriots and Turkish Cypriots were able to live side by side over the four centuries since Ottomans took possession of the island and despatched settlers to it in the mid-sixteenth century. Turkish villages and farms and Greek communities were neighbors all over the island (see map 3).

The easy explanation is that during most of this period, until 1878, peace was imposed from Istanbul and made acceptable or bearable by the time-honored *millet* system. This system gave non-Muslim communities autonomy under indigenous leaders and exemption from military service in return for obedience to the Sultan's supreme authority and payment of taxes. The peace thereby attained seems to have been fairly stable until the early nineteenth century brought an assertion of Greek identity, partial Greek independence, and aspirations to unite all neighboring Greek-speaking territories with "Mother Greece."

Cyprus passed from Ottoman to British control by the secret Anglo-Ottoman Cyprus Convention of June 4, 1878. It was the outcome of clandestine negotiations designed by Disraeli to enhance British as against expanding Russian influence in the eastern Mediterranean at the time of the breakup of the Ottoman Empire. From that 1878 Convention until 1960, the British occupied and administered the island, first under a sort of lease, then, following World War I, as ruler of a crown colony, proclaimed in 1925.[3] The British encouraged the use of English as the lingua franca, thereby establishing a most important bond between the more educated elements of the two communities. British rule vastly improved general education, health care, communications, and the legal system. Nonetheless, from the beginning, the British were aware that Greek Cypriots wanted union with Greece.

The abandonment of British rule by the London-Zürich Agreements of 1960 removed the buffer of external authority and brought the two communities face-to-face. As we shall see, they were not ready. Greek Cypriots were in the overwhelming majority, and were propelled politically toward *enosis*—a fulfillment of the traditional aspiration for Hellenistic union—and looked upon the Turkish Cypriots as impediments and inferiors. Turkish Cypriots, in turn, were quite unwilling to be governed by Greeks, just as mainland Greeks had proven quite unwilling to be governed by Turks. Recent history had set a precedent for territorial separation rather than on-the-ground cooperation. After Athens had lost the 1921–22 war to annex western Anatolia, Venezelos of Greece and Atatürk of Turkey had agreed to a swap of ethnic populations. This transfer, unfortunately, did not affect Cyprus, which remained under British rule.

The end of World War II saw a powerful resurgence of Greek aspirations for *enosis*, both on the mainland and on the island. A movement led by Lieutenant General George Grivas, a World War II hero of the Greek resistance, born in Cyprus and willing to risk all for this enlargement of the "motherland," resulted in the formation of EOKA (*Ethniki Organosis Kyprion Agoniston*, the National Organization of Cypriot Fighters). During the 1950s, this movement conducted guerrilla warfare against British colonial forces. By 1960, when the British had withdrawn, EOKA became a political force within the Greek Cypriot National Guard and an implicit menace to Turkish Cypriots.

The Turkish Cypriots demanded self-rule or, preferably, incorporation into Turkey. Turkey, while not seeking such annexation, was unwilling to see itself further surrounded on the western and southern coasts by another major Greek-held island, only forty miles offshore.[4] Even though Greece and Turkey were by this time allies in NATO, such encirclement, particularly by expansion-minded Hellenism, was unacceptable to Turkey. The only way out appeared to be by the establishment of an independent republic, guaranteed against annexation by any outside state and against partition. The opportunity came in 1959 with far-sighted leadership in Athens and Ankara.

In Zürich, a Greek Prime Minister with a Turkish family name, Constantine Karamanlis (from the Turkish Karamanlı, or the one from Karaman), and a Turkish Prime Minister with a Greek family name, Adnan Menderes (Menderes from the River Meander in the time of Greek city-states of antiquity), sat down together to negotiate away a time bomb in their bilateral relations. I remember reading the cables, as deputy assistant secretary in the Department of State at the time, and being thrilled by the good sense and geniality that pervaded these discussions. My thrill was premature.

The talks were conducted without Cypriot representation. Once they had reached general agreement, the immediate problem was to bring on board Archbishop Makarios, the ethnarch[5] and unquestionable political leader of the Greek Cypriots. He came most reluctantly to London, where the Zürich accords were laboriously refined into a series of treaties and a constitution for the republic. Britain yielded to Cyprus its sovereignty over all save two base areas on the island, and the United Kingdom, Greece, and Turkey became guarantors of Cyprus against partition or annexation. It was a statesmanlike effort at the time, and represented a monumental job of negotiating and drafting.

Cyprus had no tradition or experience of independence and its two major discordant populations did not seek that status or even desire it. It was therefore logical that the larger powers directly involved, which were also allies in NATO, should undertake joint guardianship over an untried adventure in state building and seek thereby to avert disruption of their alliance.

Let us now examine this set of agreements and the uneasy history of the new republic they created.

The Republic: Born in a Straitjacket

Cyprus is an entity with a long, fascinating, and violent history as a dependency or possession of stronger powers—not including modern Greece, which has never governed Cyprus. Since 1960, it has been recognized as an integral republic. Yet, today it is not one country but two, between which there is a formidable barrier of military, political, ethnic, cultural, religious, and linguistic contrast. There are two operative elected governments on the island: the Republic of Cyprus, which is recognized internationally, and the Turkish Republic of Northern Cyprus, which is unrecognized except by Turkey.

From the moment of its creation, the republic displayed a characteristic unique in the history of emerging states. Not only was it reluctantly accepted as an independent entity by Greek Cypriots and Turkish Cypriots, but each community leaned toward unity with a "mother country" as the focus of its national aspirations. Each has leaned also on the former colonial ruler, Britain, then on the United Nations, for protection and for the advancement of its objectives. Greece, Turkey, and the United Kingdom are all guarantors of the republic's independence. The ambiguity built into this situation is baffling and requires analysis.

Established by the London-Zürich Agreements of 1960, the Republic of Cyprus represented a compromise of clashing Greek-Turkish interests. Its constitution and the treaties binding it were never submitted to popular referendum or plebiscite. The United Kingdom as the retiring colonial ruler, Turkey as the big brother of the Turkish Cypriot minority, Greece as the sponsor of pan-Hellenic unity, and all three, as formal allies, faced with deepening intercommunal hostilities, were concerned to prevent the spread of violence into a military confrontation within the North Atlantic security system. The republic had also become a full member of the United Nations and of the Commonwealth of Nations, loosely associated with Britain, a bond that heightened British and Canadian involvement in the island. While Greece and Turkey were represented by ambassadors in Nicosia, the Commonwealth states were represented by high commissioners.

Both *enosis*, annexation by Greece, and *taksim*, partition between Greece and Turkey, were formally renounced in the 1960 agreements. The republic's charter, approved by the three guarantor powers, in turn became an integral part of several quadripartite pacts, including the Treaty of Establishment and Basic Structure of the Republic of Cyprus, the Treaty of Alliance, and the Treaty of Guarantee. All three guarantor countries contracted to prohibit union with another country or partition. All three undertook to consult should a threat materialize to the independence and territorial integrity of Cyprus. If this consultation failed, any of the three had the right "to take action with the sole aim of re-establishing the state of affairs created by the present Treaty." (The text of the 1960 agreements appears in appendix 1.)

Both Greece and Turkey were allowed to station small, lightly armed national contingents on Cyprus—950 for Greece, 650 for Turkey. Cyprus itself was entitled to a small army made up of both communities and a Cypriot Police (see appendix 1, Basic Structure, Article 14). However, as the task of combining Greeks and Turks into one force proved unworkable, this army never came into being and was replaced by the Greek National Guard. The Cypriot Police also eventually moved to become totally Greek. The Turkish Cypriots reacted by establishing a militia of their own.

Within three years, the basic structure of government outlined in the London-Zürich agreements proved unworkable, despite elaborate, perhaps excessive, safeguards to the Turkish minority. Under the constitution, Turkish Cypriots were allotted 30 percent of the seats in the unicameral parliament (the House of Representatives) and 40 percent of the positions in the projected (but unrealized) bicommunal armed forces structure. The Turkish Cypriot vice president, like the Greek Cypriot president, was granted extensive veto powers. (See appendix 1.)

Orderly administration of the bicommunal state became impossible. Makarios came to the conclusion that amendment of the constitution was imperative. Since Fazil Küçük, vice president of Cyprus and leader of the Turkish Cypriot community, resisted this adamantly, Makarios called a meeting of the guarantor powers, Greece, Turkey, and the United Kingdom, which met in London in the summer of 1963. Turkey supported Küçük in resisting change, and the conference failed to meet Makarios's objective. President Makarios then enunciated his "13 points" in November 1963, aimed at restructuring the constitional order (see appendix 2). Mainland Turkey rejected this initiative without even referring the matter to Fazil Küçük.

According to Fraser Wilkins, U.S. ambassador in Cyprus at the time, Makarios then decided that he must appeal to the United Nations. First, however, he felt it necessary to demonstrate that UN attention and action were urgent. Conditions in Cyprus at the time, however, were peaceful. Intercommunal violence on the island was therefore provoked by an incident apparently planned by Makarios. Two unarmed Turkish Cypriot peasants, returning home from working in the fields, were approached by Greek Cypriot security guards, armed and uniformed, who demanded to see their passes. The peasants carried no documentation, and, in the ensuing altercation, they were killed. In the view of Ambassador Wilkins, there was not the slightest doubt about what had happened, nor about the primary responsibility of Makarios in the affair. The incident that Makarios had staged for UN benefit quickly got out of hand, however, and intercommunal violence became a daily occurrence from then on, eclipsing constitutional change as a matter of prime UN concern.[6]

Following an unsuccessful British effort to restore peace by deployment of forces from its sovereign base areas, an international United Nations Force in Cyprus (UNFICYP) was established by the UN Security Council on March 4, 1964, to keep apart the armed militias of each community and to seek pacification of the island (see appendix 3). It is still in place as of this writing.

Both Greece and Turkey from 1960 had regarded the republic's constitution as unsatisfactory, but now Greece embraced Makarios's thesis that, as written, the constitution was a dead letter. From this it was an easy step in Athens politics to postulate that the republic itself was a mistake, and therefore annexation of this island to Greece was the logical solution. To Turkey, this was totally unacceptable, but the idea of partition or "double *enosis*" lingered in Ankara from pre-1960 deliberations and was again considered, as we shall see, as late as 1967.

In both Greece and Turkey, the sanctity of the Republic of Cyprus as a member of the United Nations was of secondary importance to the state interests of these two uneasy NATO partners, despite the provisions of the preamble and article 1 of the Treaty of Guarantee ensuring respect for the Constitution of the Republic of Cyprus. To the United States, the integrity of NATO's southeast wing was (and still is) the all-important consideration. This led the United States to focus on Greece and Turkey, and on an accord between them, as the key to a solution of the intercommunal problem. Both Greece and Turkey shared this focus and all three, together with the United Kingdom, mistakenly concluded that the fate of Cyprus could be managed from Ankara and Athens.

An anti-communist military government in Greece, headed by Colonel George Papadopoulos, had seized political control on April 21, 1967. Turkey disapproved of the suppression of democracy in Greece, as did the United States. In the interests of NATO, however, both saw little choice but to deal with the new government. Once power was consolidated in Athens, the Papadopoulos regime undertook to enlist American assistance in a settlement of the Cyprus question to be negotiated directly between Athens and Ankara, without any advance approach to Nicosia.

The clear objective of the Greek government was to negotiate a termination of the London-Zürich accords and achieve Turkish consent to *enosis* of all the island, minus the sovereign British areas of Akrotiri and Dhekelia. The regime wished to win legitimacy from its disaffected Greek populace by achieving what democratic governments had failed to do. The Cyprus Republic was only seven years old, was experimental, and had already failed to hold together. As a state, it had no prestige even within its own population. Its flag was seen only over the Presidential Palace, a few government offices, and the Hilton Hotel, whereas the colorful national flags of Greece and Turkey flew over their respective communal institutions. So little was the regard shown for the Cypriot flag that the U.S. ambassador in Nicosia often heard it referred to by Cypriots as a "dirty diaper."

Athens distrusted Makarios. It decided that if he could not be persuaded to accept an *enosis* agreement arrived at between Athens and Ankara, then he could be removed from office. It expected that the United Kingdom, in the NATO interest, would consent to dissolution of the Cyprus Republic and give over to Turkish control one of its two sovereign bases in the island, namely Dhekelia.[7] This would make possible a final Cyprus settlement and the consolidation of the Greek-Turkish alliance in NATO.

It is doubtful that Athens had concluded that it could persuade Makarios to accept this formulation. It probably counted on removing him by force, using Greek regulars in the National Guard, commanded by General George Grivas, the militant leader of the *enosis* movement.

The new prime minister of Greece, former Supreme Court prosecutor Constantine Kollias, authorized the foreign minister of the new military government, Paul Economou-Gouras, to continue bilateral talks begun in 1966 by the former foreign minister, Vice Admiral John Toumbas, with his opposite number, Foreign Minister İhsan Sabri Çağlayangil of Turkey. The secret bilateral discussions resumed in June of 1967. Apparently, Çağlayangil displayed in these carefully guarded talks a willingness to make a broad review of options, to see how far the Greek government was prepared to go. This seems to have led Toumbas and Economou-Gouras to conclude that the Turkish government was not opposed to *enosis*, providing that it received enough territorial compensation in return. Prime Minister Kollias confidently informed American Ambassador Phillips Talbot of the effort he was making and was warned by Talbot not to underestimate basic Turkish opposition to *enosis*.

Attempts to resolve a severe earlier crisis, in the summer of 1964, had included a plan put forward, unsuccessfully, by former Secretary of State Dean Acheson at discussions in Geneva that summer. There appears to have been an original and a follow-up Acheson plan. The first, accepted for negotiation by Turkey but rejected by Greece, called for *enosis* except as follows: Turkey would receive a sovereign base area on Cyprus covering approaches to Turkish ports, for example, the Karpass Peninsula. Turkish Cypriots would receive two small areas on the island for their administrative management, as well as other special arrangements for the protection of the rights of Turkish Cypriots living outside of the Turkish sovereign base area. This proposal was shown to Greek Premier George Papandreou with the express understanding that he get his own cabinet's reaction for Acheson, but not show it to Makarios. However, Papandreou had it delivered to Makarios as the archbishop was arriving by plane in Athens from Nicosia. Makarios read it and denounced it to the press.

The follow-up version of the plan would have leased to Turkey for about fifty years a base area with boundaries smaller than those of the original plan; would have provided no special administrative areas for Turkish Cypriots; would have offered less autonomy for Turkish Cypriots but would have assured them minority rights under the Treaty of Lausanne and the United Nations Declaration of Human Rights; and would have provided for a UN International Commissioner resident on the island to watch over the agreed and special safeguards for Turkish Cypriots. The

Greek government came close to accepting this as the basis for negotiation. Turkey rejected it.[8]

Ever since the 1964 failure of the Acheson Plan for a form of double *enosis*, the United States position had been that any arrangement which could be reached between its three allies would probably be acceptable to the United States. I had been told by British diplomats that the consent of the United Kingdom to the possible transfer of the Dhekelia Sovereign Base Area[9] to Turkey was not inconceivable provided that it constituted the linchpin to a final settlement. Dhekelia at that time was not being much used and appeared nonessential to British defense needs. Nonetheless, giving it up would be a serious amendment to the London-Zürich Agreements and could open the way for Greek and Greek Cypriot pressure on London to also abandon Akrotiri, which was of considerable strategic importance, hence the British insistence that its sacrifice of Dhekelia must be the key to a clearly final solution of the Cyprus issue.

2
Antecedents of the 1967 Frontier Talks between Greece and Turkey

The Johnson Letter

I had been in Ankara but a few weeks when a large chicken came home to roost on my shoulders: the famous Lyndon B. Johnson letter to İsmet İnönü of June 5, 1964, which led to the Acheson mission. I had of course read this letter before I left Washington (see text in appendix 4). It was an exceedingly tough message, designed to prevent at all costs direct hostilities between Greece and Turkey, and it had been a very close call.

Raymond A. Hare, my predecessor, had learned from then Foreign Minister Feridun Cemal Erkin that Turkey could no longer stand by and witness the killing of brother Cypriots by superior and illegally introduced Greek forces. Accordingly, an expeditionary force to the island had been decided upon by the Turkish government. Ambassador Hare asked for a delay of twenty-four hours in which to consult Washington. Erkin agreed after communicating with Prime Minister İnönü.

At the Department of State, in close coordination with the White House, an emergency drafting group chaired by Secretary of State Dean Rusk spent most of the night on a telegram that could stop the Turkish invasion. For the most part, the text was unexceptionable, a clear and strong argument for diplomacy in lieu of force and heavy emphasis on the vital importance of the integrity of NATO. But this was deemed not enough. The message added that should Turkey disregard this advice, and should the Soviet Union intervene against Turkey, Ankara should recognize that its allies would not have had "a chance to consider whether they have an obligation to protect Turkey against the Soviet Union." In other words, the message implied that the United States might not come to Turkey's aid despite the provisions of the NATO alliance.

The effect was profound. The Turkish intervention was reduced to an air raid on Greek forces besieging the tiny enclave of Kokkina. The letter was not published, but its general tenor, heavily distorted, leaked to the public and was immediately transformed into a version that the United States itself had threatened naval intervention against Turkey. Shortly after my arrival in Ankara, I was waylaid one evening by the press at the Foreign Ministry steps with the question: "Is it true that in the Johnson letter the United States threatened to use force against Turkey in 1964?" I replied that this was definitely not the case. The letter, I said, used strong language to persuade Turkey not to take an action which could lead to a Greek-Turkish war.

Unbeknownst to me, the question stemmed from a bitter parliamentary debate of that afternoon in which the opposition People's Party defended its 1964 failure to put troops ashore in Cyprus by stating that the United States had threatened to interpose the Sixth Fleet. My answer to the press was garbled in the next morning's editions: "American Ambassador says Johnson letter was only a recommendation." A People's Party delegate at once proclaimed, "The American ambassador is a liar." The press then sought my rejoinder, but I refused to be drawn in. Later, by agreement with Foreign Minister Çağlayangil, our two governments agreed to publish the letter and İnönü's reply, but the daily *Hürriyet* scooped us with a purloined copy.

The effect was anticlimactic. The letter was less severe than popularly imagined, and I heard little of it from the media thereafter. However, its impact on the Turkish General Staff was, and still is today, a matter of deep concern to all who cherish Turkish-American relations.

The Athens Position

In the aftermath of the 1964 crisis and the Lyndon Johnson letter that was credited with preventing a Turkish landing on Cyprus, Greek (and Greek Cypriot) political circles appear to have taken the position that *enosis* was obtainable, because:

1. The United States would again prevent any Turkish landing on the island.

2. Makarios's 13 points of 1963 had resulted in armed struggle, enclaves, and chaos and had rendered the 1960 Constitution unworkable and, in the view of Athens, void.

3. Pro-*enosis* sentiment predominated on Cyprus and in Greece where it was a "national cause," and Greek governments were anxious to popularize themselves by championing it. Makarios's intentions were distrusted and he, along with Glafcos Clerides, president of the Cyprus House of Representatives, and others, might have to be neutralized by Greek forces, commanded by Grivas.

4. Intercommunal talks on the island were therefore not desirable, as they would most likely perpetuate the Republic of Cyprus with special guarantees for Turkish Cypriots.

5. Unilateral *enosis* risked war with Turkey; therefore compensated *enosis* must be negotiated, but the compensation need not be great, nor at mainland expense, but rather at Cypriot expense.

6. The United States was neutral and stood for any "agreed solution."

Ambassador Alexander Sgourdeos arrived in Ankara in June 1965. He had been born in Istanbul, was friendly to Turks, and felt he understood them. He was broad-minded, easy-mannered, and ready to explore a range of compromises for a settlement. He was convinced *enosis* was possible and went far beyond his instructions in offering to Turkey:

1. Unspecified "rectification" of the Evros/Meriç frontier region in Thrace.

2. Unspecified, uninhabited Dodecanese islands.

3. A base on Cyprus (to be leased for 99 years by Turkey) in the name of NATO; or the Karpass Peninsula. Award of either to Turkey would technically require Makarios's consent. Agreements gave to Makarios first refusal of any base given up by London. Sgourdeos rejected a requirement by Hasan Işık (acting Turkish foreign minister) that Turkey be given land on Cyprus equivalent to 18 percent of the island's area, so as to conform to the percentage of Turkish Cypriots in the island's total population.

Sgourdeos was promptly taken to task in June 1965 in Athens by Prime Minister George Papandreou, who asked him whether he wanted to be recalled and shot as a traitor for offering to alienate Greek territory. However, he was not then recalled. Instead, it was Papandreou who was turned out of office by a parliamentary crisis in July 1965.

Çağlayangil took office as Turkish foreign minister in October 1965. Sgourdeos told me that he was pleased to find him broad-minded and open to various ideas for a settlement. As Sgourdeos's hopes for "compensated" *enosis* rose, he focused on negotiating a shift of one or both British sovereign areas on Cyprus to NATO status, with British, American, and other contingents as well as Turks quartered thereon, to provide an umbrella for Greek and Greek Cypriot acceptance. Greece would provide special guarantees for the rights of Turkish Cypriots. The bulk of Cyprus would then become a part of Greece, but with a special status, perhaps as a condominium or federation. Makarios would have to accept this, as he would become the hero of *enosis* and could attain high office in Athens, an objective he surely cherished.

With Sgourdeos, as I learned from several conversations, the wish was the father to the analysis. He was recalled in January 1966 and replaced promptly by Miltiades Delivanis, an experienced career diplomat who had just been ambassador to Cyprus. Çağlayangil gave Sgourdeos a farewell luncheon at the Foreign Ministry residence (Hariciye Köşkü) at Çankaya, which I attended. In his gracious, Ottomanlike style, he paid Sgourdeos compliments for his friendly attitude and his broad approach to Greek-Turkish relations. Sgourdeos in reply said that he was sure the Cyprus problem could now be solved, would indeed be solved while Çağlayangil was in office. Çağlayangil jocularly commented this was especially welcome news, as he was about to face an election to Parliament in which he probably would be defeated; so the time was very short.

As it developed, Çağlayangil won his seat easily and retained his cabinet position. Sgourdeos was out for good and the Greek government did not give Delivanis as much latitude as Sgourdeos had assumed. From the Greek embassy we later learned of some hardening of the Athens position. No motherland Greek territory could be offered for compensation unless, possibly, the tiny island of Kastellorizon.

Nonetheless, Greek interest in bilateral talks with Turkey on Cyprus developed during 1966. The Turks at first were cautious, feeling that Athens had disavowed Sgourdeos and sensing that it had hardened its demands.

Delivanis rented a house in Çankaya near the Hariciye Köşkü, across a park from the U.S. Embassy residence. We met often, and an easy, informal relationship developed. When the Greek military, led by George

Papadopoulos, seized power in Athens on April 21, 1967, Delivanis was openly embarrassed. He believed in parliamentary government as the traditional expression of Greek democracy, and felt this to be a severe setback to Greece's image. However, as Constantine remained on the throne and he was very much the king's man, he continued at his post until after the failure of the royal countercoup of December 13, 1967. He was a good colleague, broad-minded, sensitive, eager to achieve harmony between Greece and Turkey as an imperative for both countries and for NATO. He despised Makarios and made no bones about it.

The Ankara Position

There is no doubt in my mind that the Turkish government, during the period of 1965 until the frontier meetings of 1967, did weigh Greek feelers toward double *enosis* and, as an alternative, a sizable base on the island of Cyprus. One of their earliest positions seems to have been that they would be willing to entertain a cession to them in full sovereignty of some Cyprus territory if it were equal to approximately one-fifth of the total. They also referred in 1965 and repeatedly in 1966 in private conversations with me and some of my associates to the possibility of communal cantonization or federation in an independent Cyprus.

By 1966, the Turkish government had become convinced that bilateral talks with the Greek government in Athens were the best way to advance matters. This was reinforced in 1967 by the fact that they shared with the military regime in Athens a deep distrust of Makarios and did not believe that it was possible to negotiate with him. Furthermore, the Demirel government felt that its predecessor had botched the Cyprus question badly and a new approach was needed.

Some twenty thousand Turkish Cypriots were deployed in enclaves, but most of the Turkish population was scattered vulnerably in villages throughout the island (see map 3). The Turkish government desired to avoid being dragged into hostilities on Cyprus. There were many irresponsible gunmen beyond the control of the leaders of the two communities. Turkey had no ambition to annex the island or even a portion of it. Contrary to Greek assertions, Atatürkism is not expansionist by doctrine, but Turkey is allergic to Greek encirclement.

At this period, however, Ankara was alarmingly aware that Greek governments were very heavily committed to *enosis*. Public opinion in Greece left no alternative. Ankara was aware that, in a communiqué in which Makarios participated in early February of 1966, Athens declared unacceptable any Cyprus solution that excluded the possibility of *enosis*. It was also aware, however, that Makarios himself was not entirely sincere in this position. As noted, he had indicated that the only *enosis* he would concede to be proper was one that would enable him to deliver the entire island like a baby to its mother Greece, without limbs lopped off. Since the British sovereign areas, or at least Akrotiri, were lopped off for the foreseeable future, many close observers concluded that what Makarios really wanted was to be untrammeled master of the rest of the island.[10] Later on, if it developed that through *enosis* under his auspices he could also become the Eleftherios Venizelos of Cyprus and be elected prime minister of a combined Cyprus and Greece, he would welcome that opportunity and exploit it.[11]

The Turkish rejection of unilateral *enosis* did not then exclude consideration of double *enosis*, if compensated adequately by land from mainland Greece or its islands. However, by the time that the frontier talks took place, the Turkish government saw little chance of such compensation and its position hardened. Certainly, Dhekelia, even if ceded in full sovereignty to Turkey, would not meet the requirements of the Turkish Cypriot proportion of one-fifth of the island's population. It would not accommodate the livelihood of 120,000 Turkish Cypriots and would do nothing to protect the welfare of the Turks scattered over the rest of the island. Likewise, a cession of the Karpass Peninsula to Turkey, as in the Acheson formula of 1964 (rejected by Makarios), was inadequate both in space and resources to support a major regroupment of Turkish Cypriots.

At one point the Turks discussed among themselves and with us the possibility of a strip of territory about ten kilometers wide extending southeast from Kokkina on the northwestern coast, where there was a Turkish population besieged by Greek Cypriots, down to Nicosia, the largest center of Turkish Cypriot population. Although the United States gave no encouragement to such a project, this idea may have ultimately led to Turkish plans for separating off, for Turkish Cypriot use, the portion of the island which now constitutes the Turkish Republic of Northern Cyprus. At a January 1964 London conference, Turkish Prime Minister İnönü is reported to have proposed a federal state for Cyprus in which

Turkish Cypriots would be awarded a single geographical zone comprising about 38 percent of the island's total land area.[12] In early 1968, in a discussion of Cyprus in the Foreign Ministry, I was inadvertently shown a map on which was marked a boundary very similar to that of today's Turkish Republic of Northern Cyprus. A boundary of this general scope thus seems to have remained in Turkish planning as a contingency in case Greek-Turkish and intercommunal negotiations should be overtaken by a new threat of *enosis*, as eventually occurred in July 1974.

The United Nations Posture

By late 1965 when I reached Turkey, the only role the United Nations was playing was that of insuring that the United Nations Forces in Cyprus, UNFICYP, were in place and doing their job. A strong UN mediation effort under Galo Plaza had generated a published recommendation which Ankara found biased toward Makarios and the Greek position.[13] The Turkish government had rejected it angrily and refused discussions with Galo Plaza or any further UN mediation based on this report. It resented deeply the report's publication. Ambassador Belcher, since his retirement, has informed me that, in coordination with the Department of State, he had made considerable input into the drafting of that report and felt that it was sound. Galo Plaza, however, made subsequent changes, whereupon Under Secretary George Ball instructed Belcher urgently to try to persuade Galo Plaza not to release the report as written. Galo Plaza was much offended by this U.S. intervention and proceeded with the release.

The Greek Cypriot and Turkish Cypriot Positions

When it became apparent that secret talks were being held between Athens and Ankara at the subministerial level and later at the foreign ministry level, both Greek Cypriots and Turkish Cypriots became disturbed. Not being included, they felt that the two "mother" countries might be hatching something which would not accord with their vital interests. Makarios in particular predicted that the frontier talks would be a failure and that, once having failed, there would then be an opportunity for the Turkish Cypriots to negotiate with him. He was prepared, he said, to be very generous with respect to their "minority rights."

This matter of minority rights interested Ankara very much. Turkey was not yet wedded to the idea that Turks on the island must be considered as a sovereign community having a position equal and equivalent in every respect to that of the central Greek Cypriot government in Nicosia. Ankara was more concerned to restore the status quo ante, that is, the London-Zürich status of the communities as they had been formalized before Makarios proclaimed his famous thirteen points. It was ready to consider changes in London-Zürich, provided they were based on the principle that the constitution of the Cyprus Republic was fully in force until such changes had been agreed on by all parties. However, a plebiscite of the weak Turkish Cypriot community did not then appear useful or essential to Ankara.

Makarios, on the other hand, had held a much stronger position vis-à-vis the tenuous parliamentary governments in Athens that preceded the 1967 coup. In fact, he was probably the most influential Hellenic leader after Karamanlis resigned and left Greece in 1963. He had unwillingly signed the London-Zürich Agreements and looked forward to the time when he could change them unilaterally, since he could not change them by agreement with the Turkish Cypriot people.

The London-Zürich Agreements had given the Turkish Cypriot community quite disproportionate, if negative, powers. It had made the Turkish Cypriot leader, Fazil Küçük, vice president of the republic with broad veto authority, and Turkish Cypriots held more positions in the House of Representatives and the civil service and in plans for security forces than their numbers alone would have justified. The Greek Cypriots, however, through the National Guard and three private armies, held overwhelming military preponderance and were in a position to crush Turkish Cypriot resistance to measures they wished to have executed. They would simply declare, as Makarios did in 1964, that the London-Zürich treaties were dead and that Turkish Cypriot leaders had withdrawn from the government and were in a state of rebellion.

Furthermore, Makarios in 1964 had followed up his thirteen points, unilaterally amending the constitution, by declaring the end of the Treaty of Guarantee and with it the right of Turkey (1) to maintain a contingent of troops on the island or (2) to intervene with force, if consultations with the other guarantors failed. Such intervention, he maintained, would be a violation of the UN Charter. Since the United States had stopped a Turkish invasion under that treaty in June 1964, Makarios clearly felt that Turkey would never be permitted to intervene by force.

In the Turkish Cypriot community of 1963–67, frustration, fear, and anger prevailed. Makarios's actions were declared invalid by Vice President Küçük, who repeatedly wrote to the UN secretary-general that a Cyprus government without his active participation was illegal. In 1966, Rauf Denktaş, president of the Turkish Cypriot Communal Chamber, was refused re-entry to Cyprus by Makarios and was living in Turkey. He was urging that the Turkish Cypriots declare themselves a separate state. This, he postulated, was justified by Makarios's holding parliamentary elections without the participation of the Turkish Cypriots.

Meanwhile, the Turkish community on the island had regrouped perhaps one-fifth of its numbers into enclaves, including north Nicosia, defended by the lightly armed Turkish Fighters Organization (*Türk Mukavemet Teşkilâtı*, or TMT). Its lack of training and quick trigger character disturbed Ankara, which at first used its treaty contingent on Cyprus to keep it in check and train its leaders. Later, from 1964, when large numbers of Greek regulars were introduced into Cyprus in contravention of treaty limits, Turkish regular officers in small numbers were landed surreptitiously or detached from the treaty contingent to take command of TMT units.

The Political Scene in Turkey, 1965–67

In Turkey, the newly elected Justice Party at first looked on the Cyprus problem as annoying but secondary. It was not particularly interested in activating negotiations, but it wished to avoid a crisis. It planned to concentrate on Turkey's internal development, the foundation stone of its resounding electoral victory. Headed by Süleyman Demirel the party had reached power on a platform of free enterprise. It promised escape from the strictures imposed by the traditional statism of the Republican People's Party (RPP).

As Demirel often put it, the RPP believed erroneously that the "high hills" of the economy should always be in the hands of the state and that the private sector should have but a small role to play. The traditions of the RPP had come down from the time of Atatürk, when no foreign aid existed and only the state could undertake such developmental projects as building a railroad or a steel mill, digging a coal mine, or erecting a major industrial plant. Furthermore, most leading Turks of the 1930s had regarded business and commerce as beneath them. By tradition they were soldiers and administrators. Foreigners had done the trading.

Now the foreigners had long since gone, and Demirel's sense of mission lay in radically modernizing a backward, agricultural economy, unshackling private initiative, promoting industry and industrial exports, and generally raising living standards. I had many conversations with him along with our most capable AID director, James P. Grant, sorting out projects by which the United States could help to broaden not only the fundamental base of the economy, but also the geographical spread of benefits throughout Anatolia and European Turkey.

Cyprus, therefore, was not at first a problem high on the list of priorities for policy consideration by the new government. It was left to the ingenuity and diplomacy of Foreign Minister Çağlayangil and his able staff.

Exploratory conversations began between İlter Türkmen, an assistant secretary-general of the Foreign Ministry, and a Greek counterpart named Sossides. What they discussed was never made known to me. There followed conversations, also secret, between Foreign Minister Toumbas and Çağlayangil from mid-1966 until December. Conflicting stories emerged. The Greek position was that by December Çağlayangil had proposed to the Greek government that Turkey be granted the British sovereign base of Dhekelia in return for *enosis* by Athens of the rest of Cyprus, minus the British sovereign base at Akrotiri.

Whether Çağlayangil actually made such a proposition I cannot verify. In any event, in conversations with me Çağlayangil was very open-minded and mentioned the possibility that Turkey might consider: (1) double *enosis*, (2) a considerable base on the island, or (3) other forms of territorial compensation. He was also prepared to consider continuation of an independent Cyprus with adequate guarantees for the Turkish minority and with the establishment of cantons or a federated form of government. The cantons would roughly coincide with the enclaves into which so many of the Turkish Cypriots had already withdrawn. Adequate minority rights for Turkish Cypriots remaining commingled with Greek Cypriots would be negotiated with Athens.

The Political Scene in Greece

In December of 1966, the Center Union government of Stephanos Stephanopoulos fell, overthrown by Panayiotis Kanellopoulos of the National Radical Union, bringing parliamentary uncertainty to Athens. Greece entered upon an interval in which technocrats headed by John Paraskevopoulos held office subject to the general concurrence of the two leading parties. Elections were called for May 28, 1967. Meanwhile, Athens received from the Turks inquiries whether this new government was prepared to carry on bilateral conversations at the foreign ministry level starting from where they had left off in December 1966. The Greeks interpreted this to mean that the Turks had consented to discuss compensated *enosis*, including a transfer of Dhekelia to Turkish control once it was given up by the British.

Because the Athens government was without a firm political base, it took some time before the Greeks responded to Turkish inquiries. Economou-Gouras eventually replaced Vice Admiral Toumbas as foreign minister and in due time indicated that he was prepared to resume conversations with the Turks where those talks had left off in December 1966. He and Çağlayangil met in Brussels in June 1967 at a NATO ministerial meeting, always a convenient place for Greeks and Turks to get together inconspicuously in private conversation. However, when the Frontier Conference took place that September, there was not only insufficient preparation, there were also great discrepancies in Greek and Turkish expectations.

King Constantine was very anxious to settle the Cyprus problem. He personally lent a great deal of his energy to this and, as we shall later see, played an important role in the negotiations involving Cyrus Vance in late 1967.

Both Turkey and Greece at this stage were anxious to avoid a crisis between them and the resultant weakening of NATO.

American Policy in 1965

The American position on Cyprus has been one of neutrality between Greece and Turkey and willingness to support whatever the latter two could agree upon.

Before I proceeded to Turkey in early September 1965, I had a session with Under Secretary of State George Ball, who informed me of the U.S. government position with respect to the Cyprus problem. "An agreed solution" meant any solution accepted by the immediate parties—Greece, Turkey, the United Kingdom, and the Republic of Cyprus. Obviously, this meant that we had no further proposal of our own and would encourage only such initiatives as seemed to promise a consensus. The United States had been burned by the rejection of the Acheson plan.[14] George Ball was quite disgusted with the behavior of George Papandreou in reneging on his agreement to hold the plan in confidence. I was subsequently to learn from a brief personal contact with Dean Acheson after my retirement that Acheson had the lowest possible opinion of Makarios and felt that there would never be a Cyprus settlement until he was out of the picture.

On my arrival in Turkey in September 1965, I met with the caretaker government. It was the fourth coalition since the return to parliamentary government following the Turkish military seizure of power in 1960. It was headed by Prime Minister Ali Suat Hayri Ürgüplü, an elderly gentleman of distinguished lineage who had been ambassador to the United States. Under him Süleyman Demirel, leader of the Justice Party, held the nominal position of foreign minister, but left the day-to-day work in foreign affairs to Hasan Işık, a very senior career officer of the Turkish Foreign Ministry.

The Ürgüplü-Işık policy on the Cyprus problem ran about as follows:

1. Appeal to NATO allies to assist in the solution of the Cyprus problem in every possible way.

2. Work for a federation of the communities on the island of Cyprus.

3. Stand firmly for the independence of the Republic of Cyprus with adequate guarantees for the Turkish minority.

Inasmuch as the island was already semi-partitioned by the regrouping of a large part of the Turkish Cypriot population into enclaves for defense and local self-government, the federation would be based upon autonomous rights for the Turks in those enclaves and for suitable guarantees by the United Nations for all Turks not living in them.

Ürgüplü stated to me early that he feared that America's neutral position might encourage the Greeks to create faits accomplis on Cyprus in the direction of *enosis*. He was very worried about violence on the island

and desired that Turkey not be drawn into hostilities with Greece as a result of rash actions by such extremists as Grivas, a mainland Greek citizen and a man of action, uninhibited in violence. Ürgüplü said that if a single Turk should be killed, this would inflame Turkish opinion. He was very much afraid of a repeat of the events of 5–6 September 1955 in Istanbul and Izmir, when so many Greeks were subject to Turkish mob violence and to expulsion from Turkey.

Ürgüplü was of kindly disposition, reflective and far-seeing. He had fulfilled the legacy of a family celebrated for its public service. He knew he was at the end of his career and would retire from this position of prime minister, as indeed he did after the September 1965 election ended the interim regime. He died a few years later.

With Süleyman Demirel firmly in the saddle, Çağlayangil began to share with me some of his preliminary thoughts on the Cyprus problem. While it seemed that he leaned toward an independent Cyprus with appropriate guarantees for the Turkish Cypriot community, he ruled out only "unilateral" *enosis*. He did not rule out double *enosis* or partition of the island with Greece, if the partitioned part given to Turkey could preserve what he called the "balance" or "equilibrium" between Greece and Turkey inherent in the Lausanne Treaties of 1923 that had followed the end of World War I.

With a mandate from the voters, Çağlayangil went farther than Ürgüplü could in his exploration of possible avenues. He made it clear that any territory ceded to Turkey could probably not embrace all Turkish Cypriots and that those who were not included should be protected by adequate guarantees. This was a very critical point with him and became more and more important as time went on. As I remember his comments, he stated that Toumbas, foreign minister of Greece during 1965–66, had refused to spell out to him in their private conversations what guarantees he would be willing to provide for Turkish Cypriot rights. Both Toumbas and Economou-Gouras tried to insist that Turkish Cypriots living under Greek sovereignty would have a very satisfactory life, comparable to that of the Turkish population of western Thrace. This was not reassuring to Çağlayangil, who believed that ethnic Turks in western Thrace had long been denied cultural freedom.

I remember suggesting for consideration by the Department of State that Turkey might be compensated for *enosis* over a number of years, by the United Kingdom's release of both sovereign areas on Cyprus to Turkey, first Dhekelia, which the British apparently were not using, and then sometime later Akrotiri, when they found it no longer necessary for their purposes. Technically this could be vetoed by Makarios. However, if *enosis* of the rest of the island were to result, Makarios's objections could perhaps be overridden by popular acclamation in Greece and in Cyprus.

In December 1965 came a crucial test of U.S. policy. The United Nations General Assembly passed a resolution (appendix 5) favorable to the Greek Cypriot position, though with more abstentions than total votes cast. It was vigorously opposed by the Turks and was also voted against by the United States, Iran, Pakistan, and Albania. Its essence was to endorse the Greek Cypriot government's claim to the right of full sovereignty, while protecting minority rights, and to noninterference. The latter meant exemption from the guarantees against *enosis* or partition inherent in the London-Zürich Agreements, that is to say, paragraph 4 of the Treaty of Guarantee itself. Any General Assembly resolution is, of course, advisory and does not carry the force of a resolution by the United Nations Security Council. Nevertheless, it has weight in world opinion.

To the Turks this resolution meant the right of the Greek majority to rule over the Turkish minority as it wished and even to select *enosis* as the future status of the island of Cyprus, regardless of the resistance of the Turkish Cypriot community.

The United States had seen this resolution brewing and sought, along with the Turks, to substitute for it a procedural resolution relating to renewal of the mission of the United Nations forces on the island. This renewal had to take place every six months. One of the biggest problems always faced was funding. A procedural resolution introduced by Turkey with the help of the United States automatically took precedence over a substantive resolution.

Nonetheless, the substantive resolution carried, to the great chagrin of the Turks, since they did not obtain the votes of most of their Arab neighbors or the great body of Third World countries. It was regarded as a disaster by some elements of Turkish public opinion, particularly in Asia Minor, which oversimplified the result into the "loss of Cyprus." Certainly the UNGA vote was influenced by the Galo Plaza report noted earlier. It was a victory for Makarios only in a public relations sense, however.[15]

Fortunately for American-Turkish relations, the American vote on the Turkish side was well received and helped to make up for the lingering effects of President Lyndon Johnson's harsh letter of June 1964 to İsmet İnönü, which had created such a bad impression and which had reemerged in the fall of 1965 as a major factor in Turkish interparty politics. By the same token, the American vote against the resolution angered Greece and its lobby in the United States.

The Soviet Position and Third World Concerns

The United States always kept an eye on the Soviet position, but in this case the Kremlin and Washington were not totally at odds. They were at one in not wanting a war between Greece and Turkey, but for quite distinct reasons. Such a war could lead to annexation of Cyprus by Turkey or by Greece or partition between them.

The Soviet Union, its satellites, and AKEL, the communist force on the island, were particularly afraid of partition, a likely outcome of a Turkish military intervention. Cyprus could thereby become one or two large NATO bases, one Greek and one Turkish, dominating the Eastern Mediterranean. Given the Soviet policy of restricting the U.S. role in the eastern Mediterranean, *enosis*, Turkish annexation, or partition were all regarded by the Soviet Union as a threat to its interests. Moscow and its satellites therefore stood for a fully independent, nonaligned, integral Cyprus with whatever guarantees were required for the Turkish Cypriot community in order to make this work. Moscow clearly hoped for a solution that would not result in the weakening of AKEL. Nonetheless, the Soviet government was reported to be "egging on" the Turks and at the same time telling Greek Cypriots that Turkey was bluffing.[16]

Contrary to Soviet propaganda, the United States was not seeking a military base in Cyprus. It was enough for our purposes to have the British firmly in Akrotiri, or, if it helped achieve a solution, to have the Turks there as well.

The Bilateral Greek-Turkish Discussions of Early 1967

As the previously mentioned talks between Çağlayangil and Economou-Gouras proceeded with two meetings—one in May 1967 at Bonn, the second in June in Luxembourg—it was apparent that the Turkish position began to move away from compensated *enosis* or double *enosis* as the result of several factors. First, it seemed doubtful that the Turkish people would accept *enosis* in any form. Secondly, Ankara seemed concerned over a strong Soviet reaction that would result just when Ankara was trying to improve Turkish-Soviet relations for general trade and détente. Third, Ankara appeared concerned at the reaction that might occur among Arab neighbors and other nonaligned and Third World countries over a carving up by larger powers of a small member country of the United Nations. It would set a precedent objectionable in Africa and the Third World, and Turkey might lose a good deal of international diplomatic support.

The bilateral talks at the foreign ministry level were therefore difficult to conduct, despite an apparent Greek and Turkish desire to keep the integrity of their relationship as NATO allies. Serious incidents were occurring on the island, such as the Famagusta crisis of 1966 and the earlier arms deal between Archbishop Makarios and the Czech government, under which a fairly substantial amount of small weaponry had been brought onto the island in 1964 and stored in a cave for Makarios's personal bodyguard. When the Turks learned that this shipment had arrived, they became quite excited. They felt that the arms would be used against Turkish fighters.

In retrospect, I believe that Makarios's importation of Czech arms was designed mostly to beef up his own defense position against a possible coup by George Grivas. Grivas and Makarios were clearly not friends after 1964. Their policies could not coincide. Grivas was for *enosis*, come hell or high water, and was determined to obtain it by any means. He had the forces behind him to do it and to eliminate Makarios if he so wished. Makarios was a political hero to the general public of democratic Greece, especially when he "bashed" Turks, but he was no hero to the colonels.

The Czech arms shipment caused the Turks to delay resuming bilateral talks with the Greek government. For a time, they suspected that Athens had connived in the importation of the arms to the island. However, the Americans were convinced, and tried to reassure Ankara, that this was not the case, that Athens was actually quite ignorant of this shipment and distrusted Makarios. We also tried to prod U Thant, secretary-general of the United Nations, to insist that Makarios place the weapons and ammunition under UN control. U Thant was timid about this, reluctant to tread upon Makarios's prerogatives as president of the Republic. U Thant always feared a rebuff, particularly from a small country at odds with a larger power.

Gradually, the matter of the Czech arms devolved into a compromise whereby the arms were kept locked up in a cave and at rare intervals were inspected casually by the force commander of the UNFICYP. Eventually, the Turks lost interest in the issue because, I believe, they realized that the quantity of weapons did not constitute a very great threat to the Turkish Cypriots and they probably suspected, as did I, that the weapons were designed for the protection of Makarios against Grivas.[17]

Turkish public opinion was becoming very exasperated over repeated setbacks on the Cyprus question. The Justice Party, therefore, found itself in a difficult position. With a majority of votes in the Turkish National Assembly, it felt reasonably secure in proceeding with a foreign policy offensive to win more converts to its point of view on the Cyprus problem. Almost at once, therefore, the Turkish president, General Cevdet Sunay, undertook a series of visits to the Third World, in particular to Turkey's neighbors in western Asia and the eastern Mediterranean. This program was nicknamed the "foreign policy with a personality." Beginning in 1965, Turkey continued to carry forward an exchange of high-level visits, making some progress in educating many of Turkey's neighbors and many Third World countries to a degree of sympathy for the Turkish Cypriots as oppressed fellow Muslims.

3
Final Greek Efforts to Negotiate *Enosis* with Turkey: The Frontier Meetings of September 1967

By August 1967, Greek Prime Minister Kollias moved to invite Ankara to accept a conference at the prime ministerial level on the frontier of Thrace between Greece and Turkey to discuss all common problems, but especially that of Cyprus. It was to be an all-out Greek effort to remove the major cause of chronic tension in Greek-Turkish relations.

On the Turkish side, Çağlayangil persuaded Prime Minister Süleyman Demirel that Turkey could not refuse to meet the new government of Greece in direct bilateral talks, regardless of the inconclusive nature of his exploratory discussions with Toumbas and Economou-Gouros. To refuse altogether would make matters worse between the two countries and put Turkey in an intransigeant light. There might also be benefit to Turkey in a forthright clarification of the viewpoints between two guarantors of Cyprus under the London-Zürich Agreements, particularly as there now was a very authoritarian government in Athens.

The two delegations met September 9 and 10, 1967, on the Thracian frontier at what the Greeks call the Evros and the Turks the Mariç River (Maritsa in Bulgaria). They were headed by the prime ministers and supported by foreign ministers, defense ministers, and advisors. While Kollias spoke for the Greek delegation, the real head was Papadapoulos. Prime Minister Demirel led the Turkish team, but Çağlayangil took an active role. The September 9 meeting took place on the Turkish side of the line, at Keşan, while that of September 10 was held on the Greek side, at Alexandroupolis (see Map 1).

As a leading Turkish participant remarked to me later in an extensive review of the talks, he was surprised and impressed at how alike physically the two delegations were. "One could have switched members across the table," he said, and outsiders would not have known who was Greek and who was Turk. His surprise was revealing to me, for it reflected the very slender contact that had long characterized high-level relations between Greek and Turk. No one on the Greek side knew much Turkish; no one on the Turkish side knew more than a few words of Greek. Therefore, translations were made by interpreters into French or English. Despite these difficulties, personal cordiality prevailed throughout.

According to my recollection of the Turkish account, Demirel began by expressing his appreciation for this invitation to discuss basic Greek-Turkish problems. Peace with Greece was a Turkish geopolitical necessity. He invited the Greek side to present its thoughts. The opener by Kollias was jarring. He complained of rough Turkish treatment of ethnic Greeks on the north Aegean Turkish islands of Imros and Bozcaada (Greek "Imbros" and "Tenedos"). Kollias charged that the ethnic Greek population of the islands had been prevented from farming and that the Greek-speaking population of Turkey as a whole had declined (following the Istanbul riots of 1955) to less than a third of its former thirty thousand. These charges intensely irritated the Turkish delegation.

Turning to Cyprus, Kollias declared that he was not accustomed to diplomatic language. He was a man of the law, and diplomatic niceties could be set aside in a meeting of this kind where frankness, above all, was needed. The only solution to the Cyprus problem was *enosis*, and *enosis*, he said, was good for the Turks. Seeing a Greek flag flying over the island south of the coast of Turkey would be an assurance that the island was in allied hands and therefore safe. Otherwise, there was great danger that Cyprus would go communist. As prime minister of a very anticommunist government in Greece, he held strong feelings against any such eventuality, and he thought the Turks would agree that the most powerful political force on the island was that of AKEL,[18] which controlled 30 percent of all Cyprus votes. This communist labor organization would seek eventually to gain full mastery of the island and render it very unfriendly both to Greece and to Turkey.

The real question, Kollias said, was what it would take to get the Turks to agree to *enosis*. Once *enosis* had been achieved and sovereignty was in the hands of Athens, Greece could offer full Turkish control in the name of NATO over the Dhekelia base, which he said the British were going to give up anyway. Greece would acquire Dhekelia in the process of *enosis*, but would pass it to Turkey, which would then enjoy de facto sovereignty, but with a NATO label, in deference to Greek public opinion. He was even prepared to offer full sovereignty if the Turks insisted upon it.

The Turkish reply, which Kollias later explained took him greatly by surprise, was to say flatly that *enosis* was no solution. This ran counter to everything he had been led to expect from the bilateral foreign ministry talks.

The Turkish version of the September 9 discussions, as given to me, was in sharp contrast to the Greek. Çağlayangil seems to have felt that his earlier talks with Toumbas and Economou-Gouros should have made clear that the Turks were willing to explore all sorts of alternatives to *enosis*, and these could be many. These looked toward cantonization or federation of the island and toward many unspecified adjustments in the London-Zürich Agreements. In the last analysis there could even be a condominium between Turkey and Greece over the island, but not *enosis*. The Turks insisted that they never proposed or accepted double *enosis*, for it was ruled out by the basic provisions of the London-Zürich Agreements, to which Turkey was loyal.

Kollias complained that the Turks had earlier given every indication that they were prepared to consider compensated *enosis*. But, curiously, Kollias had very little to say about Makarios's position on this topic or whether His Beatitude would agree to any such trade-off of island territory, even though Dhekelia was British sovereign territory. The government of Cyprus, in any case, had the right of first refusal to either base which the United Kingdom might decide to abandon.[19] (In previous public statements, Makarios had said that *enosis* must be complete. He would then hand over the entire island to its "mother," Greece.)

The Turkish version of the Kollias presentation was that of a persistent, hard-line, and emotional insistence on *enosis*. Demirel finally remonstrated that it appeared Greece intended to implement it, if necessary, by force. In such a case, Turkey would have to respond and Turkey was not weaker than Greece.

Greek Defense Minister Lieutenant General Gregory Spandidakis immediately rejoined that if this meant war, Turkey indeed might win, but Greece would do its duty. To this Demirel replied that this was up to Greece, but had Turkey wanted war he would not have come to these frontier meetings. He had hoped to find a way to negotiate differences. *Enosis* was not a solution. At this point, according to the Turkish version as I recall it, Papadopoulos intervened brusquely to tell Kollias that his conduct of the talks had led toward a break. (Whether this was translated or someone on the Turkish delegation knew enough Greek to pick it up was not explained.) Tempers cooled enough from then on for both sides to agree to proceed with the scheduled meetings of September 10 at Alexandroupolis.

The crossing to the Greek side, according to the Turkish version, was a refreshing experience. Citizens of this largely ethnic Turk area of western Thrace had come out with Turkish flags and shouted in Greek, "*Zeta* Demirel!" ["Long live Demirel!"] Hospitality was most gracious, even though substantive progress was lacking. After dinner, Çağlayangil took Papadopoulos aside and told him that he believed Turkey and Greece were now closer than ever to a solution of the Cyprus issue. Somewhat astonished, the colonel asked why. Because, Çağlayangil stated, each side now, for the first time, knew exactly what the other's position was, what was possible, what was impossible. They could now proceed to find common ground. Papadopoulos asked for Çağlayangil's hand on that and received it. The ensuing Evros Communiqué (appendix 5) committed both sides to continue efforts to reconcile their wide differences.

In recounting all this to me, I sensed, Ankara naturally wished to present Turkey's position in the best possible light and was inclined to be upbeat rather than depressed at the failure of the talks to bridge the gap. In fact, the Turks had expected no success, whereas the Greeks had. From the reports out of Athens, it was clear that Kollias had been personally embarrassed vis-à-vis his military masters and that he sought to place the blame on Turkish reneging and obduracy. I heard little about him thereafter and noted later that he left Greece for exile with King Constantine when the royal countercoup against the colonels failed on December 13, 1967.

Tension between Greece and Turkey seemed to grow during the weeks following the frontier talks. It was not long before the Greek government registered to the Turkish government the first of a series of complaints over alleged violations of Greek airspace by Turkish military aircraft. These seemed to Athens to be designed to test limits of tolerance. Its charges were rejected by the Turkish government, which stated that its aircraft had been over international Aegean waters. Throughout the months of September and October 1967, little incidents between the two states took on added importance in view of the failure of the frontier talks and the fact that no schedule had been set for their resumption.

Situation Summary

It is worth noting at this point that Turkey had a democratically elected government and Greece did not. Nonetheless, the Turkish attitude toward seizure of power by the military in Greece was as follows. The Turkish government felt that the loss of the democratic system in Athens set a poor precedent for Turkey itself, where the military had seized power in 1960, returning it to an elected civilian parliament in 1961. Democratic Turkey felt it must await a maturing process by the Athens colonels. It hoped it had disabused them of false notions without killing hopes of better relations.

Nonetheless, as alienation deepened between Greece and Turkey during the fall of 1967, there were certain pragmatic advantages which Turkey was finally to recognize in dealing with an authoritarian Greek government that could make concessions a freely elected Greek government would have been unable to present to its public with any chance of acceptance. Memory was fresh of the Stephanos Stephanopoulos government, which had hung by a single vote in late 1966. Had the elections scheduled for May 28, 1967 been allowed to take place, any resulting cabinet might well have been too weak to enable the Vance mission of November–December 1967 to succeed in avoiding war between Greece and Turkey.[20]

The results of the frontier talks were a disappointment but no surprise to my colleague and friend, Ambassador Phillips Talbot in Athens, and to me. At Talbot's suggestion, he and I had met twice aboard the USS *America*, a carrier of the Sixth Fleet, and once also with U.S. Ambassador to Cyprus Taylor G. ("Toby") Belcher, to discuss possible avenues for a Turkish-Greek settlement. We did not keep the fact of these discussions secret from our host governments. I told Çağlayangil in each case of my intention to go to these meetings. I felt that this was required by common sense, as I would be flying out of Turkey aboard a special aircraft capable of landing on the deck of the carrier. This would be reported to him, and it was best for him to learn about it directly from me. After each trip, I gave Çağlayangil a general report of our efforts.

On the carrier, we were treated with great hospitality by the commander and his staff. The visits were enjoyable and instructive regarding the dynamo of human activity aboard such a vessel, with its complement of over four thousand men.

On the substantive side, however, and in relation to the Cyprus problem, Talbot, Belcher, and I made very little progress. It became just as apparent to the three of us as proved to be the case at the frontier talks that the gap between the two sides was too wide to be readily bridged. On the first occasion, Talbot asked whether I thought that, if offered by Athens, the Turks might accept the tiny Greek island of Kastellorizon in return for *enosis*. Said to be a waterless rock known principally as the birthplace of Greek politician George Mavros, it lay off Turkey's southwest Mediterranean coast near the town of Kaş. I told him that I could see absolutely no possibility of the Turks accepting this as adequate compensation for the annexation of so large an island as Cyprus.

For whatever one might think of the rationality of the position of either side, the Turks looked upon Cyprus from a strategic point of view as well as from a recognition of the domestic pressures in Turkey exercised by their large ethnic community on the island. They distrusted the Greek political scene. They distrusted Greek intentions. Their feeling was strong that annexation of Cyprus by Greece would surround Turkey on two sides. There was too much uncertainty in the Greek-Turkish relationship. They remembered the 1921–22 invasion of Anatolia by Greek forces to reclaim ancient Greece and were not willing to be outflanked. They could not forget that for three hundred years, until 1878, Turks had been the dominant minority on Cyprus and now were the endangered minority.

The Turkish Cypriot community's leaders had shown by many bloody encounters in 1963 and 1964 that they would not accept Greek rule. Mainland Turks were not in a position to ignore their cries for help. The violence and excesses of the EOKA movement could recur at any time. Grivas commanded all Greek forces on the island, which had a clear preponderence over Turkish Cypriots in numbers, weapons, and training. Talbot and I therefore found ourselves up against immense psychological obstacles in trying to chart between us an approach to either government which would have some chance of acceptance.

A zero option had now been explored by Greece and Turkey seven years into the history of Cypriot independence, an independence which seemed unworkable but which they had formally pledged with the United Kingdom—and with Makarios—to support.

At this juncture, appeals to outsiders for understanding and support were about to be overtaken by events.

Makarios, the unquestioned political leader of Greek Cypriots, was not as reckless a gambler as was his rival, Grivas. Makarios and Grivas envisaged the future of Cyprus quite differently. The island was Makarios's domain, and he intended to govern it. As his statements and behavior made clear, unless he could become the hero and prime minister of Greece through *enosis*, he was determined to remain where he was and to discourage competition by Turks or Greeks.

Grivas showed by his actions that he intended to sweep aside every obstacle to *enosis* and, at age 69, was prepared, militarily and paramilitarily, to carry out his mission before old age caught up with him. The three sides—Turkish Cypriots, Greeks, and Makarios with his Czech weapons—were armed, but Grivas had by far the superior force. Years of underground warfare against British rule had provided him with cadres of competent, desperate followers, knowledgeable of the terrain and of the power of surprise. Turkish Cypriots were lightly armed, poorly trained, dispersed, and isolated, and UNFICYP could be bypassed. To Grivas, UNFICYP was an intrusive nuisance, blocking Greek Cypriot and mainland Greek self-determination.

The powder keg was therefore ready and, as we shall see, the fuse already ignited.

4
Flash Point: Ayios Theodhoros and Kophinou, November 1967

The autumn chill that followed the collapse of the frontier talks was deepened by charges from Athens of Turkish Air Force violations of Greek Aegean air space. The Greeks considered these violations deliberately provocative. Whether the complaints were justified or not (they were invariably rebutted or ignored by Ankara) was less important than the acrimony that surrounded the exchange. This was worrisome to all NATO powers and especially to the U.S. government.

What transformed the political climate into a violent storm, however, were two minuscule villages on Cyprus: Ayios Theodhoros (Turkish name: Boğaziçi) and Kophinou (Turkish name: Geçitkale).[21] These neighboring hamlets in the southeastern part of the island near Skarinou on the Larnaca-Limassol road (see map 3), had traditionally enjoyed reasonably harmonious intercommunal relations. At Ayios Theodhoros, Turkish Cypriots living on the north side of the brook numbered 685. Occupying heights, they controlled normal access across a single bridge to the south, where the Greek Cypriots numbered 525. A very rough track, not ordinarily usable, provided independent entry to the Greek side for four-wheel-drive vehicles, but access by the usual northern route near Skarinou had not been a serious problem.

All this changed after intercommunal tensions rose at the end of 1963, when these two communities found themselves in the jaws of a political nutcracker. Hostility between the respective communal leaderships in Nicosia and the wildfire of violence sweeping the island generated alarm and tension. What was worse was the introduction of Turkish Fighters and Greek National Guard elements, sharpening the suspicion into confrontation.

The first clash took place without casualties on May 2, 1964, when Turkish Cypriots at Ayios Theodhoros lit bonfires to celebrate the annual Muslim Feast of the Sacrifice (Kurban Bayram) and fired off blanks. Misunderstood on the Greek side, this developed into an exchange of shooting which did not last. On June 15, 1964, a second and more serious incident was narrowly averted by the UNFICYP, which was able to persuade a detachment of the Turkish Cypriot Gendarmerie to withdraw from hill positions overlooking Ayios Theodhoros that threatened free passage by its Greek population.

From here the record is silent until December 1966, when there were three cases of Turkish Cypriot interference with freedom of movement, two involving Greek Cypriot Police and one a National Guard vehicle. In January 1967, Turkish Cypriots removed road signs at Kophinou bearing the usual English transliterations of Greek place-names and re-erected them with Turkish versions. The Turkish Fighters Organization (TMT) began to initiate local actions stemming from island-wide political bargaining or in retaliation for harassment of Turkish Cypriot buses at Famagusta. They exploited their command of Kophinou's strategic location just north of Ayios Theodhoros, astride the main junction of the Nicosia and Larnaca road links with Limassol. In Kophinou, Turkish Cypriots well outnumbered Greeks, 710 to 18.

Under a mainland Turk officer with the *nom de guerre* "Mehmet," sent from Turkey outside treaty limits to maintain discipline in the TMT but proving to be a hothead, Turks demanded that bus destination signs carry the appropriate Turkish, not Greek names. The National Guard, backed by mainland Greek officers and men introduced into Cyprus far beyond treaty limits, then moved into the area to neutralize this challenge to vital communications. After a few days of standoff, UNFICYP was able to restore the status quo. However, General Grivas, not noted for his coolheadedness, ordered a battalion of Greeks supported by armored cars to Skarinou, where it remained despite UNFICYP objections that it was unnecessary. UNFICYP then increased its own presence between the opposing forces and negotiated freedom of movement.

Just east of Kophinou and right on the Nicosia-Larnaca road fork was a police station with a family housing complex. It had been manned in common by UNFICYP and Turkish Cypriot police since the 1964 regroupment of thousands of Turks into defense enclaves across the island. Families of these police and of the TMT were housed there. UNFICYP, concerned over its image of impartiality, asked the TMT chief to keep those of his men who were in uniform away from the premises, and for a while this was done. Under "Mehmet," however, normal police functions became highly politicized. In March 1967, he provoked violent clashes with UNFICYP, which found joint occupancy of the compound impossible. Acting under its mandate, it ordered all Turkish Cypriots out of the compound. Facing superior strength, the Turks obeyed but with great resentment and open hostility by "Mehmet." By the summer of 1967 the situation again heated up.

Brigadier Michael Harbottle, chief of staff to the UNFICYP commander, Lieutenant General Armas E. Martola, relates the next sequence of events, blended here in paraphrase with the UN secretary-general's reports.[22] On July 20, 1967, a three-hour exchange of firing occurred at Ayios Theodhoros. A detachment of UNFICYP intervened and restored order. The next day, TMT fighters fired on a National Guard Land Rover on the main road at Kophinou, but the incident did not escalate. On the night of July 29, 1967, UNFICYP observers reported firing originating from National Guard positions overlooking the Ayios Theodhoros road from its local headquarters at Skarinou. This incident also did not develop, and reasons for it were not reported. Greek Cypriot buses and trucks now began to use the firm surface of the usually dry riverbed to reach Ayios Theodhoros without passing through the Turkish sector to reach the bridge.

For two and one-half years it had been customary for a Greek Cypriot Police (CYPOL) sergeant from Skarinou to visit Greek Cypriots twice weekly in Ayios Theodhoros via this bridge. He was well known to the Turkish community, who preferred his patrolling to the reestablishment of a CYPOL station in the village. However, because of the summer incidents already mentioned and the tension they generated, the CYPOL itself decided to suspend these visits temporarily to allow for a cooling off, a decision UNFICYP applauded. A permanent cessation of the patrols would have been objectionable even to UNFICYP as recognizing an arbitrary restriction of the traffic it was there to protect.

The patrol was resumed on September 7, 1967, without incident, by entry from the north, but on return it was blocked by TMT fighters and had to use the rough track to the south. UNFICYP, with a sharp reaction behind it from the Greek Cypriot government, informed the Turkish Cypriot leadership that patrols must be allowed to pass. To make the point stick, on September 16 a patrol from Skarinou was escorted by the UNFICYP. On its way south it encountered a road block, which it removed; on the return north, farm vehicles and tractors fully barred passage. Major Charles Huxtable, UNFICYP escort commander, had his men remove the obstacles, but under the order of "Mehmet," he and his company sergeant were pushed, kicked, and spat at by TMT elements. It required strong representations by UNFICYP with Turkish Cypriot leaders and the Turkish Embassy in Nicosia to get the road reopened. Soon afterward, "Mehmet" assaulted Huxtable near Kophinou and threatened to kill him. "Mehmet" was then relieved of his command by Ankara and ordered back to Turkey.

It was always clear to the U.S. embassy in Ankara that the basic reasons for TMT intransigeance and troublemaking at Kophinou and Ayios Theodhoros lay in the widespread intercommunal challenge and violent response that had prevailed on the island since December 1963. Nonetheless, TMT engaged in many brutal operations. Its reactions to Greek atrocities produced an endless chain of aggravations, which UNFICYP valiantly worked to abate.

Space here does not permit a detailed review of these events covering nearly four years between 1963 and 1967. During this time, the Turkish Cypriots, headed by Fazil Küçük, repeatedly denounced Makarios's Thirteen Points as violations of the Constitution (which they were). Being cut off from direct communication with the United Nations, they transmitted their protests to that body via the Permanent Representative of Turkey, along with charges of arbitrary decisions taken without Küçük's consent as vice president of Cyprus. Makarios, in response, charged through his UN representative that the Turkish Cypriot leadership was in rebellion against the constituted government and was being supported in its actions by the government of Turkey. He accused Turkey of deploying its treaty contingent into the Turkish enclave of north Nicosia and keeping it there contrary to the Treaty of Alliance, thus invalidating both that treaty and the Treaty of Guarantee.[23] He thus put his government on a collision course with Turkey and sought what has ever since been known as "internationalization" of the Cyprus question, i.e., the appeal of a small young political entity for UN support against threats from a more powerful neighbor. The Turkish contingent, he said, was now on Cyprus illegally, and its very presence was an aggression. The Turkish response in the United Nations became gradually sharper as these exchanges were joined by Greece on the side of Makarios. However, both Greece and Turkey were for quite some time making an obvious effort to preserve the London-Zürich Treaty structure, for the alternative could lead to military confrontation between two NATO allies.

Makarios was not so inhibited. His state was nonaligned in any case, and the local Greek Cypriot political scene was heavily influenced by the Marxist labor movement called AKEL, perhaps the strongest Communist force at the time in the entire Middle East. Internally, the power structure was further complicated by pressures from two strong men: Grivas and Makarios's interior minister, Polykarpos Georgkhadjis, a highly trigger-happy leader. It was in 1964, as the crisis in Cyprus escalated and the mainland Greek government introduced troops into the island under Grivas's command—estimated variously from 7,500 to 20,000—that Makarios had personally ordered a large supply of light-to-medium portable weapons and armored cars from Czechoslovakia, as noted in the previous chapter. At the same time, Makarios had aroused Ankara by embargoing a long list of essential imports that Turkish Cypriots needed to carry on their economy and by blocking any influx of weapons or materials that could be useful for their defense.

In May 1967, a looming military confrontation in Larnaca began to have a malign effect on the situation at Ayios Theodhoros. A small port city with an attractive waterfront boulevard, Larnaca is located on the island's southeast coast. Its normal Greek population was some thirteen thousand, its Turkish about four thousand, with the remainder made up of Maronites, Armenians, and miscellaneous nationalities. On my visit to both sectors, in late December 1967, I found the Larnaca Turkish community to be much the smaller and the poorer. It had roadblocks on the waterfront boulevard facing the Greek area to the north. Behind the city to the west was a macadamized highway running roughly east–west called Artemis Road (also known as Artemis Avenue). It led to the Salt Lake, a few miles from the city, beyond which is the Hala Sultan Tekke, a Muslim shrine and tomb dedicated to the Prophet Muhammad's aunt, Umm Haran, who had died there by accident.

Access to this shrine depended partly on Artemis Road, which was also an essential artery for Greek traffic. The land between the road and the Turkish sector of Larnaca was flat, but low hillocks rose west of it. On May 12, 1967, on Patsalo Hill on the south shore of Salt Lake facing the Turkish suburb of Scala, the National Guard under General Grivas began the construction of two coastal defenses, with the reluctant prior approval of UNFICYP, as part of Grivas's island-wide fortification program against a sea invasion (presumably by Turkey).[24] Why UNFICYP gave approval is not clear, but the original problem had arisen in May 1966, at which time, it appears, the UNFICYP saw no grounds to consider it a threat to Scala, although it would command a clear field of fire if artillery were used.

As construction began in 1967, the Turkish Cypriots took the operation as an immediate threat and began improving their more primitive defense positions east of the road. Brigadier Harbottle, then UNFICYP chief of staff, protested this action as unwarranted, but the Turkish Cypriots rejected his arguments.[25] The Greek government of Cyprus, in reprisal, tightened economic restrictions against Scala, including the blocking of imports of kerosene, and prevented access from Scala to the Hala Sultan Tekke, which Turks now complained was being defiled and damaged by Greeks.

The National Guard then reinforced its positions along the road May 12–13, 1967.[26] The situation became less explosive when UNFICYP moved in armored cars on Artemis Road to act as a buffer and a deterrent to an exchange of fire and successfully ensured free passage on the road for both communities. The situation remained calm throughout the summer and fall.

Nonetheless, Ankara, which since 1964 had become increasingly active in diplomatically supporting Turkish Cypriot positions, insisted on linking free passage for Greek patrols to Ayios Theodhoros with a withdrawal of the National Guard from positions taken May 12–13, 1967 commanding the Artemis Road and Scala. UNFICYP repeatedly argued that these situations should not be linked, since there was no question of freedom of movement on Artemis Road, but rather of fortifications and counterfortification. As the situation in Ayios Theodhoros became more threatening, I was instructed to argue for delinkage to the Government of Turkey and did so on November 7, 1967.

By then it had become apparent that patience in the Greek government of Cyprus was wearing very thin and that the Greek Cypriots were determined shortly to reopen their patrols to Ayios Theodhoros on a regular basis.

I found the Ankara Foreign Office very firm. Secretary-General Zeki Kuneralp stated the position: The United Nations on Cyprus was applying a double standard. If a simultaneous withdrawal of the National Guard from Artemis Road could be arranged, in principle, with an opening of the road to Ayios Theodhoros, Ankara would be willing to exert its influence with the Turkish Cypriots to accept. A one-sided Turk withdrawal was not fair and could not be supported. I came away with foreboding to make my report to Washington.

On the island, UNFICYP next prepared a "timetable" of gradual resumption of patrols. This was accepted by the Greek Cypriots and, provisionally, by Ankara, but with reservations that brought no decision.

Meanwhile, an entirely extraneous factor intervened, at first to complicate, then to appear to help our U.S. and UN diplomatic efforts. Rauf Denktaş, Turkish Cypriot communal leader, had been exiled from Cyprus since 1966, living in Turkey. I met him socially in Ankara in mid-1967. On October 31, 1967, he made a secret landing on Cyprus at a beach north of Famagusta and was immediately caught and held for trial by government of Cyprus security forces. His "escapade," as Kuneralp labeled it, was regarded as silly and troublesome by Ankara. Nonetheless, sympathies for Turkish Cypriots being what they were, an aroused public opinion in Turkey could exert considerable pressure on the Demirel government, particularly if Denktaş were tried and sentenced to imprisonment.

Exactly what pressures were brought to bear on Nicosia I do not know. Fortunately, they were quiet. The Makarios government did not put him on trial, but released him November 12, 1967, on condition that he leave Cyprus.[27] He returned to Turkey that day and almost at once the Foreign Ministry accepted UNFICYP and U.S. urging that it delink Ayios Theodhoros from the Artemis Road problem.

The UN special representative in Cyprus and the commander of UNFICYP now turned their full attention to the government of Cyprus and urged that the resumption of patrolling to Ayios Theodhoros be delayed to ensure that the Turkish Cypriot leadership understood and would follow Ankara's conciliatory change of stance. On November 13, 1967, UN Special Representative Bibiano Osorio-Tafall, acting for UN Secretary-General U Thant, and UNFICYP Commander Martola were informed at a meeting with

President Makarios, Minister of the Interior Georgkhadjis, and General Grivas that the Cyprus government "might not be in a position to wait any longer" before resuming patrols to Ayios Theódhoros. Both Osorio-Tafall and Martola strongly recommended that the patrols be deferred to afford time to reach an "acceptable solution."

That evening, Osorio-Tafall again saw Georgkhadjis and again requested deferral, emphasizing that the return of Denktaş without trial to Turkey the previous day had led to indications that the Turkish government and the Turkish Cypriot leadership were prepared to reconsider their stand on the patrol question and appeared ready to agree to the timetable proposed by UNFICYP for gradual resumption of patrols.

On the morning of November 14, the UN representative again drew the attention of the Cypriot government to this change in Ankara's attitude. "All along," the UN secretary-general's report continues, the Cyprus government had been informed by U Thant's representative that the UNFICYP was prepared to take measures to restore the status quo ante in Ayios Theodhoros and enable Cyprus police to resume patroling and was ready, as of September 16, 1967, to escort such patrols. However, at these meetings of November 13 and 14, the Cyprus government did not request such escort and the UN posture was that it "was out of the question to offer such assistance in the absence of an official request."[28]

This scrupulous attention to the niceties of protocol seems, in retrospect, puzzling and misplaced. I found it rather characteristic, however, from my experience in the 1962–64 Egyptian-Saudi Arabian conflict over the Yemen, which had demonstrated U Thant's excessive punctiliousness, probably rooted in threats of Soviet and French vetoes against providing UN forces with supranational authority.[29]

At 1250 hours on November 14, a local commander of National Guard troops informed the local UN commander at Kophinou that at 1315 hours (within 25 minutes) two Cyprus patrols would move into Ayios Theodhoros, one by the main road from near Skarinou, and the other over the rough track from the south. The National Guard commander asked if UNFICYP had escort to offer and said that if not, the National Guard "would be prepared to meet whatever consequences resulted." At the same time, the local UNFICYP team noted a major deployment of National Guard forces in the area of Ayios Theodhoros, which, according to U Thant's report to the UN Security Council, at once ruled out UNFICYP's joining the operation with the National Guard, since UNFICYP could not participate in any activity of one side against the other.

Osorio-Tafall and UNFICYP's command were outraged by this short-fused notice at a subordinate level of the National Guard and by the disregard shown by the government of Cyprus toward UNFICYP's dedicated efforts to solve the Ayios Theodhoros problem without a clash. Strong verbal protests went unheeded.

At 1330 hours local on November 14, 1967, the two Cyprus police patrols entered Ayios Theodhoros and were presently joined there by General Grivas, accompanied by correspondents who photographed him for the Greek Cypriot press. There was no roadblocking and no shooting. A telegram from Ambassador Belcher in Nicosia reported that for the moment we could all breathe easier.

Our relief was short. At 1000 hours the following morning, November 15, we learned that a third patrol, escorted by the National Guard, apparently without sending invitation or notice to UNFICYP, visited Ayios Theodhoros without resistance. A tractor barring the entrance to the village was removed by Turkish Cypriots without threat by the police or Guard.

Surely, we felt, this repeat performance—a clear departure from what had been the customary twice-a-week patrol—was enough to drive in whatever point the Makarios government or Grivas found necessary to make.

But it was not.

5
Massacre and Reaction

The word of heavy firing at Ayios Theodhoros was brought to me in the early afternoon of November 15 while I was putting in a necessary appearance at one of the innumerable diplomatic receptions of Ankara. I excused myself quickly and returned to the office to obtain details and consider next steps. A Cypriot Police patrol had already made an unresisted entry into the village that very morning, but now a fourth, heavily reinforced entry had been made and artillery was being used against TMT fighters.[30]

The moment could not have been less propitious. The Turkish government had just relaxed its negotiating position linking free access to Ayios Theodhoros with Artemis Road. It had also, though I did not know it at the moment, instructed its permanent representative to the United Nations to thank Secretary-General U Thant for his efforts in obtaining the release of Denktaş, and to state Ankara's acceptance of the UNFICYP timetable for the phased resumption of police patrols to the village, provided UNFICYP returned the Kophinou police compound to Turkish Cypriot police and redoubled its efforts to settle the Artemis Road situation.

The attitude of the Turkish Government was anything but warlike. For months the Demirel administration had been focusing its attention on internal development projects, many involving U.S. economic assistance. I had traveled to a number of groundbreaking ceremonies, meeting Demirel and his group, listening to his speeches, and taking stock of the upbeat mood of the countryside as communities anticipated increased employment. Cyprus was not in the news. In retrospect, I think it is clear that Ankara did not give the issues of Ayios Theodhoros and Larnaca the potential for serious conflict that they merited. However, all outside parties may well have become somewhat inured to shooting incidents on the island.

What was different here was the advance deployment of heavy weaponry and Greek mainland troops, not only, in battalion strength, around Skarinou, but throughout the island. Possibly, the reporting by the Turkish diplomatic mission in Nicosia was inadequate. In any event, the Ankara government seems to have been taken by surprise. So also, to some degree, was UNFICYP.

Who fired the first shots? From the UN record, it appears to have been the TMT. However, this time the UNFICYP had been given only twenty minutes' notice by the local National Guard commander—without invitation to participate as escort—that the Cyprus police would patrol into Ayios Theodhoros at 1400 hours from north and south and that the composition of the patrols would be the same as in the morning. In fact, the patrol included a platoon of infantry from the National Guard, with artillery from the south and from the main Guard unit at Skarinou.

This was a good deal more than a National Guard "escort." It was a provocation Grivas had been preparing and for which he had received the nod from Makarios. It worked. UNFICYP's remonstrances following the morning (third patrol) were ignored. In fact, the United Nations, according to Harbottle, was given five minutes' notice of the operation.

The patrol began at 1345 hours and came first from the north. When the unit found the road blocked by farm equipment, it waited for a companion patrol to arrive from the south, which included armored cars and the platoon of infantry. When the TMT shots began as the platoon started to remove the road block, the National Guard's response was immediate and general, involving not only small arms but heavy machine guns, mortars, and 2-pounders from the armored cars, directed at TMT positions and at the Turkish village of Ayios Theodhoros generally. Nine people were killed and nine wounded. According to Harbottle, many Turkish Cypriots fled across the bridge into the Greek sector and took refuge in homes of Greek Cypriot friends.[31]

This attack was at company strength. On what was called Tango Hill, the UNFICYP observation post was overrun and disarmed by the National Guard and its equipment stolen. Two other UNFICYP positions were later overrun.

The extraordinary behavior of Grivas is ascribed by Harbottle in part to Harbottle's earlier refusal to allow Grivas to forcibly occupy Melousha, a Turkish Cypriot village near Athienou, north of Larnaca. On that occasion Harbottle had spent an entire night trying to persuade Grivas not to engage in this operation and finally informed him that the intervening UNFICYP unit, a Swedish contingent with superior firepower, positioned to prevent hostilities pursuant to its mandate, would resist if an attempt were made to overrun it. Grivas was furious and withdrew, apparently determined to humiliate UNFICYP at the next opportunity. That opportunity was afforded by the action of the TMT under "Mehmet" at Ayios Theodhoros.

Grivas's forces, having gained control of the Turkish village on the heights, then turned their attention to Kophinou, two and one-half miles away. Kophinou had not been involved in the problem of access, but nearby Turkish Cypriot fighter positions had long since faced the National Guard at Skarinou. Employing 75-millimeter and 25-pounder guns, as well as the equipment used earlier, the Guard bypassed the police compound from the north on either side, bringing the UNFICYP headquarters under fire, but without UN casualties. By evening, twenty-two Turkish Cypriots had been killed, nine wounded, and considerable destruction of Kophinou had been accomplished. One National Guardsman had been killed and two Greek Cypriot policemen wounded.

Throughout these engagements, the UNFICYP observers reported the action in detail by radio from their observation posts within the fields of fire, showing great courage, never evacuating a post. Through Osorio-Tafall, they provided the secretary-general with solid facts as he vigorously sought in New York to bring about a cease-fire. By 1800 hours, the Turkish Cypriots, whose positions had been overrun, accepted the cease-fire; but the Cyprus Government was giving "consideration" to the matter until about 2030 hours, when the Guard was already in Kophinou, although not in complete control of it, and general firing had stopped of its own accord.

In New York, U Thant sought peace through the Cypriot, Greek, and Turkish permanent representatives. When the news reached Ankara of the massacre of civilians in Kophinou, Çağlayangil sent a telegram to the secretary-general saying that if the UNFICYP could not immediately clear the Turkish areas of Ayios Theodhoros and the village of Kophinou "of both Greek and Greek Cypriot armed forces—a crisis which will go beyond the borders of the island will be unavoidable."[32] U Thant at once relayed this message to Cypriot Foreign Minister Kyprianou, who replied at 2145 hours that a cease-fire had been ordered, effective immediately. It was not entirely effective, however, for firing continued until the early morning of November 16 as the Guard conducted house clearance operations in Ayios Theodhoros, after the cease-fire, until orders were received to withdraw to original positions.

The secretary-general reported to the UN Security Council that before these mopping-up operations, civilian Turkish Cypriots were moved out of danger by the Guard and "well looked after." A Greek major in command of a company of the National Guard had negotiated the exodus of Turkish Cypriot families to Skarinou.[33] This was certainly not the case at Kophinou, as I was able to confirm by a visit there in late December, and could only have occurred in Ayios Theodhoros after the above-mentioned casualties reported by Harbottle had occurred. Harbottle's statement that the TMT fighters broke and ran rather early in the Ayios Theodhoros engagement may account for the small number of their casualties.

Losses were proportionally severe in Kophinou's civilian population, however, and were of such a nature as to generate an eruption of feeling in the illustrated Turkish press, representatives of which were quick to visit the villages and fill the mainland weekend editions with bloodcurdling stories of attacks on the mosque, of the killing of civilian noncombatants in cold blood, and of the soaking in gasoline and burning alive of an eighty-year-old man. Turkish public opinion, which had been bored with the dreary Cyprus syndrome, flared like dry sawdust to which a match had been set.

At the embassy in Ankara, we knew we were in real trouble and that matters might already have passed the point of no return. Such was not yet the case, however, nor had the crisis yet played itself out on the ground. Grivas had not had enough.

On November 16 at 1550 hours, the UNFICYP commander at Kophinou was informed by the National Guard that at 1615 hours that afternoon a fifth patrol into Ayios Theodhoros would be made from Skarinou composed of Cypriot Police and National Guard. There were apparently no Turkish fighters left to offer resistance and the mission took place without incident, leaving three Land Rovers and about a dozen policemen in the Greek sector, one of whom seemed to be a member of the National Guard. This occurred despite the urgings of Osorio-Tafall to the Government of

Cyprus that after the November 15 fighting the UNFICYP timetable of patrols should be suspended temporarily. At the United Nations in New York, the Turkish permanent representative informed U Thant that Ankara looked on this November 16 patrol as a clear provocation.

A sharp dispute now flared between the UN forces and General Grivas over responsibility for the killings. U Thant had already protested vigorously to the Cyprus Government the overrunning of the first UNFICYP observation post, the disarming of its men, the theft of some of its equipment, and the destruction of its radio. Grivas now addressed its commander with two notes holding UNFICYP responsible for what had happened, since it had not helped the Cypriot Police exercise their rights! He warned that the operation then under way would require the Guard to move through certain areas, including UNFICYP positions.

All this was categorically rejected by UNFICYP's commander and by U Thant to New York representatives of Cyprus and Greece, who were urged at once to ensure termination of "all excesses" and to order a cease-fire and a pullback. U Thant concluded his report to the Security Council by saying, "the magnitude of the Ayios Theodhoros operation and the speed with which it was carried out clearly indicate that the National Guard had planned in advance to carry out this operation in the event of any show of opposition by the Turkish Cypriots."[34]

Two more patrols went into Ayios Theodhoros on November 17 and encountered no resistance. Two more patrols took place the next day, also unopposed. Altogether this made nine patrols in three days.

Makarios was much taken aback when he learned of the full extent of the damage and casualties, but his reaction was to authorize release of building materials which the Turkish villagers could use to rebuild their homes. There was no word of compensation or of reprimand for those who had committed "excesses." Never did Makarios express public regret for the killing of his Turkish co-citizens, although he was urged to do so by Americans and British as a means of cooling the atmosphere at a critical moment. This was noted by mainland Turks with deepening resentment.

Stricken Ayios Theodhoros and Kophinou now were quiet. Not so other points of confrontation on the island, where Turkish Cypriots, in anger and frustration, sniped at Greek Cypriots and manhandled an UNFICYP patrol near Kyrenia. More ominously, Turkish military aircraft from the mainland began low flights over Cyprus. Turkey now was aroused, its slumbering nationalism awakened and its sympathy for its cousins exceeded only by its anger over the overbearing use of force by large mainland Greek troops that had no treaty right to be on the island. The crisis generated by a bloody but relatively minor fracas now threatened Greek-Turkish peace.

In Ankara, Turks who had traditionally been most friendly to the United States warned me that if we intervened again, as in 1964, to prevent Turkey from rescuing its ethnic brothers in Cyprus, we would never be forgiven.

On the official front, I had been in constant communication with Kuneralp and Çağlayangil since November 14th. By November 15, Secretary Rusk, Defense Secretary McNamara, and President Johnson had weighed in with urgent messages to the Turkish government to exercise restraint, and to Makarios and the Greek Government to restore the status quo ante in Ayios Theodhoros. That meant suspending the patrols and removing the National Guard from the occupied positions, as well as permitting displaced Turkish Cypriot villagers to return to their homes. It was a race against time.

The Greek government complied, but events moved too fast. The Turkish cabinet met in emergency session throughout the nights of November 15 and 16. Kuneralp warned me that if UNFICYP (which at this stage was being primarily blamed by the Turks for negligence) could not restore the situation, Turkey would have to react, possibly by the use of aircraft. Indeed, we learned separately that twenty-five Turkish fighter-bombers were being loaded for action at Inçirlik, the base near Adana shared under NATO agreements between the United States and Turkey, with administrative command in the hands of the Turks. All principal airports in the country were now closed to civilian traffic. Six frigates and two additional naval craft left Gölçük Naval Base that day for the Aegean.

In Athens, my colleague Ambassador Phillips Talbot worked tirelessly to bring a sense of urgency to Prime Minister Kollias, who seemed always to retreat to a legalistic posture, drilled into him no doubt by many years of judicial training. Defense Minister Spandidakis was also not much help, since he tied the Turkish Cypriot resistance at Ayios Theodhoros into the entire sequence of Greek complaints over Turkish military overflights of the Aegean that autumn. These two phenomena had absolutely no connection except in his mind, and yet the fixation rendered him difficult and obdurate in Talbot's attempts to urge action upon Athens to restrain Grivas.

Fortunately, Talbot had excellent relations with King Constantine, and here I must pay tribute to the young monarch for his contributions, absolutely vital, to the avoidance of an all-out Greek-Turkish war. Constantine seemed to grasp at once the importance of restoring the status quo ante in Ayios Theodhoros and Kophinou. He acted quickly to secure an order for the National Guard to withdraw, despite Kollias's position that the National Guard was the defense organization of the government of Cyprus and that Grivas was under the orders of Makarios. Constantine accepted Talbot's point that while that might be the legal position on paper, in fact Grivas was a Lieutenant General in the Greek Army, seconded to Cyprus, and identifiable to the Turks as subject to the ultimate discipline of Greece. The orders were issued from Athens to Grivas to cease all hostilities, to withdraw his forces from the two villages, and to restore the situation as it was before.

I was able to convey this news to Kuneralp just in time, and it helped that I was able to cite King Constantine as the prime mover. Kuneralp informed me that the Turkish Air Force had been ready to depart for Cyprus at 0600 hours on the 16th. Independently, he had received word of the Greek instruction to restore the status quo ante and now, he said, we could exchange congratulations that the crisis was past. Prime Minister Demirel pronounced it finished in a press conference at 11 A.M. on November 16.

Their rejoicing was premature. There had been an intense battle of wills on the nights of the 15th and 16th in the Turkish cabinet between the hawks and the doves. Later, I was to learn that the line-up was between Demirel, Çağlayangil, and Defense Minister Ahmet Topaloğlu, who sought a peaceful solution, and provincial-minded ministers who occupied secondary cabinet positions. The latter were jingoistic in the extreme, and continued to be so until the end of the crisis. They had little notion of the larger issues involved and gave full rein to their built-in prejudice against all Greeks, a posture always popular in their constituencies. Mirror feelings against all Turks had long prevailed in Greece but, fortunately for our efforts, public opinion there could not take to the streets. The Greek military regime also censored news.

What turned the relief of the Turkish government into anger and frustration was the use by Grivas of regular Greek forces above treaty limits and the provocation of repeated patrols. Perhaps because he was, after all, a Greek general officer, Grivas avoided direct disregard of the orders of Athens. However, he apparently persuaded Makarios and Georgkhadjis to undertake the follow-up patrols, and the latter, as minister of the interior, to authorize them.

This decision was an expression of Makarios's penchant for demonstrating his independence and his deep frustration over the mess that had been created by the hostilities, with nothing to show for them. He realized on November 16 that out of twenty-three dead, twelve had been Greek Cypriots. Since Athens had demanded a return to the previous situation, the Turkish Fighters could now return to dominate the heights in their part of Ayios Theodhoros and again be able to interdict patrolling to the Greek village. Grivas swore that, in such case, he would "blast them out." Accordingly, the follow-up patrols were authorized, and it was their action that tipped the balance in the Turkish National Assembly.

In Athens, Grivas's transparent end run around his orders quickly put the government on the spot. King Constantine acted again. He ordered Grivas's recall, and Kollias was persuaded that while Grivas was technically under the orders of Makarios, he could be summoned to Athens "for consultation" and kept there. Grivas received his orders on November 17, and it was first bruited in Cyprus that he would depart on the early morning of the next day. I hastened to so inform Kuneralp, for the information of Çağlayangil (then totally absorbed with battling extreme opinion in Parliament), but urged that the news not be allowed to leak before it became public knowledge in Greece. Otherwise, the order might be cancelled, for no Greek government could appear to be bowing to Turkish pressures.

In fact, Grivas did not leave on the 18th, and two more National Guard patrols went into Ayios Theodhoros on that day in further disregard of Athens's orders. This seemed to confirm Turkish suspicions that Athens had lied and had no intention of restoring the status quo ante, despite my and Washington's representations that Greece was indeed moving decisively to do so.

It became clear also that Makarios himself was not always aware of every move, much less the extent, of National Guard activities, but that he bore the primary responsibility as head of state in not taking a position and sticking to it. He was swayed by Grivas and probably feared him. He took the occasion to order a partial distribution of the Czech arms, for his own defense. Here, Athens acted again, under American, UN, and British urging, and demanded that the Guard collect them all and turn them over to the commander of UNFICYP, General Martola. Makarios reluctantly agreed to place them where UNFICYP could inspect them on November 20. I at once brought this news to Kuneralp's attention, as a sign of Greek goodwill.

Grivas left Nicosia on a commercial flight November 19 at 0955 hours and arrived in Athens early that afternoon. But all this was too late for Turkish parliamentary and public opinion. Ankara now held Greece primarily responsible. It took the position with primary third parties, such as the United States, the United Kingdom, and Canada (but not yet publicly with Greece) that Greek forces introduced since 1964 into Cyprus (which Demirel estimated to total twenty thousand and Çağlayangil placed at twelve thousand) must be withdrawn. Otherwise Turkey would land its own forces on the island to "equalize" their strength and protect the Turkish Cypriots against further brutalization.

In Ankara and Istanbul, parades of students took on a somewhat anti-American cast, but no violence was evidenced against Greek residents or, in Istanbul, the Patriarchate.[35] Perhaps this was due to general satisfaction with Turkish military deployments already initiated. We began to learn that the Turkish First Army, normally stationed for the defense of the Bosphoros in accordance with NATO Command directives, was now being moved toward the Evros River frontier carrying bridging equipment and artillery. At the U.S. embassy we evaluated this as precautionary, in case a direct clash of Turkish and Greek forces on Cyprus should spread into general hostilities.

Situation Summary

Both Phil Talbot and I now faced the threat we had long feared most. A situation was developing where neither Greece nor Turkey could back down, and a tiny republic, whose two main communities were unable and unwilling to negotiate coexistence, would now be in a position to trigger a war that could destroy the southeastern flank of NATO. Threats to NATO, however, were clearly of no concern to Makarios.

Thus, while Ambassador Talbot and I had some, if diminishing, leverage, as representatives of the major NATO ally, on the desire of both our host countries to seek a way out of the impasse, Ambassador Belcher in Nicosia faced a chief of state much more concerned with his own authority and its consolidation in an immensely volatile and complex situation than with larger issues of regional or global peace. Makarios's superb talents lay in exploiting external pressures for his own purposes, but the opportunities were now reduced. He had skillfully manipulated Athens before the colonels took over in April, but he had little influence there now. The scenario at Ayios Theodhoros had made headlines in U Thant's reports to the UN Security Council. With both Greece and the United Nations displeased with his actions, he was isolated. Nonetheless, he was a master of resistance to pressures. He was the wild card in the pack.

Belcher labored tirelessly at every level of the higher Cypriot political structure, in closest liaison with United Nations Representative Osorio-Tafall, the Greek ambassador, the British and Canadian high commissioners, and the Turkish chargé d'affaires, while his staff worked the secondary levels. The information that poured out of his mission was indispensable to Washington, the U.S. mission to the United Nations in New York, to Talbot in Athens, and to us in Ankara. We were fully synchronized with one another and operated our embassies around the clock, but Grivas and Makarios moved events faster than Turkish public opinion could handle, or the colonels could evaluate.

On Sunday afternoon, November 19, 1967, I received a phone call from the Foreign Ministry, asking me to meet privately with Çağlayangil and his assistant secretary-general, İlter Türkmen at the Hariciye Köşkü—the foreign minister's official residence and reception halls—at 6 P.M. As it was to be two-on-two, I phoned my deputy, William C. Burdett, Jr., and we immediately went into a quick review of our strategy. The parameters and the facts were clear, but we had no way of knowing what the Turkish approach would be. I found it slightly encouraging that we were not called to the ministry itself, which had a formal atmosphere and was always surrounded by an alert and intrusive press. We sensed Çağlayangil's desire for privacy and welcomed it, but we were sure the meeting would be a maximum test of our resources if war was to be avoided.

Part 2
Crisis Diplomacy

6
The Five Points

In the main hall of the Hariciye Köşkü, İhsan Sabri Çağlayangil and İlter Türkmen welcomed us cordially and informally. Çağlayangil directed us to a corner of the room and took orders for the usual tea or Turkish coffee. He spared us a recitation of the gravity of the situation, well known to us from many sessions with him, including one earlier that very day. Could I suggest a way out of the current crisis? The question was direct and personal.

Burdett and I were immediately aware that this was the foreign minister's last chance for a peaceful approach, for he had been under tremendous pressure from party and cabinet hawks and his public statements had been very tough, in order not to lose his credibility. Çağlayangil was eloquent on the floor of the National Assembly. He had been educated in the Eastern classics, including Arabic script and Persian poetry, and he spoke with an Ottoman elegance forgotten by most Turks but admired. His philosophy was that, with patience, all problems could be worked out short of violence, that the possibilities of accommodation by give-and-take were limitless.

We were dealing therefore with an eminently reasonable man, caught up in the interplay of powerful forces. It might well be his last chance for an alternative to a Turkish military action, which would at once meet mainland Greek forces in Cyprus commanded by Grivas and trigger general war between Turkey and Greece.

We had gone over this ground innumerable times within the embassy and with the Department of State. All sorts of ultimate solutions had been explored. None were relevant at this juncture. The imperative was to show that military intervention was *unnecessary*, instead of trying to persuade Turkey that it was not in its interest to risk war.

Çağlayangil well knew that script and how to use it in the National Assembly, but he could only use it effectively if practical alternatives were offered and fully supported by the United States, Turkey's most important ally. At once, therefore, I responded to his request to suggest a way out by giving him my own distillation of a peaceful alternative. I was confident that even without advance clearance by Washington it would be generally approved. In any case, that risk was now to be taken, and I knew Washington had nothing better immediately at hand.

I emphasized to Çağlayangil that it was of utmost importance not to issue an ultimatum to Greece or otherwise humiliate that country. He at once interjected that no ultimatum had been sent. (This referred to the Turkish note we knew had been dispatched but had not ourselves seen.) I said that I hoped Turkey would consider how counterproductive it would be to put Greece into a corner where resistance to military threats would become a matter of national honor. Çağlayangil at once agreed, and I felt encouraged.

I said that a withdrawal of the excess Greek troops must therefore be balanced with a withdrawal of over-treaty Turkish military personnel, who we knew were present on the island, albeit in far less numbers than the Greeks. Çağlayangil at first asserted that he knew of none, but Türkmen said there were about thirty-five. While I felt this was probably very low, and perhaps Belcher's estimate of three hundred to four hundred was closer to the mark, the point was to seek equilibrium in an agreement and not to quibble over numbers at this stage.[36]

After a Greek withdrawal, I said, something would have to be done to disarm the bands and militias which operated irresponsibly and outside of the treaty limits and to strengthen the role of UNFICYP to do this and to keep order. Again he agreed, and I went on to propose that the Cyprus Police be reconstituted on national Cypriot lines as a mixed Greek-Turkish force. Çağlayangil was less enthusiastic about this, but seemed to weigh it. The security of Turkish Cypriot communities must be protected by special measures, he said.

Discussion proceeded for about two hours, at the end of which we had a draft proposal of five points, more or less as follows:

(1) The Government of Turkey would reassert its commitment to the inviolability and integrity of the Republic of Cyprus.

(2) All Greek and Turkish troops over those permitted by the London-Zürich Treaties would be withdrawn.

(3) UNFICYP would supervise these withdrawals and would collect arms from unauthorized civilians and militias. Its role on the island would be greatly strengthened by an enlarged mandate from the United Nations, to enable it to keep the peace. The regular Cyprus police, now divided and deployed on confessional lines, would be reconstituted and strengthened as a mixed Greek-Turkish Cypriot force, to replace the irregular bands.

(4) Payment would be made of an indemnity to the Turkish Cypriot victims of Ayios Theodhoros and Kophinou.

(5) Security measures of a special kind would be devised to protect Turkish Cypriot communities not now protected by Cypriot police or the National Guard.

The essence of this proposal was to retain the London-Zürich Agreements as the foundation stone of the Republic of Cyprus and to stop violence, giving the United Nations a central role in domestic peace until the two communities had settled down and learned to live together. The guarantors of the Republic would continue to be, in addition to Turkey, the United Kingdom and Greece, which would have to be approached with all persuasion and speed—the United Kingdom first, then Greece. With Greece would come the critical test. It was therefore agreed that I would present this formula to Washington at once, to seek U.S. government backing and help in obtaining the support of the other guarantors.

I left the meeting with a feeling that we had a fighting chance for peace, but the next hours were crucial. Burdett and I entered into an accelerated tempo and hardly left the office from then on, day and night. We delegated to others all embassy business unrelated to the crisis.

Our first job was to draft and send by the fastest means a summary of the meeting and the five points agreed upon. This was on its way in about fifteen minutes. Burdett then drafted a more detailed account, which we edited with the utmost care and sent out by highest precedence. Our communications were direct, and self-contained in the chancery.[37] There was no secret about these facilities. Some ten years earlier, when such systems were first installed in embassies, they were unacknowledged, and this applied to embassies of all countries that could afford to have them. Not now. Before the end of this affair, the Turkish government itself was to ask to use our equipment for a FLASH message in the clear.

I urged the secretary of state to wire back the same day for the personal attention of the foreign minister a statement that he found the tenor of Çağlayangil's five points to be positive, thus giving him something to use to forestall military action. Rusk did so at once, to my relief, and said there would be a follow-up within hours. This was vital to enable Çağlayangil to fend off the mounting impatience of the hawks. The shadow over us all was the Johnson letter to Ismet İnönü of June 5, 1964, and the clear determination of the Turkish public not to again be "threatened" away from what was profoundly felt to be a duty of national honor, to protect their ethnic brethren on the island.

It was now November 20, and in Washington the strategy took on a tripartite form: the closest U.S. coordination with Britain and Canada.[38] This was done for the very good reason that these two were not only members of NATO but fellow associates with the Republic of Cyprus in the Commonwealth of Nations. They also had troop contingents in UNFICYP and Britain, as the former colonial power and keeper of the peace had retained two sovereign areas on the island.

Canada had long been restive under the unpopular burden of its contribution of men to UNFICYP and wanted a settlement of this irritating problem so that its men could be brought home. To that end, in coordination with planners in our State Department, it had drafted a "Declaration of Reconciliation," which it now sought to bring into play. It was agreed that such a document could not be used until after emergency measures to forestall war had been accepted by the parties, who would then be willing, it was hoped, to sit down and discuss fundamentals.

Action between the three was swift. As I recall events, we in Ankara received instructions on November 21 to present, with our British and Canadian colleagues, a proposed formula for Greek acceptance which, with preambular references to the seriousness of the crisis and its significance for NATO, proposed the five points intact, embellished a bit and improved upon by reference to the "spirit of Evros," with an eye to Greek acceptance. At the end, the hope was expressed that, assuming acceptance of the proposed steps, the governments of Turkey and Greece would subsequently meet face to face, perhaps in a third country, to discuss a basic settlement. Canada would then pass to Turkey and to Greece the draft "Declaration of Reconciliation" and verbally offer to host such a meeting. (In the end, the draft declaration was offered informally by Canada as a "working paper" in Athens, then Ankara. By then, however, it had been overtaken by events.)[39]

My colleagues for the approach to the government of Turkey were Sir Roger Allen, ambassador from London, and Klaus Goldschlag, Berlin-born ambassador from Ottawa. Allen was a veteran of the Middle East branch of the British Foreign Service. As he and I had similar backgrounds, we had been on very easy and friendly terms from the time he arrived. He had been absent when the crisis broke, but returned quickly for tripartite duties. Goldschlag was a former aide to Canada's prime minister, Lester Pearson. Highly motivated and full of energy, he was new at the post and eager to play an active role.

After preliminary consultation, we three met with Çağlayangil at the Hariciye Köşkü and presented back to him his embellished five points. He made two editorial amendments, both easy to accept. One clarified that the non-Cypriot forces to be removed were those introduced after the end of 1963. This covered the start of major violence. The other stated that direct talks between Athens and Ankara would begin only after Greece had agreed to the withdrawal of its forces introduced after the end of 1963 and after such withdrawal had actually started. I remonstrated that for the wording to be acceptable, it would have to be general and not apply to Greeks alone. Once again, Çağlayangil attempted to assert that no mainland Turkish troops were on the island, but I said that I had in mind the thirty-five officers mentioned earlier and also some publicity in the Turkish press regarding a mainland Turkish officer who had been captured, tortured, and then released. The matter was dropped and the language kept general. Otherwise, the five points bore his approval for presentation to the Greek government.

In Greece, the aging Panayotis Pipinelis had been sworn in as foreign minister on November 20. He was not eager to take on the job. Having served as one of Greece's top diplomats under democratic governments, he apparently did not relish being called back from retirement to serve the colonels. Yet, being a patriot, he accepted, on the condition that he have a free hand and not be subordinated to the prime minister. Papadopoulos accepted and kept the cabinet well informed. It was a favorable sign as far as it went, for Kollias had been anything but helpful since his rebuff at the Evros talks.

On the same day, Manlio Brosio, secretary-general of NATO, who had been watching the developing tension with understandable alarm, offered his good offices to Athens and Ankara. NATO headquarters was being kept fully informed, but a central role for him, as matters developed, was never found.

My Greek colleague in Ankara was haunting my phone and office with understandable anxiety and impatience. A career diplomat very loyal to the king (and not to the colonels), as well as very anti-Makarios, Miltiades Delivanis and I had had an excellent relationship. He had been frank with me, and now I had to be less than forthcoming with him. Prior to the setting up of the tripartite initiative, I was by no means at liberty to tell him about the five points and thereby alert his government. I did, however, obtain Washington's permission to give him a general briefing on the flavor of my frequent discussions with Çağlayangil and to recommend "personally" that he suggest to Pipinelis that, as new foreign minister, he communicate at once with his colleague Çağlayangil and say that he would like to pay him an immediate call in Ankara, to become acquainted and to exchange views on a situation he personally felt should never have been allowed to get out of hand. I felt sure that Çağlayangil could not refuse. Delivanis agreed and undertook to transmit the advice.

But the clock was ticking too fast—too fast also for another act of appeasement to have much effect. On November 20, as scheduled, the UNFICYP commander inspected the cache of Czechoslovak arms acquired by Makarios and verified that most, if not all, were in place. A raindrop on a forest fire.

On Cyprus, the high commissioners of Britain and Canada were sensitive to their Commonwealth relationship with Makarios and proposed to show him the five points at once. Belcher recommended against such action in advance of approval of the points by Athens, pointing out that Makarios had wrecked the Acheson Plan in 1964 by revealing it to the press and at the same time denouncing it. The State Department agreed and instructed him that if his colleagues called on Makarios for that purpose, he was not to accompany them.

The instruction arrived too late. Belcher did accompany the British and Canadian high commissioners and, to our general relief, Makarios at once took a positive view of the five points, except for reservations regarding compensation to the Turkish Cypriot victims and the special security measures to be taken to protect Turkish Cypriots not now effectively covered by adequate means. These items, he said, related to internal considerations and he would have to discuss them with his cabinet. As far as non-Cypriot forces were concerned, he had long wanted them out, no matter their origin.

This emphatic expression gave clarity to something many of us had suspected, that Grivas and his Greek troops were almost a state within a state and were a threat to Makarios's clear and untrammeled authority, something more important to him by far than union with Greece. I had asked Kuneralp on one occasion if he really bought the thesis that Makarios was for *enosis*. "Of course not, Pete," was his immediate reply. It also cast light on the order for Czech arms that had caused so much disturbance in Ankara but were probably destined to provide Makarios with a Pretorian Guard of his own.

In Athens, the five points were presented to Pipinelis by Ambassador Talbot and his British and Canadian colleagues. They learned that only then were the Greeks replying to the Turkish note of November 17, which neither the U.S. government nor the others had yet seen. We were to learn that Çağlayangil's message to Pipinelis's predecessor had been toughly worded. True, it was not an ultimatum, but it came close to having that flavor. It made Pipinelis's job more difficult and eliminated the likelihood that he could accept my recommendation of a quick visit to Ankara. It would look too much like panic.

As it developed, the Greek reply in no way met Turkish requirements, since it did not agree to an early draw-down of over-treaty troops, but to a dialogue which could only be conducted in an atmosphere free of threats. This was November 22. The texts were wired back to us in Ankara, in translation. What had seemed to be progress was now stopped cold, and the likelihood of Turkish military action on the island appeared almost a certainty. Nonetheless, the tripartite group immediately urged Pipinelis to accept the Çağlayangil five points forthwith. He made no promise.

Prior to the démarche in Athens, the State Department wired me urgently seeking confirmation of certain reports which both they and I had received, namely that the Turks were planning a landing on Cyprus for November 23. I had replied that this could well be the case, but I felt that at this stage they would wait until a Greek reply to their earlier note had been received. Now it had been received, and Athens had not demonstrated any haste to embrace the five points.

It was obvious that the mood in Turkey had not impressed Athens with its deadly seriousness. Either Delivanis was not reporting it effectively or he was not believed, and that despite some very tough talk to him by Çağlayangil, which Delivanis reported to me, to the effect that unless those extra Greek forces were withdrawn, the Turkish Army would go in to create a balance. If this were opposed, Turkey would fight its way in. Delivanis hoped that peace could be preserved. Çağlayangil replied that he hoped so too, but that hope was almost dead.

On Cyprus, Belcher was unable, despite all his best efforts, to convince Kyprianou and Makarios that the United States could not possibly stop the Turks if they decided to move. Some ten days earlier he had sent U.S. dependents and nonessential staff to "safe haven" in Beirut, but there were still over one hundred at the embassy and at U.S. official radio stations elsewhere.

In Turkey we now had practice blackouts and the installation of antiaircraft on the edges of the city. We sent guidance to our consulates general in Istanbul and Izmir and to the consulate in Adana the essence of which was to put them on alert, to avoid crowds, but not as yet to call for implementation of evacuation plans. Such plans are standard around a troubled world and are routinely checked and updated in most areas where war could start.

Troop movements became far more intensive, and there was nothing secret about them. Nor, we felt, were they done for effect. Rather, they were businesslike, encompassing mobilization of naval forces with landing craft from Gölçük; the loading of Turkish aircraft with napalm, as well as bombs, at the U.S.–Turkish Air Force combined facility in Inçirlik; and much activity at the NATO-shared facilities in Çiğli, near Izmir. Troop ships were being loaded at Mersin, where we estimated fifty thousand of the Army had been mobilized. The napalm, loaded in the morning, had to be expended in the desert near Konya every evening. Another batch was loaded the next morning.

In Greece, we learned that the Royal Hellenic Air Force was readied for one-way missions against Turkish troop ships—one-way because it was assumed that Rhodes airport would be taken out by Turkish forces and post-strike refueling, therefore, denied. The RHAF would thus have almost no time over target, or it would be unable to return to Crete or other Greek bases.

Time, however, was running out.

7
Shuttle Diplomacy: The Mission of Cyrus Vance

By November 22, only hours counted, not days. Public positions were being taken in Turkey from which it was increasingly unlikely there could be a retreat. Demirel had sent a much-publicized, supportive telegram to Fazil Küçük, the Turkish Cypriot leader, which was very tough in tone but nevertheless called for "common sense" and "endurance" by the Turkish Cypriot community. In Greece, the press was controlled by the regime. We were relieved that mobs were not in the street, as might have been the case had a democratic government been in power. It would have been under irresistible pressures to take a defiant stance. The mood in Ankara was brittle enough as it was, and anything but a forthcoming Greek reply was sure to ignite an angry "I told you so" among the hawks in Ankara's cabinet and in the Grand National Assembly. The Justice Party was being shaken to pieces by radicals within its ranks and by opposition taunts.

In New York, an incredibly lethargic attitude prevailed in the office of the secretary-general of the United Nations. When the five points were presented to U Thant with the urgent recommendation that he use them in some form to make an appeal to the parties beyond generalities, he refused to do so unless it was made clear that the details would be accepted in advance by all the parties and that the funding would be guaranteed for the enlarged mandate of UNFICYP. He had no such funds at hand and required a pledge. Indeed, he had just gone through a financial problem with the UN Observer Team in the Yemen civil war. (I knew this story firsthand from my participation in the diplomatic efforts to resolve the Yemen crisis, as ambassador in Jeddah, where I had witnessed the reluctance of the secretary-general to take action for peace unless he had everyone on board and all arrangements agreed upon. I often reflected on how differently a Dag Hammersjöld might have handled it.)

U Thant also had another problem. Neither the Soviet Union nor France—both with veto power in the Security Council—would permit funding, if they could prevent it, of a more effective peacekeeping role for United Nations forces. It was a matter of principle for both. Furthermore, Makarios had expressed objections.

The able U.S. ambassador to the United Nations, former Justice Arthur J. Goldberg, was wrestling with this problem. He kept up the pressure on U Thant, who finally moved to send an emissary to the area—José Rolz-Bennett, a Guatemalan diplomat of great ability and experience. The trouble was that Rolz-Bennett had only his good offices to offer and no specifics. What was needed was a mediator with full powers and the ability to take action.

At this point I received instructions from Secretary of State Rusk to inform the Turkish government that President Johnson wished to send to Ankara and then to Athens his personal representative, a man in whom he had absolute confidence, Cyrus Roberts Vance.

Vance, until shortly before, had been deputy secretary of defense and had made a reputation as the president's troubleshooter. I was to inform the Turkish government that Vance would embark by presidential aircraft that very afternoon about 5:00 P.M. EDT. The wording of the message was a request to receive Vance, but made clear it was too late to stop him. The Foreign Ministry was very courteous about it and, after checking with the prime minister, gave their approval.

İlter Türkmen has authorized my inclusion in this book of his version of the Turkish government's reaction to President Johnson's move: When he received the message from me by phone, Türkmen at once informed Çağlayangil and Kuneralp, who were much concerned. Çağlayangil said he would discuss the question in a forthcoming cabinet meeting. Türkmen responded that there was nothing to discuss; Vance was already en route. Kuneralp took the position that Vance was a "living Johnson letter" (referring, of course, to the letter of June 5, 1964, to Prime Minister İnönü) and that the mission should be rejected. Çağlayangil took the matter at once to the cabinet, which provisionally agreed with Kuneralp.

When Çağlayangil emerged, a lively argument ensued with Türkmen, who stressed that the Turkish government could take any position it wished after Vance's arrival, but it was not possible to tell the president of the United States to turn the aircraft around, saying that it would not receive his envoy. Voices rose, and Prime Minister Demirel, whose office was adjacent, came out to learn why they were shouting. Çağlayangil and Türkmen each stated his case. Demirel finally agreed with Türkmen, called back his cabinet, and obtained its concurrence. Later that evening, Kuneralp (who was and is a man of great integrity) came to Türkmen and apologized for shouting at him, saying that, on reflection, he agreed with him. (This, I would add, is characteristic of the integrity of Kuneralp, one of the finest men I met in thirty-one years of foreign service.)

As Vance told me later, he had been reached in his New York law office at 11:30 A.M. that Wednesday morning, November 22, by order of the president. The call to Vance came from Deputy Secretary of State Nicholas deB. Katzenbach on the recommendation of Lucius D. Battle, assistant secretary for Near East and South Asian affairs.[40] Vance had been planning a Thanksgiving weekend with his family, beginning the very next day, and had packed for that purpose and was clearing his desk. He now called his wife and asked her to grab his suitcase and meet him at Kennedy Airport, where Air Force One would be standing by.[41]

In Washington, four other people were mobilized with equally short notice and made similar arrangements for delivery of baggage: John P. Walsh, executive secretary for Secretary of State Rusk and a court reporter; John Howison, the Foreign Service officer holding the post of country director for Turkish affairs in the Department of State; Captain Edward Hollyfield USN of the Bureau of International Security Affairs, Department of Defense; and Ellen Johnson, top-flight typist, carrying a new portable electric typewriter with a small transformer with which to handle Vance's correspondence. Battle accompanied this group to Kennedy Airport, where he gave Vance an indispensable, greatly condensed briefing before take-off, then returned to Washington to backstop the mission.

The pilot of Air Force One had just received his orders, totally changing his previous instructions, and had had time only to fuel the plane, not to lay in food for the trip. On board were coffee and cornflakes with some milk. Howison, Walsh, and Hollyfield had brought briefing materials, including all my recent reports from the embassy to the department, and were fully primed for the long trip. Vance gave the order to forget about food and get underway. It was a long twelve hours in that chilly KC-135, a converted Boeing 707 tanker without windows.

In Ankara, November 23, Thanksgiving Day, dawned. Weeks before, my wife Jane had invited a few guests to share our fat American turkey, purchased from the Air Force Exchange and now being cooked under her supervision by Hasan "Usta," our Bolu chef. (Almost all good cooks in Turkey traditionally come from that mountain village on the road to Istanbul.) I went out to Murted Air Force Base just before 2:00 P.M. to meet the plane. A landing at the Ankara civilian field, Esenboğa, had been scratched to avoid a student demonstration against Vance, who was rumored to be bringing another "Johnson letter threatening Turkey."

At Murted, the Turkish commander greeted me cordially and informed me that the plane was on schedule. Under a high overcast and chill wind, Vance disembarked wearing a very light overcoat and battered felt hat, smiling cheerfully. He was followed by his team who did not look at all bedraggled but indicated they could use some food. I told them that Thanksgiving dinner was still on the table and we made haste over the twenty-odd miles to Ankara and the residence at Çankaya. On the way I brought Vance up to date on developments.

Our guests had eaten, and Jane had discreetly moved them to one of the large living rooms well away from the dining area. The turkey and fixings were kept warm. I seated my party and then made my apologies to my friends. They did not ask for details, not even the names of my hungry group, but they understood the nature of the situation. I phoned İlter Türkmen to say our team had arrived and asked to take them to the prime minister as soon as they had eaten.

We made it hurriedly through the main course, whereupon Vance said that we had best get about our business. We set off at once for the Baş Bakanlik, a structure linked with the Foreign Ministry. It was surrounded by Turkish newsmen. I had primed Vance before his departure that the local press corps were very excited and would zero in on him about whether he was bringing another "Johnson letter." Fortunately, we managed to avoid any sort of comment as we entered the building.

We found Prime Minister Demirel in his outer office, surrounded by several aides, including Çağlayangil and Türkmen. Unlike the jolly, relaxed and cordial personality I had come to know very well, Demirel was now extremely tense, his eyes red from lack of sleep and his expression haunted. I introduced Vance and his group.

Vance opened by saying that President Johnson sent his personal greetings and was naturally very concerned over the tension that had developed and had asked him to make the journey to see if there was some way in which he might be helpful. He was anxious to hear the prime minister's views. Walsh took out his notebook and recorded verbatim all that followed.[42]

Demirel launched into an uncharacteristically emotional monologue which reflected the mood of cabinet members in the room. He described the plight of the Turkish Cypriots and how intolerable their situation had become. Their oppression by the Greek Cypriots and the mainland Grivas forces, which he said numbered twenty thousand, had been going on for years and had now reached the point at which it could no longer be endured.[43] This was plain brutality and enslavement. The presentation to Turkey of the Tripartite Proposal of Five Points had come to nothing and was worse than useless, because it called for Greek-Turkish talks on generalities and had served Greek ends in preventing Turkey from reacting militarily. The proposal was a bad idea in the first place.

At this point I intervened to straighten out the record. I recounted how I had been invited by the foreign minister on November 19 to propose a course of action alternative to war; that Çağlayangil and I had at once agreed on the principle that there was to be no ultimatum to Greece and no diplomatic victory or defeat; that the five points were approved in outline by Çağlayangil; and that my British and Canadian colleagues had then joined me, on instructions, in a proposal faithful to these points, which was edited by Çağlayangil for presentation to Greece with the full backing of the governments of the United States, the United Kingdom, and Canada.

There was a moment of tension in the air between Demirel and the foreign minister, who asked me very carefully if I had made clear in my message to be passed to Athens that the crisis required action in hours, not days, and that there could be no negotiations until after the excess Greek troops had begun their withdrawal. I replied that I had, and that, as he and I had agreed, the message was that no direct Greek-Turkish talks could begin until a start had been made on the withdrawal. This seemed to end the controversy. It was now clear that Demirel had not been fully briefed or had not absorbed all that he had been told.

Throughout the discussion Vance raised only a few questions. One of these was whether Demirel would agree to a formula by which Turkey would begin demobilization as Greece began withdrawals from Cyprus. Demirel rejected this. At the end of an hour or more, when Demirel had finished, Vance thanked him, said that he felt he now had a grasp of the situation, and proposed to go at once to Athens to see what he could do. First, however, he wished to pay a call on President Sunay, if that could be arranged. Demirel responded affirmatively and gave instructions. We then took our departure. As we left, I wondered whether I had created trouble between Çağlayangil and Demirel and between Çağlayangil and the cabinet. I decided I had not, but that it was profitless to worry; the stakes were too high.

We were admitted promptly to the office of President Sunay and found the atmosphere there very different. Cevdet Sunay was an imposing, calm, and kindly figure. He was a full general of the Turkish Army and had been a defender of Jerusalem in World War I against the British forces led by Allenby, who had taken him prisoner. Over the years of the Turkish Republic, he remained in the Army and rose to be Chief of Army Staff. When I first met him, he had become chairman of the Joint Chiefs. He had succeeded to the presidency in 1966 by overwhelming vote of the Grand National Assembly, after it was determined the incumbent president, General Cemal Gürsel, had suffered permanent brain damage from a stroke and could no longer function. Sunay's duties as president were largely honorary and ceremonial, but his prestige was so great that if he took a position on an important matter, it was unlikely that he would be contradicted.

Our visit with him was brief but reassuring. He was accompanied only by an interpreter. Fully informed and with a very reflective demeanor, he wished Vance success in Athens and pointed out that time was of the essence. We felt we had a window of opportunity, small though it was.

In the late afternoon of that November 23, an unpleasant event had occurred—a student demonstration in the Kızılay section of downtown Ankara against U.S. Cyprus policy. It focused on the United States Information Service offices, and several windows had been broken, people hurt, and the office closed. Informed of this, I decided that it was time to evidence impatience and not just concern. My representations to the Foreign Ministry were therefore heated, and I used strong language.

It registered, and was useful, I was to learn years later, in confrontations by irresponsible hawks in the Turkish cabinet with the prime minister and the foreign minister. Demirel argued that my "loss of temper" was that of a friend of Turkey and that I had made a valid point in stressing that matters could get out of hand if Turkey did not protect Americans. Together with the Vance mission, it figured in renewed debate over the American relationship, which continued vigorously over the following days, a reflection of aroused nationalism in the general public. Çağlayangil was asked to assuage and reassure me and did so. Although we had no further demonstrations in Ankara, I was to learn that the student right was moving to join the opposing left in challenging the NATO, as well as the American, connection as not consonant with Turkey's vital interests. Aggravation of this trend was directed against my successor, Robert Komer, in 1969.

After refreshment, Vance and party were off for Murted and were airborne by about 10:00 P.M. I returned to the office to make my own report on the day's events. Then a bit of sleep seemed to be the best possible use of my time, for the hours ahead would be crowded.

Vance and party were not to enjoy such rest. They were met in Athens by Phillips Talbot and began a strategy session, lining up appointments for that very night.

Vance reported to Foreign Minister Pipinelis on his talks with Demirel and Sunay. Pipinelis's reaction was at first very negative, but in due time he got down to practical consideration of Çağlayangil's five points and the necessity of providing Vance with something he could carry back to Ankara. He appeared unaware that Greek forces on the island greatly outnumbered those of Turkey. His chief concern with withdrawals seemed to be the prospect of wholesale violence between Greek and Turkish Cypriots once non-Cypriot forces pulled out. This could trigger a Turkish military intervention. He was also unwilling to appear to be making major concessions in the face of the Turkish buildup of forces on the Thracian frontier. What therefore emerged from strenuous negotiations with Vance throughout November 24 was a modification of the five points.

Vance now decided on a significant reinforcement of the approach.

Concluding that neither side would give in on a purely bilateral basis, he sought the Department of State's assistance through the permanent representative of the United States at the United Nations, Ambassador Goldberg, to prepare the ground for personal appeals by the secretary-general to the parties, to be issued when Vance gave the signal. The essence of the appeal to be addressed to Greece, Turkey, and Cyprus would be that they take no military action, and to Greece and Turkey that they undertake to withdraw all non-Cypriot troops above those authorized by the London-Zürich treaties. The United States would seek endorsement of such an agreement by all UN Security Council members, by members of NATO, and by contributors to UNFICYP. Vance therefore formulated his proposal with Pipinelis as a Greek-Turkish undertaking to respond favorably to an urgent appeal by the secretary-general. When such bilateral agreement was reached November 25, he would fly to Cyprus.

Vance and Pipinelis therefore worked on an embodiment of the five points in a more elaborate appeal to the three parties to concur in a phased withdrawal of *all* non-Cypriot forces, including national contingents authorized by the London-Zürich treaties, to be synchronized with the reconstitution of a more effective Cypriot Police and its deployment with new duties. A key point for Vance was to induce the Greeks to agree to an initial withdrawal of some forces with minimum delay and without awaiting the start of Turkish demobilization, in order to show a will for peace and to avert a precipitous Turkish military move into Cyprus. It was made clear to Vance in Athens that such a move by Turkey would involve hostilities with regular Greek forces on the island and a quick escalation into an all-out Greek-Turkish war.

To reach this vital agreement, Greece needed an arrangement that would appear to be not a surrender but, rather, an act of cooperation with the United Nations in bolstering the Republic of Cyprus in its requirements for law and order. A particularly sensitive point for Pipinelis was *simultaneity* in the start of the Greek withdrawal with a beginning of the standdown of Turkish mobilization on the Thracian frontier. This deployment was a direct threat against which Greece was only partially, and with reluctance, mobilizing its own forces. I read this to mean that Greece did not want to risk a hair-trigger confrontation, for the colonels knew that a war would be a disaster. Every step would therefore be taken to avert it unless Greece was humiliated or its forces directly attacked.

Vance made clear to Pipinelis that he could not sell exact simultaneity to Ankara in the present state of Turkish public excitement and outrage. Pipinelis therefore agreed to a provision whereby simultaneity would be observed on paper, but Pipinelis would authorize Vance to say verbally that Greece would consider simultaneity to be satisfied if, within four hours after the start of a Greek withdrawal, Turkey would begin a standdown of its mobilization. (This point, along with the text as a whole, had to have cabinet clearance, and it caused much argument. In the end, it was King Constantine who swung opinion to its acceptance.) From there on the phased withdrawal-standdown would be tied to the UNFICYP's progress in training, reorganizing, and effectively deploying a reconsitituted CYPOL.

It took all of the night of November 24 for Vance to work this out and for the Greek cabinet to clear it. Vance made calls on Prime Minister Kollias and King Constantine (who had insisted on the withdrawal of Grivas, now back in Greece). He also called on Rolz-Bennett, whom the UN secretary-general had sent to the area after concluding that the situation was critical.

Finally aroused, U Thant also despatched during November 24, on his own, an appeal to Greece, Turkey, and Cyprus in very strong terms to exercise restraint and to avoid all acts or threats of force, or they would bear responsibility for war. He urged all three parties to agree upon a "substantial reduction" by phases of all non-Cypriot forces, other than UNFICYP, leading to their total withdrawal from Cyprus. This would make possible the "positive demilitarization of Cyprus." He assured the parties that UNFICYP would be available to help carry out this withdrawal and maintain calm on the island. He ended by invoking the obligations of the UN Charter, including respect for the "sovereignty, independence and territorial integrity of the Republic of Cyprus," and called on all governments concerned to refrain from any military intervention in the affairs of that republic.

The Greek government informed Vance that he could tell the Turkish government that Athens was willing to put its proposal, if accepted, into effect by 2000 hours of November 25.

Meanwhile, Çağlayangil summoned me on November 24 to say that a decision of the ruling Justice Party, now virtually final, had been reached to send forces into Cyprus without further delay and that the only chance to avert this would be a quick and favorable answer from Athens to his five points. He felt that it was vital to receive this by 6:00 P.M. that day. I relayed this to Vance at once and he replied, asking me to tell the foreign minister that he found this position most disappointing. It bore the flavor of an ultimatum and jeopardized his mission. He was about to meet again with Pipinelis to finalize a proposal which he would submit in Ankara and asked for a meeting with Çağlayangil for November 25 at 10:00 A.M.

Çağlayangil agreed immediately to see Vance, but as he was scheduled to participate in a National Security Council meeting at 9:30 A.M., he set the time for Vance at 8:00 A.M. and invited us all for breakfast at the Hariciye Köşkü.

I met Vance's plane at Murted at 5:30 A.M., November 25, and read his points over carefully as we drove into Ankara. Vance had not slept in three days but was buoyant and encouraged. Retaining a Greek-Turkish commitment to the inviolability of Cyprus, the personal appeal of the secretary-general to all parties would call on them not to threaten one another, but to act to reduce tensions; and to agree to a total disarmament of Cyprus, with the phased withdrawal of all non-Cypriot forces, including the national treaty contingents, in favor of a reconstituted CYPOL endowed with an enlarged mandate for the protection of all minorities. Greek withdrawals would begin at once and consist of a negotiable number, say five hundred, to be matched by a progressive Turkish standdown from its present mobilization. This apparent simultaneity of action was qualified by the private verbal message authorized by Pipinelis.

The proposal that Vance carried was therefore quite in tune with U Thant's November 24 appeal, but moved it several important steps farther, some of which would require the consent of Makarios. However, Vance was certain that a bilateral Greek-Turkish agreement must be achieved before he visited Cyprus, in order to stop the impending war and forestall a possible Makarios move to wreck the agreement, as he had the Acheson Plan of 1964.

Meanwhile, we learned, U.S. Ambassador Goldberg was to brief the UN secretary-general in New York on the broad principles being sought by Vance, especially those requiring UN assistance to a reconstituted CYPOL. U Thant had already heard from Rolz-Bennett and indicated to Goldberg that funding for such an enlarged UNFICYP role would have to be guaranteed in writing by the U.S. government; that the agreement should be endorsed by all three parties before he would issue the appeal; and that he doubted that the Turks would accept this Greek proposal. It was vintage U Thant; but on the last point, he was right on the mark.

At 8:00 A.M. on the 25th, we found the Hariciye Köşkü all set to serve a Western-style scrambled eggs breakfast to the entire U.S. team and several members of Çağlayangil's staff, headed by İlter Türkmen. Vance immediately tabled his proposal, with the optimistic statement that he felt he had something the Turks could accept. He read the full text, then added that five hundred Greek troops would begin the withdrawal at once, as soon as U Thant's appeal was accepted and publicly announced. Turkish military standdown could begin four hours later.

Çağlayangil gave the proposal very cursory treatment. He rather derided the four hours and declared that the proposal was totally unsatisfactory. While the breakfast cooled, Vance remonstrated and attempted to stress what it had taken for the Greeks to reach the terms now offered. To my astonishment, Çağlayangil hardly seemed to be listening. His attitude and manner were totally out of character. He said that it was possible that the NSC might decide otherwise, but he could not recommend this document. He left abruptly for the National Security Council.

I told İlter Türkmen that I would be grateful if he would phone Çağlayangil at the NSC and tell him for me that, if this proposal were rejected out of hand, I would personally conclude that we never had a chance from the beginning. Türkmen started for the phone, and Vance reinforced to him my sentiments. In addition, he asked for a meeting with President Sunay on an urgent basis. Türkmen made the phone call.

Many years later, he told me how it had gone. Çağlayangil had not yet reported to the NSC. Türkmen told him that his rather dramatic rejection had aroused the American side and caused all to be very upset. Çağlayangil wanted to know how upset. Türkmen said "plenty upset" and repeated my and Vance's words, saying that Vance wanted a meeting with Sunay as soon as possible. Çağlayangil said that he would call back. When he did, Türkmen appeared to have obtained authorization to discuss the Greek proposal with us. He suggested we eat and then go over the terms. Famished, we were glad to comply on both counts. During the discussion that followed, notice was delivered to us that President Sunay would receive Vance around noon.

The Turkish and American military teams managed to do much more than edit. With Vance and Türkmen going over the text article by article, a considerable amount was accomplished in the direction of acceptance of most of the Greek-Vance proposal, but not on simultaneity.

Vance, Walsh, and I met with President Sunay, Demirel, and Çağlayangil soon after noon at the presidential palace. Vance presented to Sunay the personal good wishes of King Constantine. Sunay was obviously gratified and asked Vance to convey his appreciation and warm greetings to the king. Vance then asked Sunay if he could be assured that, during his mission, Turkey would not initiate military action. The president replied that Vance could have his word on that, but should count the time available in hours, rather than days. Subsequently, he reconsidered and removed that qualification, to our vast relief.

Vance then reviewed the history of the negotiations to date, emphasizing the U.S.–Turkish agreement that no humiliation of Greece or diplomatic victory was being sought. He asked whether he could take it that the formulations of a Turkish response worked out that morning with Türkmen and his aides constituted the position of the Turkish government. Sunay looked to Demirel, who responded that the cabinet had reviewed the language and had problems with the concept of a phased withdrawal. It was necessary to ensure expeditious withdrawal, or the Greeks could delay indefinitely. He also said the cabinet had trouble with the simultaneity of the start of Greek withdrawal with a Turkish standdown. This, too, invited trickery. After a short conversation between Sunay and Demirel (Çağlayangil remaining silent throughout), Demirel said the cabinet would meet again. Vance's insistence on language that would not humiliate the Greeks seemed to have led to this reconsideration.

We had a quick lunch at the embassy residence and waited for a call. It came in the late afternoon, affording Vance and his group their first rest in about 36 hours. At about 5:00 P.M., we were at the Hariciye Köşkü where Vance, Walsh, and I found the foreign minister alone with Türkmen. The change in Çağlayangil's attitude from the early morning was striking. He was his old self, relaxed, genial, offering refreshment and finding a joke where he could. What was more important, he was cooperative. The cabinet had given approval to a private letter from him to Pipinelis, which Vance could deliver along with a text of the proposed appeal by the UN secretary-general. The text of the appeal would require the Greeks to expeditiously withdraw such forces as they had introduced into Cyprus after December 1963, following which (in Turkish: *ondan sonra*) the Government of Turkey would take the necessary measures to restore the peace. The letter, on the other hand, would say that in parallel with this expeditious Greek withdrawal, Turkey would take steps to return its military posture to that prior to November 15, 1967.

Vance asked whether this letter could be made public. Çağlayangil replied this was impossible, whereupon Vance, with considerable heat, declared that the provision of the appeal as it stood was a public humiliation of Greece. It meant the end of Vance's mission, and it meant war.

Çağlayangil was silent for several minutes, then said there was an Ottoman expression that could perhaps be substituted, if the cabinet agreed, for "*ondan sonra*"; it was "*bulunla murâfik olarak*," which could be translated "in parallel with." He would try it out on the prime minister. He returned in a few minutes from the phone and said that Demirel had considered the phrase, which was old Turkish, to be too problematical for the cabinet (whose education, like Demirel's, had generally been in the modern idiom) and would require an individual, person-by-person explanation and clearance. Çağlayangil therefore had an alternative to suggest: "*bunun üzerine*" (literally, "on top of this"). He explained the difference by placing his glass of water on the table. The glass was on but also with the table. I suggested that the English translation might be "accompanying this." Çağlayangil again phoned Demirel (whose English is excellent), returned and said that "accompanying this" could be regarded as a very loose translation indeed, but that Demirel was prepared to seek cabinet approval to substitute "*bunun üzerine*" for "*ondan sonra*." Çağlayangil quipped that if objection arose in Turkey over the English, which would be official, he would say that İlter Türkmen had made a bad translation. As Türkmen's English was (and is) outstanding, this caused laughter in which was heavily mixed our sense of relief. We were back in business.

Over the years I have wondered about the reasons for Çağlayangil's uncharacteristic behavior on that morning of November 25, 1967, and his reversion to type the same afternoon, and have concluded that it was deliberate. I speculate that in the morning meeting with the National Security Council he had to establish his toughness and, at the same time, oblige its more hawkish members to face the probable consequences of their intransigeance. It worked; and after the crucial meeting with Sunay, he and Demirel had recovered the mandate to be flexible, patient, and statesmanlike. Had Vance not demanded an audience with the president, the gambit might well have failed.

Vance and party, collected at the embassy, flew to Athens that afternoon with a revised text in English of the proposed appeal by U Thant to the parties, Greece, Turkey, and Cyprus. It invited them to adhere to the independence and integrity of the Republic of Cyprus in the framework of the London-Zürich Treaties of August 16, 1960; Greece and Turkey to withdraw all forces introduced into Cyprus after December 1963; Greece to initiate expeditious withdrawal of its forces; and Turkey, accompanying this withdrawal, to take the necessary steps to remove the crisis. The private letter to Pipinelis would define removing the crisis to mean taking steps to a standdown of Turkish forces to the posture which prevailed on November 15, 1967.

The rest of the text of the proposed appeal was unchanged from the Athens proposal and related to the development by UNFICYP of a new, reconstituted Cypriot Police capable of protecting all minorities, meaning Turkish Cypriots. This was going to require the consent of Makarios; but despite an earlier notice to him by Vance of his impending arrival in Nicosia, it was imperative right now to see what could be done in Athens with the Turkish negotiating position on simultaneity.

Vance was met by Talbot and taken at once to see Pipinelis, who seemed to approve most of the modifications. He indicated, however, that the cabinet would have problems with the reference to the London-Zürich Treaties and the withdrawal only of those forces introduced after December 1963. It appeared to me that this meant Athens still wanted to leave open the future possibility of *enosis*, for the public line of Greek governments had long suggested, without formally declaring, that the 1960 treaties were dead. Makarios furthermore wanted all Turkish and mainland Greek forces out of Cyprus, including the national contingents, a major abrogation of the treaties, and Greece had agreed with this objective.

We were therefore by no means out of the woods. The deliberations of the Greek cabinet on November 26 were to prove it.

8
Deadlock, the Vance Formula, and a Break

The events I have described were not taking place in a vacuum. NATO members had come to realize the danger of war and the possible destruction of their organization that hung in the balance. NATO Secretary-General Manlio Brosio flew to Naples, where he consulted with the American commander of CINCSOUTH, then on to Athens. There, on November 24, Vance asked Brosio for his support with the Turks of the proposal Vance would carry to Ankara the following day. He was most helpful in reinforcing Vance, at this stage and later, as negotiations moved on. The governments of France and the Federal Republic of Germany urgently appealed to Turkey and Greece to exercise restraint. So did the Soviet Union, which sent notes urging against war.

The attitude of the Soviet government from the start of this crisis was most interesting. Soviet long-range objectives clearly included, and include today, constant pressure for British return of its sovereign areas to the government of Cyprus. They might also include a post-Makarios electoral triumph of AKEL and the subsequent award of base rights to Moscow. Therefore, while one might have assumed that a fratricidal struggle within the southeast wing of the NATO alliance could have been very much in its interest (and would seem to be so today), the Soviet Union and its Warsaw Pact satellites were making it clear to me that what they feared most was either a partition of Cyprus between Greece and Turkey or an outright conquest of the island by Turkey. In either case, Cyprus would become the potential site for NATO bases and the strongest Communist Party in the Middle East, the Greek Cypriot Progressive Party of the Working People, AKEL, would go down the drain. AKEL would be tolerated neither by the

Greek colonels, who were strongly anti-Communist, nor, in case of Turkish conquest, by any government of Turkey, where the Communist Party was proscribed. Communism seeks the overthrow of the Atatürk principles, which are more fundamental than any constitution.

Both the Polish chargé and the Romanian ambassador, in calls on me, therefore sought my confirmation (which was easy to give) that the United States stood for the survival of the Republic of Cyprus. Unsought by them was the U.S. conclusion that, at this juncture, the republic's survival meant disengagement and, it was hoped, peace between Greece and Turkey.

Callers were indeed numerous during the November 26 interval, while Vance worked with Pipinelis in Athens. Belgian Ambassador Robert Fénaux, dean of the diplomatic corps and a NATO colleague, was kept generally informed and was very supportive. Greek Ambassador Miltiades Delivanis was desperately trying to keep abreast of negotiations, but I could tell him little, fearing that he would report even fragments of a fast-changing scene to Athens, thus roiling the waters and creating expectations that could be damaging.

By this time, it was also the case that my British and Canadian colleagues, Ambassadors Allen and Goldschlag, so helpful before the Vance mission and with whom I had worked in the closest confidence, could not be informed of the details of these kaleidoscopic discussions. Delivanis could not be on the same basis as they were, but would sometimes arrive at our embassy while they were there for such debriefing as I could give them. As I was up to my ears in cables, I would put him in a separate room promising shortly to return, say a few words to Allen and Goldschlag in my office, excuse myself for a moment to draft a message in the communications room, then return to all my visitors in sequence. The setup reminded me of that time-worn farce, "Charley's Aunt," where the most undesirable encounters are averted by split-second timing.

Catnaps during the long nights were occasionally possible, and Jane brought me blankets and a pillow for my office couch. Bill Burdett, my deputy, hardly slept at all for ten days, covering all cable traffic in and out and tending, as well, to administration and to all embassy business not directly related to Vance's mission. He was later to have a mild heart seizure and be hospitalized. The entire embassy staff, attachés and all, devoted their utmost energies to meeting the crisis. I was proud of them.

We steadfastly avoided the Turkish press, which was very aggressive and sensational. Its reporters shadowed Vance's movements with all resources at their command and attempted to waylay him on one occasion over the transom of the men's room in the Hariciye Köşkü. There was a time, however, when I felt that I had to provide some general background on Turkey and Cyprus to certain distinguished members of the nonresident American press, who would otherwise obtain poor orientation from dubious sources.

Even such veteran correspondents as Winston Burdett, out of Rome, I found totally unconversant with Turkey and with the background of our problems. I finally asked where they had all been these last few years. The reply was that, with limited travel budgets, they had funds only to pursue crises, not to study a country that was not in flames. As I write these lines, I find that situation not much changed today. Except in specialized periodicals and in scholarly books, read by a very few, Americans are still poorly served in their reading diet for a country that has pretensions to leadership in world affairs.

Vance had a long wait on November 26 for a Greek cabinet decision on the text he brought from Ankara. When it came, as he had foreseen from Pipinelis's first reaction, it was devoid of reference to the London-Zürich Treaties and to the withdrawal of non-Cypriot forces introduced above the national contingents permitted by these accords. Vance, therefore, during the day, had made up his own formula of synthesis, perhaps to be a last resort. He held it in reserve. When Pipinelis showed him the cabinet's approved changes, he remarked that he would present them as they were to the Turkish government, but he felt sure that they would be rejected. This, despite the fact that Pipinelis, in a separate message addressed to Vance for copying to Çağlayangil (which Vance had requested), promised a complete withdrawal of Greek forces within three months.

Pipinelis had found the Turkish draft generally satisfactory, but his cabinet's exclusion of any reference to the treaties of August 16, 1960 carried the implication at this particularly sensitive juncture that Greece continued to regard those agreements as overtaken in Cyprus by Makarios's Thirteen Points and largely a dead letter. Even national contingents, those mainland Greek and Turkish forces authorized by the 1960 treaties, were to be withdrawn, a Makarios objective.

Vance arrived back in Ankara for an 8:00 A.M. meeting with Çağlayangil on November 27. Others present in his ministry office were Türkmen and, for our side, Walsh and myself. Vance delivered a copy of the letter by Pipinelis offering complete Greek withdrawals within three months. He also delivered the Greek text. Çağlayangil at once spotted the omissions in an otherwise reasonably satisfactory proposal. He remarked that Athens appeared to be attempting a ploy which would permit it to say that Turkey had abandoned the London-Zürich Agreements. This the Turkish cabinet could not accept.

Vance said he understood. He had promised to deliver the proposal as a mediator. Up to now he had been acting somewhat as a postman, trying to get the parties to see their best interests and build their own bridges. However, he now believed that the time had arrived for him to put forward on his own responsibility a synthesis that he had personally and privately developed. It left out some items that had been desired by each side; but, given the experience of the last few days, he felt it served the basic interests of both. He showed it to Çağlayangil, who read it without voicing objection, then asked whether the Greeks had approved it. Vance replied that they had not seen it. He had discussed the general tenor with them and felt there was a better-than-even chance that he could bring them to accept it.

Çağlayangil was worried about the length of time indicated for completing the Greek withdrawal. Three months was long, and the Cabinet was sure to object. Vance argued that it was a reasonable period for a complicated operation, as he knew from his experience in defense matters. It was a forthcoming gesture by Pipinelis, who had greatly appreciated Çağlayangil's private messages and who sent him his personal regards.

Vance's proposal, in its general thrust, called for expeditious Greek withdrawals and an accompanying Turkish standdown. The Greek and Turkish forces to be withdrawn were all of those introduced into Cyprus after 1963. There was no mention of the London-Zürich Treaties. The portion on beefing up UNFICYP was very carefully worded, on advice of the U.S. mission to the United Nations, so as to include this within UNFICYP's existing mandate. This would get around U Thant's demands for a special U.S. written guarantee of additional funding and also be acceptable to Makarios, whose assent, along with a Greek-Turkish agreement, was a precondition set by U Thant for making his appeal. UNFICYP would be available not only to assist the Cypriot Police in reorganization and new security measures for all citizens, but also to assist in disarming forces introduced after 1963. While the withdrawals were keyed to the enlarged role of UNFICYP, they were not to be held back pending full UNFICYP deployment in that role, but only until finalization of the *arrangements* for UNFICYP's additional duties. The three parties were to agree that they would accept the appeal by the UN secretary-general immediately upon receipt, and the agreement as a whole would forthwith enter into effect.

Çağlayangil seemed pleased with Vance's proposal. He excused himself to attend a midmorning cabinet meeting, saying that he would be in touch with us as soon as he had its reaction. We returned to the embassy to wait.

The wait was long. As the hours dragged on, we were informed that the National Assembly was the scene of vigorous debate. There was nothing to do but eat and rest, and I encouraged Vance and his party to get some sleep. We would awaken them as soon as we had a call. As the afternoon went by, Vance had three uninterrupted hours of deep sleep, for the first time since his mission had begun. He had severe back problems and wore a complicated harness, but had not allowed himself any intervals, as every hour counted in the race against war pressures within Turkey and the absolute necessity of bringing down the temperature through realistic Greek responses. Now that he had tabled his own proposal, the matter for the moment was out of his hands.

The call came in the very late evening. We met with Çağlayangil about 2:00 A.M., November 28. He was cheerful but tired. He told us he had been on his feet since the previous morning. The president and cabinet had required that he and Demirel explain their position to all opposition parties, and he had gone on the floor to do so, meeting a barrage of vitriolic criticism. He had been charged with promising that there would be no negotiations with the Greeks until they had fully withdrawn their troops from Cyprus, but had now been negotiating with Athens for several days. Some members called him a traitor. He had offered to resign, but this had not been accepted by his party. He now had a revised text to show to Vance.

It was a big disappointment. The three months had been cut to thirty days, and that with great difficulty. Vance argued that it was totally unreasonable, that at least sixty days should be allowed, but Çağlayangil said it was the best he had been able to do. Vance asked to see Demirel, whose office was almost adjacent, and it was quickly arranged. A vigorous argument ensued during which Vance asked for at least sixty days, saying that was reasonable and that on this hung the success or failure of his mission. History would never justify war over such a detail. Demirel agreed to refer the matter to his cabinet, assembled nearby, and came back with an extension to forty-five days. Vance did not like it, but undertook to carry it to Athens.

The language regarding the role of UNFICYP so carefully worked out with USUN had been badly mangled. Vance sought restorations, knowing that U Thant's appeal might otherwise be derailed and that a Makarios rejection, made more likely by these changes, could also abort the appeal. Çağlayangil, saying that the cabinet had seen more than enough of his face during the last twenty-four hours and might react negatively to any further changes he might propose, asked İlter Türkmen to take them into the cabinet room. Time after time, Türkmen returned to the lions' den with Vance's efforts to improve language critical to acceptance in New York and Nicosia. Good-humored, tireless, he made progress as the night wore on, but the results by no means made Vance happy. The cabinet hawks were becoming more and more frustrated and intransigeant.

Finally, as dawn was breaking, Çağlayangil called a halt. Addressing Vance with great courtesy and obvious personal admiration, he expressed warmest gratitude for his efforts for peace. He hoped that Vance would some day in the future be a guest in his home; he would be honored if he would do so. Now, however, any further efforts to modify texts would surely result in the cabinet throwing out the entire negotiation. Vance must therefore consider this to be the final Turkish position and so tell the Greeks. He must not return to Ankara in official capacity.

The time had come to put the final text into type and make copies. No typists were yet on hand at the ministry, but Türkmen quickly summoned four or five from its pool. As English was not their language, but was to be the official one, we also needed embassy staff. I called Burdett to supply the best typists we had, with typewriters and paper. Soon, at about 7:30 A.M., we had a collegial array of Turkish and American young women who seemed to have no trouble in communicating despite the language barrier. Texts began to roll out in Turkish and English.

In Çağlayangil's office, we were famished and tired of drinking the sweet tea which had been the only refreshment available during the long night. Out in the street we could hear early morning vendors of *simit*, a large and nourishing pretzel studded with sesame seeds, hawking from large trays which they carried on their heads. Türkmen went out and brought in a goodly supply. Presently ministry staff was able to brew coffee, and we felt human once more. Our labors were completed as office workers began to make their way into the various ministries of the Bakanlıklar.

As we were leaving, Çağlayangil asked Vance to try to obtain Greek agreement by 6:00 P.M. that same day. Vance ruminated over this on the way to the airport and asked me to relay to Çağlayangil his best wishes and to say that he would do his level best, but that the time given was unreasonable and he doubted it could be met. After all, the Turkish authorities had debated his own formula for nearly twenty-four hours and had changed it in directions he would find hard to sell. Çağlayangil later replied through me to Vance in Athens that the time limit was not set by him and therefore could not be changed by him. It was simply a fact of the political situation in Turkey.

Vance carried with him a letter addressed to himself by Çağlayangil, but to be given in copy to Pipinelis, reaffirming the readiness of the Turkish government to accompany the initial Greek withdrawals with a standdown of the current Turkish military posture and to pace further Greek withdrawals with steps to revert the posture to that which had prevailed November 15. He also suggested (but there was no doubt that it was more than a suggestion) shortening the time of total Greek withdrawals to forty-five days.

As Vance and his party took off from Ankara for the last time, one could see that a Greek-Turkish agreement was tantalizingly close, but a severe gap remained, and acceptance by Makarios was a very large question mark. The U.S. embassy had done just about all that lay in our power, as Vance was not to come back. Still, we did not rest.

In Athens, at a meeting immediately arranged by Ambassador Talbot with Pipinelis, Vance described the mood in Ankara and declared that no further changes in text could be expected from the Turks. War or peace hung on Greek acceptance. He felt it was acceptable.

Pipinelis at first reacted very negatively, but he listened. It had to be obvious to him that today's decision was crucial to the future of his country and that Vance had accomplished an almost superhuman task toward bridging the gap. He could see that in the Turkish draft there was no mention of the London-Zürich Treaties; an immediate relaxation of the threatening Turkish posture on the Thracian frontier would occur with the first Greek withdrawals; and, while forty-five days for completion of those withdrawals was short, the Turkish demobilization and Greek withdrawals from the island would keep pace. It was not a dishonorable formulation for Greece. He pointed out, however, that Makarios was not subject to control by Athens, and the Turks could not hold Greece responsible for the latter's decision regarding the role of UNFICYP. Furthermore, Pipinelis saw chaos and killings on the island if, as in the Turkish text, there was no keying of Greek withdrawals to the training and reconstitution of the Cypriot Police that "should" be instituted.

At this juncture, Talbot made what I consider to have been a decisive intervention. He pointed out that the language "should" in this paragraph was not mandatory; it expressed a *desideratum*, a need. Pipinelis looked at it again. True, it would be up to Makarios and U Thant to work out the practicalities, and Greece could only hope that the Archbishop would not reject the entire agreement and thereby lead U Thant to refuse to make his appeal (as he had so stipulated on more than one occasion). Against this consideration must be weighed the vital importance of an accord between Greece and Turkey, which now seemed close. Pipinelis then took the Turkish offer to his cabinet and the king.

In New York, our ambassador, Arthur Goldberg, had been working very hard to keep U Thant informed and to ensure that he would make his appeal. U Thant had demanded a U.S. guarantee of the funding of additional UNFICYP personnel and duties. Goldberg's study of the original UNFICYP mandate of March 1964 showed that the existing mandate could be invoked to cover the enlarged responsibilities, thus avoiding the guarantee, as well as French and Soviet vetoes in the UN Security Council. The language also had to be permissive (which it was), for a demand on Makarios would certainly be met by a rejection.

The possibility of an appeal to the three parties without reference to UNFICYP and matters internal to Cyprus alone was also being weighed. However, U Thant's position had been and still was that his appeal must be cleared in advance with all three parties and be directed to all three. The secretary-general had his own emissary in the area, Rolz-Bennett, and was ordering him to go to Nicosia. This alarmed Vance when he learned of it; he felt instinctively that the results would be negative and U Thant would thereupon refuse to issue his appeal.

Late on November 28 the break came. Pipinelis called in Vance and Talbot and informed them Ankara could be told that Greece accepted the Turkish text with the understanding that the Turkish standdown would be carried out in good faith. It had been an emotional cabinet session, and the king had played a very positive role. Vance expressed to Pipinelis his deep gratification and told him that he had his admiration for a courageous decision.

Vance flashed the news to me, which I communicated immediately to Çağlayangil via Türkmen, along with Vance's warm thanks to both.

A vital turning point had been attained and the prospects had greatly improved—this despite the heavy-handed intervention in the negotiating process by the National Assembly of Turkey and the intractability of a large element in the cabinet. Progress at this advanced stage had replaced deadlock, thanks to several fundamentals.

First, there were strong forces for peace in both Ankara and Athens. In Ankara, Çağlayangil had the invaluable help of Türkmen and the broad support of Prime Minister Demirel and Defense Minister Ahmet Topaloğlu. The draft Vance carried to Athens, a mangled version of his own final proposal, was nonetheless a basis for negotiation. Pipinelis was a realist and had the support of the king and Papadopoulos. Fortunately for peace, there was no need or place for parliamentary approval in Athens, where decisions could be made in secret. Lastly, after Vance had delivered his best and final shot in Ankara, he knew that he must take what he had. He therefore carried a firm message to Nicosia with an ingredient previously lacking, the backing of Pipinelis.

Would he have the support also of U Thant? The desirability of a UN endorsement of the Greek-Turkish understanding was immeasurable. Makarios, it was known, would be difficult, and if he could sway U Thant away from the agreed formula as constituting a derogation of sovereignty of a small Third World power, the agreement might fall apart. It was necessary to get to Makarios fast and to isolate him as much as possible.

Vance therefore asked Talbot to do what he could to dissuade Rolz-Bennett from visiting Makarios at this moment, so as not to undermine his mission. Talbot was successful. Vance flew off to Nicosia very early on the morning of November 29.

9
A Rose Garden in Cyprus

Vance arrived in Nicosia by Air Force One well before daylight November 29. The presidential plane had been entirely at his service at every hour of the day or night throughout his mission, its pilot and crew always at his command. Met by Ambassador Belcher, Vance and his party had a strategy session in the embassy before meeting at about 8:30 A.M. with Foreign Minister Kyprianou. Walsh attended to record all discussions.

Kyprianou was informed of the Greek-Turkish accord and reacted very negatively, particularly toward paragraph 4, dealing with the enlarged role for UNFICYP. Vance bore down hard on the immediate threat of war, which the agreement had merely delayed. A military landing on Cyprus by the Turks was not to be avoided if the Government of Cyprus refused to approve without change the text which he now brought.

Vance then met with Makarios and Kyprianou together, Belcher and Walsh participating. While softening his tone just enough to make it more palatable to a head of state, he described the mood in Turkey in unvarnished terms. He informed the archbishop flatly that if the agreement were rejected by Cyprus, he estimated the Turks could and would put fifty thousand men ashore on the island within forty-eight hours, along with heavy equipment and complete mastery of the air. As if to emphasize this point, Turkish overflights at low level occurred repeatedly over Makarios's office while Vance was speaking.

Makarios responded that he was grateful for the efforts that President Johnson and Vance had exerted to save the peace (Vance delivered him a letter from Johnson), and he was aware of the Greek-Turkish Agreement. He saw the first three paragraphs relating to acceptance of the UN secretary-general's appeal and the withdrawal of troops as a bilateral concern between those two countries. Of course, paragraph 4 raised matters which he would have to discuss with his cabinet. In any case, it was essential that all non-Cypriot forces be withdrawn from Cyprus, including the national contingents, as they poisoned the situation. What was needed was complete disarmament. This would permit the disbanding of the National Guard, which had become a heavy financial burden on the state. There would then remain only the Cypriot Police, carrying the responsibility, however enlarged and improved, for the protection of all citizens.

Vance said that he was aware of these considerations and had insisted that the withdrawals be a first step, along the lines of the secretary-general's appeal of November 24. (This provision was in Vance's "synthesis," handed to Çağlayangil November 27, but keyed to the withdrawal of all forces introduced after 1963.) However, the Turks were in no frame of mind to discuss withdrawal of national contingents and complete demilitarization at the present time. Approval of the text as it stood, agreed upon by the Turks and the Greeks, was imperative to stop a war. Acceptance by Cyprus in no way jeopardized later steps to complete demilitarization, including removal of the national contingents. The measures the archbishop had in mind could be worked out later.

To avoid tampering with the text, Vance suggested that the archbishop might address a letter to him approving the Greek-Turkish agreement while reserving his views on the points that troubled him. Such a letter should be worded carefully so as not to be seen by the Turks as a rejection. When Makarios asked if the United States would guarantee Cyprus against a military attack, Vance replied that such a guarantee would have to be sought in the United Nations. He had no authority to extend such a guarantee from his president.

Makarios spent most of the day with his cabinet, while Vance and his party waited at the embassy. They were received by the archbishop about 8:00 P.M. There followed more than six hours of intense discussion with Makarios, Kyprianou, and Parliamentary President Glafcos Clerides, at the end of which Vance had a letter to himself, thought up and drafted by Clerides but signed by Kyprianou, commenting on the Turkish text of paragraph 4 without attempting a revision.[44]

The letter acknowledged (and, as Kyprianou explained, this meant accepted) the first three paragraphs of the Greek-Turkish accord as a matter between those two countries. The Cypriot position on paragraph 4, however, was that it would press the point that withdrawals of all forces introduced after 1963 would be just a first step toward the phased withdrawal of all forces on the island except the Cypriot police. This would include the national contingents.

The letter also responded to the November 24 appeal of the secretary-general and added that Cyprus would seek UN Security Council guarantees against military intervention in Cyprus. It was a clever move by the archbishop and would carry weight with U Thant, since the secretary-general had gone rather far in that appeal in urging demilitarization, to the point of barely skirting a revocation of important features of the London-Zürich Treaties. The secretary-general's appeal of November 24 (appendix 7) had called on "all governments concerned" to "refrain from any military intervention in the affairs of that [Cyprus] Republic."

Vance found this letter to be a commentary and not a rejection. He took it to Athens before dawn November 30 and wired it at once to Ankara, Washington, and USUN, New York.

His interpretation was not shared by Zenon Rossides, Cypriot ambassador to the United Nations. Rossides proceeded to tell the secretary-general that the Makarios position amounted to a rejection of the Greek-Turkish agreement.

It was now clear that the United Nations was becoming a major scene for the success or failure of the effort for peace. Goldberg did his best with U Thant to correct the impression transmitted by Rossides, and in Athens Pipinelis showed his goodwill by telephoning Kyprianou and obtaining his promise to set Rossides straight.

Vance wired Washington that he believed the locus of coordination should now be shifted to New York. He had tentatively planned to fly back to Washington December 1 to report to the president, as he felt the Makarios letter to be a tolerable substitute for a damaging rewrite of paragraph 4. But on reflection, he felt uncomfortable about leaving until the secretary-general had issued his appeal, based on the Greek-Turkish Agreement, and until it had been accepted. He wired his urgent hope that the appeal be issued sometime on November 30. He asked Talbot and me to ask our foreign ministers at Athens and Ankara, respectively, to urge their ambassadors to the United Nations to establish and maintain a close contact with Goldberg to ensure that U Thant understood the sensitivity and importance of fidelity to the text.

In Ankara I learned from Çağlayangil that Turkish instructions for coordination with Goldberg had already been sent, but that the foreign minister was very disturbed over the wording of Makarios's letter to Vance. He saw it as a conspiracy between Athens and Nicosia to annul that portion of the London-Zürich Treaty of Guarantee that provided, in case of a breach and failure of consultation among the guarantors, that any one of them (Greece, Turkey, or the United Kingdom), individually, had the right to intervene in Cyprus. Ever since the publication of the Galo Plaza Report, the Turkish government feared a bias by the secretary-general against Turkey. Çağlayangil was worried that by implicitly recommending the withdrawal of national contingents in his appeal of November 24, U Thant was also being drawn by Nicosia and Athens into supporting a major derogation of the Treaty of Alliance, another pillar of the London-Zürich complex.

I argued that any UN secretary-general could hardly sponsor a violation of treaty rights; that Makarios had not specifically expressed himself against the Greek-Turkish agreement, but was registering his long-term political objectives; and that injection of these objectives into discussion could be neutralized for the present if Greece, Turkey, and the United States could quickly agree with the secretary-general on language for paragraph 4. I also bore down hard that the United States had no reason to believe that the Greeks were not entirely loyal to their accord with Turkey.

Çağlayangil was not easily dissuaded from his theory of an Athens-Nicosia collusion. He drily remarked that if a young man and a young girl spent three days together alone in a room, it could not necessarily be established that they were not praying the whole time.

As the discussion wore on, Çağlayangil seemed to become partially reassured, less perhaps by me than by Türkmen, who emphasized the importance of crafting a text which Orhan Eralp, Turkey's ambassador to the United Nations, would recommend and which U Thant could support. Çağlayangil would consult the cabinet.

Later in the day he gave me the cabinet's decision. Accepted were the following points: The existing mandate of the UNFICYP was sufficient for a broader and improved role in the disarmament of all armed elements constituted after 1963. Turkey reserved the right to return to the UN Security Council for an upgraded mandate if the existing one proved to be unsatisfactory. Turkey called on its NATO allies to support the secretary-general's appeal from the moment it was issued, especially paragraph 4, and to support it again on December 15, when the Security Council would meet for its semiannual decision on the renewal of the mandate for UNFICYP. This converted what had been a concise text into a long one subdivided into various paragraphs. I had no alternative but to pass it to Vance.

The Department of State and White House now agreed with Vance that he should remain in the area to clear up problems. Vance recommended to Pipinelis that he transmit to the Turks immediately a detailed, specific Greek schedule for a start in withdrawals from Cyprus. Pipinelis agreed at once and shortly was able to send to Ankara a message that within four hours of joint acceptance of the secretary-general's new appeal, a ship would leave Piraeus for Cyprus to pick up the first load of Greek troops. This unquestionably had a calming effect, reinforcing Çağlayangil's position with the cabinet, as it reinforced my arguments with Çağlayangil.

Vance meanwhile flew back to Nicosia on the evening of December 1. He had learned that Makarios was now submitting to the Greek and Turkish ambassadors at the United Nations and to U Thant a new text of paragraph 4. Makarios had succeeded in breaking open the negotiations. Vance also knew from Çağlayangil via my messages that Turkey would not accept the option of the complete elimination of paragraph 4 from the secretary-general's appeal.

The new Makarios version was crafted with skill. It stated, in effect, that the three parties would "discuss" in the Security Council an improved mandate for UNFICYP, including the disarmament of all forces constituted after 1963. It said nothing about this being a "first step" toward total disarmament or about the withdrawal of national contingents. It commended itself therefore to Ambassador Eralp and to U Thant. In Ankara, however, it did not commend itself. The hawkish cabinet saw the word "discuss" as a trick for encouraging endless debate rather than action, and it went right back to an insistence on its earlier formulation of paragraph 4 that there "should be" an improved mandate for UNFICYP. I recall receiving a message from Vance in the middle of the night asking whether I felt I could try again to change this language, and I had to tell him I was afraid it would smash the negotiations as a whole.

In fact, the negotiations seemed to be heading for collapse, for Makarios would not budge. He had the upper hand with U Thant on that paragraph, in its reasonable wording of respect for the sovereign right of Cyprus to make final decisions on affairs closely affecting internal order, combined with respect for some of the most sensitive points that had been raised by the Turks. Vance held three meetings with Makarios from the night of December 1 to December 3, marshalling every conceivable argument: that Cypriot sovereignty was completely covered; that "should" did not mean "must"; and that for peace to hang on such nit-picking was incredible.

A slender hope now lay in Goldberg's efforts with U Thant to get the secretary-general to relax his insistence that every small word be fully accepted by all three parties before he would issue his appeal. Goldberg seemed to be making progress. The real question seemed to be how quickly U Thant would act, especially on a weekend. On Sunday, December 3, came the crunch. In Nicosia, Vance was informed that U Thant would issue an appeal that day. The wording was not known and the secretary-general had made clear that he was selecting his own phraseology and not clearing it with the parties.[45]

Vance and his group now had what Vance knew would be the final session with the archbishop, who was likely to make a public announcement of his position. In the morning of December 3, while it was still the middle of the night in New York, Vance did his best to drag out the discussion, going over the ground with Makarios again and again as the minutes ticked into hours, trying every new angle he could devise to use up time and keep Makarios from taking a public stance that would discourage U Thant from making his appeal.

One angle was to ask for a breather in the archbishop's fine rose garden, just outside their meeting place. It was His Beatitude's special conceit. They walked together as Vance asked detailed information about every plant and blossom, admiring the care shown and the results. The archbishop saw through this maneuver, and whenever the conversation turned to substance he quietly—even sweetly—said that his decision could not be changed. Even Clerides, who had been more flexible in earlier talks, was now unmovable. If Turkey went to war over a single phrase, said Kyprianou, the world would know who the aggressor was.

There were several walks in the rose garden, until it was no longer possible to continue what would shortly become a charade. Vance took leave of Makarios and his aides with the request that he reconsider and let him know at the embassy, where he would be until it was time to leave a few hours hence. Makarios bade him goodbye with the warmest of thanks to President Johnson and to himself for his efforts for peace. There would be no change in his position.

It was now about noon and there was nothing to do but wait and hope. From New York, messages from Goldberg indicated that the appeal had been formulated and would shortly go out, the text still not available. Perhaps because of confidence that time was on his side, Makarios did not go public. U Thant's appeal came through about 7 P.M. Cyprus time, on the air and to the world.

In Athens, the appeal was accepted within minutes and without change or reservation. Flashed to Ankara, I rushed this news to Türkmen, who was delighted and within the hour gave me the Turkish agreement, very brief and also without qualification. Could I transmit it for him to New York for Eralp? The Turkish transmitter was down. We had been at the office all night and a staff member was standing by, ready to go. Burdett shouted "Hallelujah." Within minutes we had the message on its way.

Vance had departed for Athens after the appeal but before the acceptance. Indeed, acceptance by Turkey was considered unlikely. In Nicosia, Belcher felt that war was close and decided to consult Vance by radio to his plane whether he should proceed with further evacuation of Americans and close out the radio stations. Vance responded that he could not in good conscience recommend against these actions. Shortly after, Belcher decided to send all but ten of the staff to the British sovereign areas for onward travel to Beirut; but by a very happy coincidence, Greek Ambassador Menelaos Alexandrakis phoned fifteen minutes later to report that his government had accepted the Turkish position and that the Greek forces would shortly begin to leave Cyprus. The closing of our vital communication link in Cyprus was avoided by this close cooperation between Belcher and his Greek colleague.

The text of U Thant's appeal on December 3, 1967, to the heads of government of Cyprus, Greece, and Turkey follows:[46]

> I have the honor to address you once again on the matter of Cyprus. You will recall that, in an effort to avert war, I addressed urgent appeals on 22 and 24 November to the Governments of Cyprus, Greece and Turkey. In recalling and reiterating the substance of those appeals, I express appreciation for the generally favorable reactions of

the three Governments to them and for the avoidance of resort to force. My Personal Representative, who arrived in the area on 23 November and has since returned to United Nations Headquarters, has kept me informed of the talks he has had with the parties and about the course of other and separate discussions and developments.

In addition, since those appeals, the Security Council, on 25 November, adopted unanimously its consensus which noted with satisfaction my efforts to avert war over Cyprus, which called for utmost moderation and restraint by the parties and for other courses of action by them in the interest of peace and a permanent settlement in accordance with the Security Council's resolution of 4 March 1964.

I am aware, of course, that subsequent to my appeals there have been consultations and discussions involving the parties which, according to reports reaching me, hold promise that a way can be found to the resolution of at least the current crisis. In the light of this prospect, I feel encouraged to issue this further appeal to the parties to take prompt and positive action for the preservation of peace. Particularly do I appeal to the Governments of Greece and Turkey to take immediate measures to end any threat to the security of either one by the other as well as of Cyprus and, as a first step in response to my second appeal dated 24 November, to carry out an expeditious withdrawal of those of their forces in excess of their respective contingents in Cyprus.

With regard to any further role that it might be considered desirable for UNFICYP to undertake, I gather that this could involve, subject to the necessary action by the Security Council, enlarging the mandate of the Force so as to give it broader functions in regard to the realization of quiet and peace in Cyprus, including supervision of disarmament and the devising of practical arrangements to safeguard internal security, embracing the safety of all the people of Cyprus. My good offices in connection with such matters would, of course, be available to the parties on request.

I am confident that actions of the kind I have referred to will remove the threat of war over Cyprus and thereby win the gratitude of an anxious world.

U Thant's appeal impresses me even now, after the lapse of twenty years, as a masterpiece of synthesis, though no reader of it would know

On the brink of Cyprus independence in 1960, the outgoing British governor of Cyprus, Sir Hugh Foot (later Lord Caradon), flanked by the incoming president, Archbishop Makarios III, and vice president, Fazil Küçük, at Government House in Nicosia.

Cypriot officials attending UN Security Council meeting on the Cyprus problem on February 17, 1964. From left, Foreign Minister Spyros Kyprianou; Glafcos Clerides, president of the House of Representatives; and Ambassador Zenon Rossides, permanent representative to the United Nations. (Credit: UPI/ Bettmann Newsphotos)

King Constantine and members of the Greek military government, Athens, April 26, 1967. Front row, from left: Col. George Papadopoulos, Premier Constantine Kollias, King Constantine, and Gen. Gregory Spandidakis. (Wide World Photos)

İsmet İnönü, left, with U.S. Ambassador Parker T. Hart at airport in Ankara, February 1966.

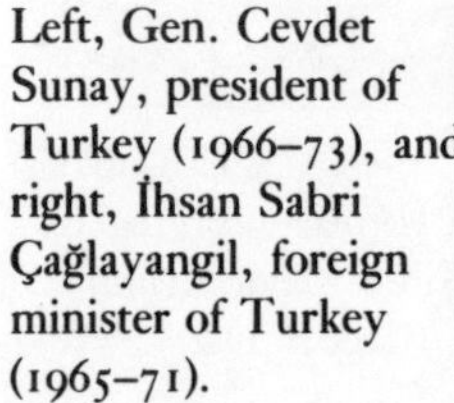

Left, Gen. Cevdet Sunay, president of Turkey (1966–73), and right, İhsan Sabri Çağlayangil, foreign minister of Turkey (1965–71).

EOKA founder and commander-in-chief of Greek Cypriot forces, Lt. General George Grivas, left, with fellow EOKA ministers, including Polykarpos Georgkhadjis, right foreground, shown on Cyprus street in mid-1960s.

UN Under Secretary for Political Affairs Ralph J. Bunche, right, being briefed by Brigadier Michael N. Harbottle, OBE, UNFICYP chief of staff, east of Nicosia, July 1966. (Credit: United Nations/PAS)

Kophinou (Geçitkale), Cyprus, December 1967, showing Turkish Cypriot homes ravaged in November 15, 1967, fighting. Right, home burned out by Greek troops in which a woman was killed. Below, war-damaged home in which occupants were killed. (Photos by Parker T. Hart)

Cyprus, December 1967. Above, Kokkina beach, encampment of Turkish Cypriot refugees in American arctic tents and mud houses. Below, Paphos, abandoned Turkish Cypriot shops in old city. (Photos by Parker T. Hart)

Left, UN Secretary-General U Thant (Credit: UN Photo/Y. Nagata), and right, Ambassador Arthur J. Goldberg, permanent representative of the United States to the United Nations, 1965–68. (Credit: United Nations/YN/ARA)

Greek Foreign Minister Panayotis Pipinelis, right, with U.S. Ambassador Phillips Talbot in Athens, January 1969.

Post-crisis meeting in Rhodes, December 1967, of three U.S. ambassadors. From left, Parker T. Hart (Turkey); Phillips Talbott (Greece); a local resident; and Taylor G. Belcher (Cyprus).

An informal President Makarios, without his usual ecclesiastical vestments, at his summer residence in Troodos with UNFICYP commander Lt. General A. E. I. Martola and UN Special Representative Bibiano Osorio-Tafall.

Cover of *The Economist* (London), December 9–15, 1967, showing Archbishop Makarios (left center) with Cyrus Vance. (Courtesy of *The Economist*)

Opening of joint high-level meeting on Cyprus at UN Headquarters, January 17, 1985. From left, Spyros Kyprianou, president of Cyprus; UN Secretary-General Javier Pérez de Cuéllar; and Rauf Denktaş, president of Turkish Republic of Northern Cyprus. (Credit: UN Photo/Y. Nagata.)

there had even been a Vance mission. Since it was his personal language, kept private until release, it was not a transmittal to any party for approval of content. By its very nature it was very hard for any recipient to refuse. Its quick and bare-bones acceptance by Greece facilitated prompt approval by Turkey, assisted by Pipinelis's earlier promise of a fast departure of the first evacuation ship from Piraeus. The cabinet hawks were quieted, for the immediate objective had been accomplished and paragraph 4, subject to near-fatal wrangling, was sufficiently covered in the last part of the appeal.

The response of Makarios became a secondary consideration in this effort to avert a war, instead of being a primary requisite. In a sense, he was isolated. Nonetheless, Turkey's formal note to U Thant of December 3, which followed the brief message of acceptance I transmitted to Eralp, added the following paragraph expressing Turkey's continuing concern for the security of its brethren on Cyprus and for the Treaties:[47]

> In view of the recent tragic events on Cyprus my Government fully supports an enlarged mandate and a broader function for UNFICYP including supervision of disarmament which should extend to all forces constituted after 1963. As you point out in your appeal, an action of this kind will remove the threat of war over Cyprus. My Government fully shares this view and considers such measures as an indispensable guarantee to ensure the security of the Turkish Community and to prevent new menaces to peace in the island and in the region.
>
> As you have also stressed, the purpose is now to resolve the current crisis. Consequently, the measures which would be taken in pursuance of your present appeal cannot of course affect the validity of existing treaties or prejudge the modalities of a final solution. (Signed) Süleyman Demirel, Prime Minister of Turkey.

The reply of Cyprus to U Thant on December 3 was positive but provisional, Rossides saying that Foreign Minister Kyprianou asked him to convey that the Cyprus Government "finds your appeal particularly constructive, and that the written reply will be following very shortly, within the next twelve hours." The formal reply, dated December 4, accepted the appeal but treated it as "a first step, thus being in line with your previous appeal of 24 November 1967, namely towards the ultimate and complete withdrawal from the Republic of Cyprus of all non-Cypriot armed forces other than those of the United Nations." It also cited the last paragraph of the secretary-general's appeal of November 24 as requiring "effective guarantees against any military intervention in the affairs of Cyprus . . . (which) should be ensured through the Security Council."

Makarios thus laid the ground, invoking U Thant, for an effort to marshall Security Council action to secure a modification or a nullification of the London-Zürich Treaty of Guarantee and the Treaty of Alliance. Makarios welcomed consideration of a further role for UNFICYP by the Security Council "with due regard for the sovereignty of Cyprus, as provided in the Security Council resolution of 4 March 1964" and looked forward to "measures to be taken, with the contribution of UNFICYP, for the establishment of permanent peace and security for all the people of Cyprus." Lastly, Makarios accepted U Thant's offer of good offices.

Warm messages of thanks from Vance, President Johnson, and Dean Rusk were now sent out to the heads of government and foreign ministers of Greece and Turkey and to other key participants, including ambassadors, as Vance took off for the United States. Air Force One took the route to the Azores, at his request, where U.S. base facilities were available for some of these communications, drafted en route, and where he allowed himself and his staff a few hours of rest. He then pushed on to the United States.

Before Vance left Athens, late Sunday evening December 3, and after Greece and Turkey had accepted the appeal, a phone message was received by Talbot at the embassy that the triumvirate who ruled Greece, and who had remained in the background throughout these critical days, wished to come and meet the mediator who had done so much. Colonels George Papadopoulos and Nicholas Makarezos, along with Brigadier General Stylianos Pattakos, arrived at the embassy while Talbot was giving dinner to Vance and party. They spent an hour expressing to Vance their deep appreciation that peace had been salvaged.

To Talbot alone, Pipinelis had earlier affirmed that Greece's action in this crisis represented a fundamental shift in its attitude on the Cyprus problem. Never again would Greece be dependent on the policies of Makarios.

• • •

In Washington, Vance reported to President Johnson and had breakfast with him, Rusk, and McNamara at the White House on December 4. Typically, he then avoided the press and went quietly back to his family and his law practice. In Ankara, we felt that we had met and worked with a man of great strength, humane, direct, persistent, resourceful, tireless and, only when necessary, very tough. In his letters of appreciation to heads of state, prime ministers, and foreign ministers, there was one major difference in treatment. While to the Greek and Turkish leaders he gave warm praise for their wisdom and courage, to the Cypriots his message was a courteous but plain recognition of profound differences in approach. He wished them well in their personal lives.

Situation Summary

The immediate danger of war between Greece and Turkey had been averted. The problem of Cyprus remained, and, as these lines are written, is still a major issue in Greek-Turkish relations. What therefore had been gained, and by whom?

It has been an article of faith with me that success is only achieved when there is no clear diplomatic victory or defeat. The defeat of a country is a serious matter. It carries the seed of profound resentment, magnified by those collective pressures we call nationalism. This is especially true when "triumph" is publicized. Each side must be led to perceive that certain concessions produce a situation which is more endurable than the existing state of affairs. The mediator, if there is one, must find this common ground so that each government, if publicly challenged (as it usually is), can proclaim some kind of achievement.

Vance succeeded not only because the Department of State and the White House left him alone in a fast-moving situation,[48] or because of his personal qualities, but because he never lost sight of a common need shared by the parties. Neither Greece nor Turkey wanted a war, and the fact that Makarios was quite willing to risk one (believing that the United States would be able to stop it at the last moment, as in 1964) dictated a strategy between Greece and Turkey of groping for the commonality of vital interest between them. An evaluation of Makarios's brinksmanship seems also to have penetrated the Secretariat of U Thant, through the help of

Arthur Goldberg, to make possible public issuance of the appeal before Makarios moved to block it.

Vance took a critically important step when he won the agreement of Pipinelis to send Çağlayangil the message that within four hours of a joint Turkish-Greek acceptance of the awaited appeal by the UN secretary-general, a Greek ship would leave Piraeus for Cyprus to pick up the first load of mainland Greek troops, thereby initiating the withdrawal. Thus, Greece and Turkey placed their bilateral interests in the foreground of the dispute and made them, to an important degree, independent of the manoeuvres that Makarios might undertake.

It was a telling advantage that Vance was able to operate in a near vacuum of world publicity, particularly in Greece, where the media were controlled. His instincts and his natural modesty dictated avoidance of the press.[49] In any case, the world press placed higher priority on events elsewhere, and the aggressive Turkish press seems to have had little outside impact. Vance was able, therefore, to orchestrate full cooperation by the White House, the Departments of State and Defense, the U.S. representation to the United Nations, NATO, the foreign offices of the United Kingdom and Canada, and the U.S. embassies at the scene of the crisis. In a charged atmosphere, he was able to keep Greece and Turkey to their pledges of confidentiality and to play, as necessary, on their dread of diplomatic isolation and the consequences of war.

Turkey won Greece's agreement to the prompt withdrawal of mainland Greek forces above treaty limits, and Turkey temporarily lost motivation for a military intervention in Cyprus. Grivas was out of the picture, and Turkish Fighters now had only to face a National Guard deprived of its massive backup. Turkey had not received another Johnson letter, had not caved in under U.S. pressure, and had been saved heavy human losses in what would have been an all-out encounter with Greece. It also avoided a powerful and probably uncontrollable reaction in the U.S. Congress, which (as proven eight years later) would have to cut off all U.S. aid.

Greece won an honorable peace, given the Turkish standdown and the general consensus everywhere that demilitarization of Cyprus was a valid long-term objective. It saved itself from a disastrous conflict with a more powerful neighbor which would have occasioned the loss of thousands of Greek and Greek Cypriot lives. It also freed itself from the grotesque political control that Makarios had exercised in Cypriot matters over earlier Greek governments. As Talbot told me later, there was a "sea change" in Greek public opinion, discernible notwithstanding censorship by the colonels. *Enosis* would still be regarded in Greece as a natural and indeed inevitable course of history, which would come about some day because of the ties of Hellenism, of common language and culture, shared by the large majority of the population of Cyprus with "Mother Greece"; but it was not to be gained by war with Turkey. Such a war risked Greece itself, as well as NATO and the protection which NATO offered to Greece. The colonels knew the cost, and they were profoundly anti-Soviet.

Makarios won UN recognition that under his own leadership matters concerning the enlargement of the powers of UNFICYP were primarily his business as head of a state with a seat in the United Nations. There he had the broad support of a large number of fledgling states sensitive to pressures and threats by larger powers. His insistence on an eventual complete disarmament of the island, involving total withdrawal of Greek as well as Turkish treaty contingents, leaving only a Cypriot police, remains the position of the Vasiliou government of Cyprus as of this writing.

Makarios played successfully in the United Nations on the theme of David versus Goliath until mid-1974. The way had been open for him, at the end of 1967, to select his course toward pacification, disarmament, and reconciliation between the two communities. He stood to have the warm cooperation of the United Nations Security Council. He failed to exploit this golden opportunity over the next seven years until de facto partition finally occurred.

Part 3
Extinguishing the Fuse of War

10
Withdrawal, Standdown, and Détente

Both Pipinelis and Çağlayangil carried out their promises. On 8 December, 411 mainland Greek troops were lifted from Cyprus by the passenger liner *Margarita.* Shortly thereafter, the readiness of the Turkish forces was reduced in Çiğli and in İnçirlik, both bases dedicated to NATO as well as Turkey.

Tension surrounded these early movements. In Ankara, at least, the Turks were deeply worried over verification. Pipinelis had rejected as humiliating a formal undertaking to the Turks that UNFICYP, along with Turkish observers, monitor all Greek withdrawals. Çağlayangil had heard that the Greeks planned to take out their troops via Boğaz, a military port secured against outside observation. He told me that he would not stand for a "James Bond" operation. It must be aboveboard. The government of Cyprus would have nothing to do with the verification program. However, the Greeks suddenly decided to use the port of Famagusta, where not only the UNFICYP but many Turkish Cypriots could observe the movements, since the old walled part of the city was a Turkish Cypriot enclave.

On December 13, fifteen hundred more Greek troops were lifted, and the NATO partners began to breathe more easily. That same day, however, high-level events in Greece itself diverted concentration on verification. King Constantine, who had played so constructive a role in the negotiations mediated by Vance, decided to move against the colonels and restore a democratic regime with the help of certain senior officers of the Greek Army, Navy, and Air Force. The operation was hastily planned and it leaked. In a matter of hours the coup failed and the king, his pregnant queen, and a small retinue that included Prime Minister Kollias left by plane for Rome, a temporary exile from which they have never returned. According to Talbot, "The king, in the guise of inspecting the readiness of Greek units to respond to the escalating threat of Turkish military action against Greece, had in fact been testing the readiness of his generals for a countercoup. From them he got a positive response, of course, but unfortunately he failed to draw in the staff colonels who, in the event, interjected themselves in the chain of command and derailed the generals' movement orders to armored and other units."[50]

Pipinelis remained with the military regime. The undertakings which he, the cabinet, and the king had made to U Thant and the Turks were in no way interrupted. By December 20, a total of 3,211 troops had been lifted from Cyprus, along with 200 truckloads of equipment and ammunition, by the *Margarita*, the *Minos*, the *Phaistos*, and various LSTs carrying tanks and vehicles. The pace was sustained, and by January 6, 1968, it was publicly reported that these vessels lifted on that day 1,572 troops plus 150 vehicles, including 18 tanks, while an LST took 157 vehicles and 20 truckloads of ammunition. On January 16, the Greeks notified the Turks, the United Nations, and the Americans that all Greek troops in excess of the national contingent and those seconded to the National Guard, numbering 8,000 to 9,000 men, had been withdrawn before the 45-day deadline, which was to expire January 18, 1968.

In the more relaxed atmosphere generated by the prompt start of the withdrawals, Talbot proposed to Belcher and me a tripartite ambassadorial meeting in Rhodes to compare notes on the latest events and to try to look ahead. With the State Department's full agreement, we assembled with our wives at a small hotel opened for us on an otherwise off-season and tourist-free island. Our presence as customers was most welcome, and there was no press corps at hand. The weather was rainy and cold, but between lengthy sessions we managed to sandwich in the beautiful ancient monuments and the picturesque city so richly embellished by Italian administrations from 1912 to the close of World War II. I noted that two thousand Turks lived on Rhodes, but there was no "Cyprus problem."

After two nights, we returned to our posts with a clearer idea of what lay ahead. I also gained details of the final hours in Nicosia of the Vance mission related in the previous chapter. Now absorbing our attention was the outlook for pacification and for intercommunal cooperation in government—how, that is, to apply paragraph 4 and how to avoid a future international crisis. During Christmas week, beginning December 26, I therefore obtained the department's consent to accept Belcher's invitation to visit Cyprus, with my family, for an on-the-spot appraisal of the situation of Turkish Cypriots in their enclaves.

The first protocol requirement was a courtesy call with Belcher on Archbishop Makarios, to be followed by a call on Vice President Fazil Küçük. I had expected the call on Makarios to be brief and private, but on arrival at the Presidential Palace I was surprised to find the full Cypriot and foreign press on hand. Television cameras whirred as Makarios greeted us outside the steps. They were not allowed, however, to follow us inside. The publicity of my call did not worry me as far as the authorities in Ankara were concerned, for I had discussed my trip in advance with Çağlayangil. He in turn had notified the Turkish embassy in Nicosia and the "Küçükery," as the top-level entourage of Vice President Fazil Küçük was popularly called. There were no public statements.

Makarios opened by remarking that I must have had some tense moments during recent days. I replied that indeed this was the case, and I wanted to state with no ambiguity that the Turks had not been bluffing. If it came to another crisis like the one just passed, I was absolutely sure that the United States government would not be able to restrain the Turks from a landing on the island.

The archbishop made no comment on this but turned to the problem of long-term prospects. He was prepared, he said, to allow the Turkish Cypriots their own police force in their communities, but not "of course" a federation, as the structure of the republic must be a unitary state. We went over this ground for about forty-five minutes, at the end of which I excused myself to call on his vice president.

It was not my business but Belcher's to argue the future of the Cyprus Republic with Makarios. I knew he had the most sensitive touch on such matters of anyone in the U.S. government, having served in Nicosia as consul, consul general, and later chargé d'affaires before his present post as ambassador. He knew both communities well and spoke fluent Greek. There was little in the history of the intercommunal relationships which could have escaped his attention.

I felt let down by the attitude of Makarios. It seemed to me that he had learned nothing from recent events. The Turkish Cypriots living in enclaves (some 25 or 30 percent in all) already had their own police, indeed their own defense system. A de facto fragmentation already existed. Did Makarios think this would melt away?

My call on Küçük brought up nothing of significance that I can remember. I told him of my plans to visit certain Turkish enclaves, and he undertook to alert them. We then traveled to Famagusta, where all was quiet in and around the Turkish enclave in the old walled quarter of the city.

The next evening at the Belcher's residence, guests included Judge Michael Triandafylides, a disarmingly frank Greek Cypriot who engaged me in fundamentals. Remarking on what a beautiful island this was "if its inhabitants were not so stupid," he asked for my views on a structure for a unitary state that might have a chance. I asked if he considered Switzerland to be a unitary state. When he replied in the affirmative, I suggested that the three principal Swiss ethnic groups among whom I had lived as a student many years previously had achieved a harmonious balance by their system of cantons. Cyprus, of course, was not the same, but the concept, with adjustments, could be useful. Somewhat to my surprise, Triandafylides appeared never to have considered this model, and he became very reflective.

At this point, however, the news burst upon our relaxed group that during that very day a "Provisional Turkish Cypriot Administration" had been formed in northern Nicosia in the presence of Zeki Kuneralp, secretary-general of the Turkish Foreign Ministry. Küçük was made president and Rauf Denktaş, in absentia (still in involuntary exile), had been made vice president. The statute comprised nineteen articles and resembled a constitution. The move appeared to presage formation of a separate state and to diminish the chances of reconciliation and unity. It cast a pall over the evening, and the judge immediately asked me why the Turks had done this. I was embarrassed to have to say that I hadn't the least idea nor had I received forewarning. At the end of the dinner party, however, as he was leaving, the judge turned to me and said that he was glad of the suggestion about cantonization and would weigh it further.

The next day my family and I made a tour of the major Turkish Cypriot enclaves of the island. In Larnaca and the confrontation zone on Artemis Road, all was quiet. We were briefed in the confrontation zone by UNFICYP officers on duty. We then drove to Ayios Theodhoros and Kophinou, also quiet, but in Ayios Theodhoros it was the calm following tragedy: homes destroyed by Greek artillery, a mosque pockmarked with shell fire, a courtyard where an old man had been incinerated alive. In

Kophinou, where damage was less, Turkish Cypriot men lounged at tea tables in open air and remarked on the partridge hunting.

We went on to Limassol for the night. Waiting for us in the hotel lobby was the district commissioner, Khristodoulos Veniamin, a Greek Cypriot greatly admired by our embassy in Nicosia for his broadmindedness and who was later to play an increasingly significant part in the affairs of the republic. He talked with me alone for well over an hour regarding intercommunal relations in his area. It appeared that they were good, if higher authority merely left the locals alone.

I later learned that he was personally popular with Limassol Turkish Cypriots and had once taken a Greek Cypriot friend to Nizar's Restaurant in the Turkish Quarter for dinner. They were cordially received and seated by Nizar himself, but then someone notified the Küçükery by phone and the orders came not to serve them. Nizar, totally embarrassed and chagrined, had to make his apologies to Veniamin and to ask his friend to leave. I related this story to Çağlayangil after my return to Ankara as an example of just what it would be useful to avoid if intercommunal relationships were to have a chance for improvement. He had little response to make, as the story was new to him, but he was obviously taken aback.

In Paphos I found a quite different situation. The district commissioner there was a rigid constructionist. Intercommunal relations were virtually zero. After calling on him, I visited the Turkish enclave, Ktima. On the borderline between the Greek and Turkish sectors, vacated Turkish Cypriot homes were pointed out to me by my embassy escort. The Turkish Cypriots had been crowded for defense into the poorest quarter of the city, which reminded me of simple Anatolian villages we had encountered during the past two years of travel in remote parts of Turkey: the central square with its bust of Atatürk and its municipal building painted white and marked "P.T.T." (post, telegraph, and telephone); the small coffee shops and the little general stores, often unlabeled but fragrant with the smell of freshly baked bread. The scene had a static, clean, and impoverished look, as did the old men sitting in the sun, exchanging few words and drinking their coffee. Homes were small and inadequate compared with those vacated beyond the "green line" in the Greek sector. The leadership was cordial but disconsolate. The outlook promised no return to homes or resumption of businesses or professions.

We then drove on to Lefka in the northwest, a very narrow enclave with tight defenses. We had little conversation there and none with Greek Cypriot authorities, who had no access even to drive through the village. On then to Kokkina, the tiny hamlet on the northeast coast which had become a flashpoint in the summer crisis of 1964. Here Greek Cypriots had surrounded and besieged the defenders to prevent resupply from the sea and were about to assault and overrun them when the Turkish Air Force, operating from the nearby mainland, bombed their positions and discouraged further advance.

We were met here by a uniformed officer in command, who declared himself to be a Cypriot but betrayed his mainland identity by his accent and by his reference to kilometers instead of miles. He was one of the thirty-five (or three hundred) from the Turkish Army not yet withdrawn—and perhaps to be rotated—under the Greek-Turkish accord. Like the mainland Greeks who had likewise not been withdrawn from the National Guard, where they stiffened discipline, so Turkish officers among the TMT kept their trigger-happy militias under tight control.

It was a leftover problem of the mutual withdrawal program, never made clear between Greeks and Turks. Vance had left it to be discussed by the three parties. Pipinelis had claimed that the "excess" of Greek forces did not apply to the National Guard, since that body was under the Government of Cyprus and required mainland officers for proper training. It was a matter for discussion under paragraph 4, i.e., pacification. Çağlayangil, on the other hand, was to insist at first that the excess included all Greek forces beyond the treaty contingent. In the end, the point seems to have been quietly forgotten when some eight thousand Greek troops had been actually counted out, with equipment, by UNFICYP and by Turkish observers.

Kokkina presented a dramatic situation. The ring of blockade around it was tight. We could pass through the Greek Cypriot barrier only by virtue of our embassy escort and earlier official notice. Once inside, it was clear that supply from the open sea was coming in, presumably at night, for the people were housed, camp-style, enjoyed fresh bread, and no one looked underfed. Nonetheless, the siege was real, with no future there even for farmers, the site being rocky and barren. The people of Kokkina could do nothing but wait for a general settlement, and the prospect of returning to their homes looked dim. They were caught in an island-wide deadlock which they had no power to influence in the slightest degree.

Back in Nicosia we pondered the fate of that divided capital, with its stark contrast between the modern, prosperous-looking Greek south and the early nineteenth-century look of the Turkish north. The two sectors were divided by barriers of oil drums filled with sand, revetments of concrete blocks and adobe, with rifle embrasures visible. One could pass around the drums with permission, as we did, accepting an invitation to dinner by the Turkish chargé, Ercüment Yavuzalp.[51]

In the Turkish sector, vendors of vegetables and fruit sold their produce from donkey-drawn carts. Atatürk's statue dominated the square. Most traffic was by foot. On the Greek side, automobiles filled the streets and the pace of commerce was intense. On the road to Kyrenia, a Turkish Cypriot strong point extended a bit east from fortified positions on Mount Saint Hilarion, but was prevented from completely blocking the north-south traffic by UNFICYP. Kyrenia itself was in Greek Cypriot hands, and a total disruption of this major artery would have brought about major action by the National Guard.

Following New Year's Day, we flew back to Ankara, my head stuffed with impressions of intercommunal complexities. I called on Çağlayangil and gave him a fairly detailed account, noting his receptivity to the idea of cantonization, which he had apparently had under consideration for some time. Later, it was to become a cornerstone of his proposals for a solution to the problem of the enclaves, which were to be the kernels of the future cantons. A degree of self-government within them was already apparent. However, not every Turkish Cypriot could live in a canton. Two-thirds of all Turkish Cypriots still lived in hamlets and villages scattered about the island, surrounded on all sides by Greek Cypriots. Protection by other than regroupment had to be worked out for most parts of the island, or the individual families would lose their farmlands and their means of livelihood. There was an urgent need for a reconstituted Cypriot Police and a system of justice that rose above ethnic considerations.

Meanwhile, I protested vigorously the "Provisional Turkish Cypriot Administration" and related how embarrassing and counterproductive I had found it to be while in Cyprus. I was not alone in this view. Officials in Washington were very disturbed about the move and remonstrated particularly regarding its timing.

The Turkish riposte emphasized that its purpose was not to create a Turkish Cypriot government, but to pull together discordant factions of the community who were at serious cross-purposes and to strengthen leadership in preparation for tough negotiations with the Greek Cypriot community toward pacification and intercommunal political cooperation. Apparently Ankara's earlier view of Denktaş as irresponsible (particularly when he precipitated a crisis by his surreptitious landing on the island and arrest) had yielded to a new estimate of him as a mature leader. Unspoken, but implied, was the conclusion that Fazil Küçük did not have the capabilities required to lead his community in the new phase and that Denktaş, as president of the Turkish Cypriot Communal Chamber, was the man on whom they must rely. Küçük was not removed, but he was dealt out of the future negotiating process.

The Cyprus government reacted swiftly to the announcement of the Provisional Administration. The Foreign Ministry, headed by Kyprianou, issued notes on December 28, 1967, to all embassies in Nicosia forbidding their ambassadors to have any contact with the Turkish Cypriot leadership. This, in turn, was protested vigorously by the United States and other governments as unrealistic and extreme, but the ministry would not yield. Consequently, Washington decided to refuse to recognize Nicosia's position and see what would happen. It instructed the embassy to have the deputy chief of mission make New Year's calls on both Makarios and Küçük and report the reaction. It was done, and no one was declared persona non grata.

In New York, the UN secretary-general also deplored the establishment of the "Provisional Administration." On January 8, bolstered by this, Makarios announced new elections, leaving up in the air which Cypriot law would apply, that of 1963 or that of 1965. If the latter were to apply, the Turkish Cypriots would be excluded.

While all this maneuvering was going on, muddying the never very clear waters, bilateral Greek-Turkish relations were improving as the withdrawals progressed on schedule and the standdown of Turkish readiness kept pace. The problem of how many Greek "illegals" there were to be withdrawn continued to cause difficulties in Ankara, where the government had a very exaggerated concept of the numbers involved.

It was settled by Pipinelis and Çağlayangil as follows: On January 18, 1968, Pipinelis publicly stated that the Greek withdrawal of excess units in fulfillment of the UN secretary-general's appeal of December 3 was now complete and that the lifting of Turkey's military readiness pursuant to that appeal was now advancing in accord with the Greek-Turkish agreement. To ensure recall of all excess Turkish forces and to avoid disputes, Greece had proposed to Turkey that confirmation of the numbers of troops withdrawn by both sides be entrusted to UNFICYP. The Foreign Minister of Turkey had concurred by telephone, and the government of Greece had accordingly asked the UN secretary-general for the assistance of UNFICYP to accomplish this task.

This confidence-building move by Pipinelis and Çağlayangil disposed of the question of how many illegal Greek and Turkish forces, outside the National Guard and the national contingents, there were on the island. On March 8, the secretary-general's permanent representative, Bibiano F. Osorio-Tafall, reported that UNFICYP had instructions from New York and consent from the government of Cyprus to verify the presence of foreign troops in all but ten of sixty restricted areas and that, in those ten, the commander of UNFICYP, General Martola, personally, with one staff officer, must make the inspection. By this time, the pressure was off in Ankara regarding mainland Greeks in the National Guard, and I heard no more about this matter. Attention had turned toward Greek-Turkish cooperation to ensure that Cyprus would never again bring the two states into military confrontation.

In the search for a long-term but urgently needed Cyprus settlement, the Department of State, the UN Secretariat, UNFICYP, and the foreign ministries of Turkey, Greece, and Cyprus all had ideas to float. Makarios's interest appeared to lie primarily in ensuring that decisions regarding Cyprus were not made for him by others. In the UN Secretariat, the emphasis seems to have turned to initiating direct intercommunal talks chaired by Osorio-Tafall.

In Washington, Charles W. Yost, a career ambassador of great distinction, had been charged with forming a study group even before the Vance mission finished its work. In fact, it was Vance who had recommended its creation. Basing its efforts on the Canadian Declaration of Reconciliation, the group seems to have urged that the United States take the leadership in pressing for direct negotiations between the governments of Turkey and Cyprus. The report was no doubt a good one, as was just about anything coming out of the mind of Yost, but it never materialized into a program of action. It marked the close of a U.S.-Canadian chapter in their joint effort toward long-term solution of this common NATO problem.

In Athens, the mood of detachment from involvement in Cypriot affairs continued to grow, with preference shown for direct Turkish Cypriot-Greek Cypriot conversations or Ankara-Nicosia discussions. In any case, bywithdrawing its military support from Cyprus, Athens had lost most of its leverage in the island. However, as Phil Talbot observed, the withdrawal ended the very awkward hold Makarios had exercised over Athens from the time those Greek troops were first introduced.[52] This was a positive result from the standpoint of the Papadopoulos regime, as previously noted.

In Ankara, the mood was one of intense distrust of U Thant and his supposed bias against the Turks. There was an insistence that the secretary-general's role be confined to paragraph 4, i.e., pacification and disarmament, not mediation in a long-term search for a solution as U Thant apparently desired. The ghost of Galo Plaza and his report hung in Turkish minds. Ankara preferred not to see the early start of Turkish Cypriot-Greek Cypriot direct negotiations, being convinced that the disparity in strength would operate to the disadvantage of the Turkish Cypriots and perhaps to that of Turkey itself. It sought, first of all, direct mainland Turk-Greek discussion to establish ground rules for the two communities. Cyprus and its fate were bound up in treaties affecting Greece and Turkey as guarantors. Decisions might otherwise be made by a weak Turkish Cypriot leadership under pressure from Makarios, with consequent prejudice to Turkey's security interests. Therefore, Turkey favored a series of Athens-Ankara discussions, to be followed by Turkish Cypriot-Greek Cypriot negotiations on matters purely internal to the island.

In Nicosia, Makarios and Kyprianou opposed Greek Cypriot-Turkish Cypriot talks, although these were favored by Parliamentary President Glafcos Clerides. All such positions were to be modified as time passed.

On February 2, 1968, in Geneva, Switzerland, Pipinelis met with Çağlayangil in the first of a series of very private discussions designed for personal rapport and to chart a general course for future relations on all matters, including Cyprus. Pipinelis was supported by Byron Theodoropoulos, while İlter Türkmen assisted Çağlayangil.

What was said was not revealed to me, and my instinct was not to probe. As I saw it, this was a new era in the relations between two old adversaries who were, for us and for NATO as a whole, extremely important allies. Success in diplomacy often depends on total privacy, the fruit and the germinator of confidence.

For Makarios, however, the existence of these talks was deemed a threat to his autonomy and perhaps to his aspirations to recover lost leverage in Athens. In Ambassador Talbot's view, Athens had never had enough influence on Cyprus to silence Makarios, and what was demonstrated was a reaffirmation of the imbalance between Turkey's virtual control of the Turkish Cypriot leadership and the repeatedly frustrated Greek efforts to tether Makarios and his subordinates.[53] Makarios apparently felt that a real entente between Turkey and Greece would be at his expense. So he denounced the meeting and served notice that any agreements reached would not be binding on the government of Cyprus. He thus advertised the loss of Greece's influence on Cyprus and forecast the failure of any Greek-Turkish dialogue on the Cyprus problem.

As this was a very negative stance to take in view of his need for a good image in the United Nations, Makarios accompanied this declaration on March 8 by yielding to the pressures of the secretary-general for steps toward normalization on the island. He had to move quickly to avoid adverse mention in U Thant's forthcoming report to the UN Security Council. He therefore lifted most, if not all, restrictions on Turkish Cypriots, such as the Strategic List (items barred from import or delivery), and all bars to freedom of movement, including the return to Cyprus of Turkish Cypriot students in Turkey. This shrewdly shifted to the Turkish Cypriot leadership the obligation to respond in kind by opening the enclaves to Greek Cypriot travel. That response did not come, as the Turkish Cypriots, conscious of their relative weakness, did not want the Trojan Horse, and Küçük in any case took a negative stance toward such moves by Makarios.

On March 9, Makarios removed all barricades on major roads into the Turkish sector of Nicosia and many Turkish Cypriots came out for their first look in four years, using passes required by their own Turkish Cypriot authorities. On March 16, the Turkish Cypriot leadership dropped the requirement of passes except for TMT fighters, and thousands came to Nicosia from all over the island for the four-day Bayram Festival and the Nicosia-Famagusta soccer match, which they had not witnessed in four years. There were no incidents. A few Greek Cypriots were allowed in Turkish Cypriot enclaves. The atmosphere was greatly improved, but by

April 2 there was still no real "normalization" in the behavior of Turkish Cypriot enclaves.

By March 19, Ankara had begun to relax a little on the subject of direct Turkish Cypriot-Greek Cypriot discussions, provided they were merely convened, not chaired, by the United Nations. Turkey emphasized that such talks could not produce decisions affecting treaty rights of Turkey, Greece, and the United Kingdom. By March 22, Adnan Bulak, director general for Cyprus affairs in the Foreign Ministry at Ankara (later to be a leading ambassador in the Turkish Foreign Service), had a first round of talks with Greek Cypriots in Athens on minority questions and indicated that the next round would be in Ankara.

On the same day, Osorio-Tafall reported progress in his verification of the numbers of mainland Greek and Turkish troops on Cyprus, and on March 27, the Turkish Cypriot leadership was reported to have accepted a convening by the United Nations of direct talks by Turkish Cypriots with Greek Cypriots, but without a UN presence.

More important, responsibilities were now being carried by Turkey and Greece in direct and secret communication with one another, an enormously refreshing shift from the distrust and hostility which had prevailed a few months earlier. Çağlayangil, in particular, took initiatives. In early May he inaugurated meetings with Kyprianou, thus recognizing his status as foreign minister of the Republic of Cyprus and erasing, to some degree, the implication that, by sponsoring a Provisional Administration, Turkey was setting about creating a Turkish Cypriot state within a state.

The first two meetings were in Strasbourg and totaled four to five hours. It was reported in the press that Çağlayangil had told Kyprianou that conditions were now favorable for a settlement, as the *enosis* idea no longer existed, and that two steps could be taken: (1) intercommunal talks could be started, and (2) follow-up discussions could be organized among the other concerned parties (Greece, Turkey, and the United Kingdom) regarding the political status of Cyprus. The implication was of Turkish flexibility regarding the London-Zürich Treaties and of a new era of confidence in Greek-Turkish relationships.

Kyprianou was said to have come away from these meetings very pleased. In June, Turkish chargé Yavuzalp made a courtesy call on Kyprianou in Nicosia, the first by a high embassy official since 1963. On June 27, Çağlayangil again met with Kyprianou, this time in

London. At the same time, his relationship with Pipinelis continued in its confidential and friendly course. Less widely noticed was the developing rapport between Türkmen and Theodoropoulos, two extraordinarily talented and dedicated career men who could carry the details and probe the depths of the Turkish-Greek syndrome with good humor, honesty, and total discretion. (Türkmen later became ambassador to Greece, his first post as chief of mission, then to Moscow, later the United Nations and then to the post of foreign minister. At this writing, he is Ambassador to France.)

On the island during the early spring, Osorio-Tafall was struggling to advance normalization and get intercommunal talks under way. It was tough going. There was no sign of a Turkish Cypriot move to match Greek Cypriot measures until May 20, when six unmanned barricades in Nicosia were finally dismantled. However, manned barricades were retained. Osorio-Tafall was discouraged over the rigidity shown by both sides regarding procedures and a venue for the start of intercommunal talks. On April 16, Denktaş returned to Cyprus with the full consent of the Government of Cyprus and held a press conference. He was conciliatory in his remarks and was handled in a friendly way by the Greek Cypriot press.

Throughout April, arguments dragged on over venue. Finally, on May 16, Osorio-Tafall managed to break the ice. He invited Denktaş and Glafcos Clerides to dinner, and a compromise was reached. On June 3, the Cypriot press reported that both men had departed for Beirut on June 1 and would hold initial meetings at a hotel until June 5, then return to Nicosia. Meanwhile, Osorio-Tafall made a quick visit to his New York headquarters and returned to open "full talks" in Nicosia and then leave Denktaş and Clerides alone. They would alternate their venues between the Turkish and Greek sectors.

Both Denktaş and Clerides made public statements on June 6 characterizing their contacts in Beirut as "very useful and constructive," explaining that no time limit was set for the discussions now to begin, but that much time would be necessary and it was far too early to speak of a five-party conference. Clerides added that Beirut represented the first time since 1963 that Greek and Turkish Cypriots had been able to talk directly. UNFICYP's mandate was renewed during June for another six months, and it was noted that there had been no serious intercommunal violence on Cyprus for the first half of 1968.

Situation Summary

A diplomatic process was now in full swing, one that did not require or have place for a mediator. The Yost Report was not launched, as it was felt to be outdated and inappropriate. The United States, the United Kingdom, and Canada could do little but urge compromise and flexibility and above all keep the UNFICYP in place. Its presence was desired by the Cypriot communities and was certainly needed, but its deficit stood at $10 million. There were strong pressures to reduce its size and its mandate, from six to three months, and even to eliminate it altogether. Somehow it was kept alive and retained for periods of six months. There is no doubt that it proved vital to the maintenance of general peace until the fateful summer of 1974. It even survived that crisis and remains in operation as I write these lines, a factor for peace since 1964.

The intercommunal talks began well, although Fazil Küçük was jealous of Denktaş, who had taken over his turf. He expressed himself privately in totally negative terms, predicting the total failure of the discussions. It was a self-fulfilling prophecy for which he was partly but by no means solely responsible. Clerides and Denktaş had a warm personal rapport from the start. They were both graduates of Grey's Inn, London's great law school, although they were not classmates.[54] Years later, Clerides told me that there had never been an angry word between them. Separately they made it clear that, left alone, they could have reached a basic and sound agreement in short order. Their trouble almost from the start was with their constituencies.

Indeed, the start of Phase Two was reported to be promising, Denktaş offering to agree to no more than 20 percent Turkish Cypriot representation in all branches of government, including the military and CYPOL, while the Greek Cypriots offered to increase their financial support of secondary Turkish Cypriot education from 50 to 100 percent. There was much discussion of the justice system, and here some of the best legal minds on both sides joined the talks. Progress was made.

The real stickler after the first exchanges came to be, and remained, the degree of autonomy of the Turkish Cypriot enclaves. It was not only a matter of recognizing local self-government where it already existed and where Greek Cypriots, without permission, could not penetrate; it was also a question of *area* versus village-level self-government for the large number of tiny Turkish Cypriot hamlets and villages which dotted the landscape of the island. The Küçükery demanded jurisdictional clusterings of these otherwise isolated and helpless communities under a Turkish Cypriot constabulary, which would report to an assembly or council of Turkish Cypriots in the Turkish sector of Nicosia.

Makarios, however, was keeping Clerides on a very short rein and, with his cabinet, insisted upon introducing into the deliberations, one by one, the famous Thirteen Points of his 1963 campaign to modify drastically the 1960 Constitution. He regarded the enclaves as anathema. As the archbishop's moves became increasingly radical, the response by the Küçükery steadily hardened. By the end of August, the mood of the negotiators was no longer cheerful, although their personal rapport remained intact. The Küçükery was seen by Makarios as demanding two parallel administrations, with the House of Representatives in the middle holding very limited powers. This was totally unacceptable to as proud and defiant a brinksman as Makarios had already proven himself to be.

Clerides then decided to put aside the toughest issue and focus on matters more susceptible to fruitful discussion, in order to show progress and dissipate some of the negative atmosphere. Osorio-Tafall quietly suggested compromises in private meetings. By September, a worried Pipinelis was urging Kyprianou to prepare for discussion items likely to be productive and to forget about scoring points.

Çağlayangil, who seems to have been far less worried, concentrated on setting the tone for the talks by continuing personal contacts with both Kyprianou and Pipinelis throughout the balance of 1968. By August, he was expressing privately the view that Turkey would accept any constitutional arrangement that the Turkish Cypriots found tolerable and was even flexible on the matter of the Turkish military contingent and Turkey's right of intervention as guarantor. He expressed the view that Turkey's geographic situation and its recently demonstrated concern for its island brethren might be sufficient guarantee in itself, if pacification and security of Turkish Cypriot rights were adequately provided. In September, Kyprianou was reported to have forecast an agreement within twelve months.

In fact, pacification was gradually taking hold on Cyprus. The number of shooting incidents had declined radically. The UN Secretary-General's Report of June 1968 listed 106 apparently minor shooting incidents between December 7, 1967, and June 7, 1968, compared with 346 between December 6, 1966, and June 6, 1967, and 348 between June 7, 1967, and December 6, 1967. An early June 1968 incident, involving the shooting of Turkish Cypriots by uniformed Greek Cypriot police and members of the National Guard, was defused by a quick apology from Makarios to the Turkish chargé and an investigation. The subject was not even brought up by the government of Turkey, and Cypriot news on June 10 reported that Clerides accepted an invitation by a Turkish Cypriot to dine in the Turkish sector of Nicosia at a public restaurant, to the delight of Turkish Cypriots generally. This time the Küçükery did not interfere.

Détente was uneven, however. The Küçükery rejected in October an UNFICYP proposal for a mutual pullback at the Artemis Road confrontation zone, despite terms which would appear to have favored their side. These would have required Greek Cypriot troops to fall back three miles, while the Turkish Fighters would pull back only fifty yards. UNFICYP would have manned the vacated positions. In general, throughout the fall of 1968, it appeared to be a standoff between Turkish Cypriot intractability and suspicion and Greek Cypriot refusal to recognize that a confederation or cantonization of much of the island already existed and would not be abandoned to satisfy Makarios's desire for a unitary state under Greek majority control.

Yet Ankara continued to take an optimistic view of the intercommunal talks even by year's end, perhaps partly out of wishful thinking as an election year was approaching and partly to radiate a sense of security to the Küçükery. Not so Pipinelis, who worried that time was passing with a loss of momentum and who felt that the regime of the colonels, which could not last forever, offered a unique opportunity for compromises which would never be possible under a democratic government in Athens. He worked on Kyprianou, as did Çağlayangil, as late as December, in separate meetings with him in Athens and elsewhere in Europe.

Pipinelis seems to have felt strongly that this was a historic moment for him to stand by Greece at a time when others, who like him disapproved of the colonels' regime, had fled or were in prison. Pipinelis was near the end of his career of public service and had no apparent ambitions beyond saving his country from disaster. He believed that once decisions were made regarding Cyprus, they would not and could not be reversed by a future democratic government. However, Pipinelis's leverage with Makarios was very slight.

The archbishop saw little need, according to reports from reliable sources, to make real concessions as long as the United States and Britain set such great store by keeping Turkey from a landing on the island, and as long as Turkey itself was turning its national attention away from Cyprus in the new atmosphere of détente. In other words, Makarios apparently believed that time was on his side.

Pipinelis met with Çağlayangil in Brussels on November 13 and agreed to try to expedite the talks by special meetings respectively between Pipinelis and Clerides in Athens and Çağlayangil and Denktaş in Ankara. This was done, but the results were not visible.

So ended the second phase of the intercommunal negotiations, not without some progress on the least sensitive issues and with agreement to enter a third phase in 1969. So ended, incidentally, my direct concern with these problems in the change of administrations in Washington and my access to official information and participation. The outlook was neither encouraging nor discouraging, but it was clear that a mediatory U.S. role was indefinitely shelved. We had nothing to say or do at this juncture that could induce the parties to narrow the gap in their basic positions. To avoid raising the ante, we could only urge flexibility and realism, and we could backstop advice from the United Nations Secretariat and its closely observant representatives in Cyprus. This we did.

The Role of an Embassy

It is appropriate at this point to reflect on the role played by U.S. Government agencies in this phase of the ongoing Cyprus problem. I have told the 1965–68 story in detail with two purposes in mind. In terms of space, I have given more attention to the issues involved than to the mechanics of "crisis management." I have done this because the problem of Cyprus is so complex and so widely misunderstood and because this phase of its evolution has been largely ignored. So also, however, has been the range of capabilities of the Department of State and the U.S. Foreign Service to act in crises of this kind. I have sought to provide an illustration of that range of capabilities.

To be effective the Service must shun publicity, and this applies particularly when supporting a mediator such as Cyrus Vance in a fast-moving and dangerous situation. In Turkey, as in many posts where severe problems lie in wait, preparations in the embassy were rehearsed for the crisis that might or might not occur as the result of external threat or internal tension. We must remember that Turkey lives in an environment of not very friendly neighbors. In 1965, it had just restored parliamentary government after the 1960 internal military intervention that led to the execution of a popular prime minister, his foreign minister, and his finance minister; the proscribing of an entire political party that had enjoyed grassroots support; and the establishment of a new constitution.

The U.S. embassy had an unusually able staff, largely unknown to the world press and to the U.S. Congress, but highly respected within the confines of the U.S. intelligence community (State, Defense, CIA, NSA, and others) for its dedication and sound judgment. This staff gave exemplary service during the height of the crisis of 1967, as described in this case history, but prior to that time and afterward it never flagged in its attention to the preservation of NATO, sound relations with Turkey, and peace in the area.

When speaking of "crisis management," this book uses a popular term that is easily misunderstood. Most factors in an international crisis are beyond "management." Rather they must be met, and dealt with. Training, experience, and intuition are brought to bear. The "management" comes in martialing all the tools at hand. The embassy is managed so as to subordinate other work and to apply manpower under new priorities. In Washington, every appropriate agency may participate in a task force, chaired in this case by the State Department. The help of friendly governments is enlisted as well as the good offices of the UN Secretariat and other international organizations that might assist in moving the situation out of danger and into an atmosphere where calm and reflection can prevail. Thus an interagency and even an international team is mobilized, but the embassy remains on the front line of action, reporting, and analysis. It is expected not simply to carry out orders but to use its best judgment in line with well-understood policy, to take timely initiatives, and to handle press inquiries with skill and discretion.

Secrecy in this case was imperative to avoid public reactions beyond those already faced. An aroused citizenry can be highly irrational. We were assisted somewhat by competition for news space from other world issues, and by the cooperation of the Turkish Foreign Ministry in handling the aggressive Turkish press. It was also an advantage that only a slender international news force resided in Ankara.

Part 4
Epilogue

11
Aftermath and Beyond

In the final chapter, we review events subsequent to my period of direct involvement and attempt a look into the future.

The withdrawal of Greek forces in response to the appeal of the UN secretary-general expressed a fundamental change in mainland Greek attitudes toward Cyprus—unwillingness to go to war with Turkey to achieve union with the island. It also produced shifts and crises in the Greek Cypriot political arena. Greece had ceased to be a credible champion of *enosis*. The intercommunal negotiations, encouraged by the United Nations, Athens, Ankara, the United Kingdom, and the United States, centered the attention of both communities on the means whereby Turkish and Greek Cypriots might live together in a "unitary" republic. With excellent legal and political talent supporting them, Denktaş and Clerides pursued their often frustrating discussions with poor results on the fundamentals of power sharing and Turkish Cypriot self-rule. So it went until mid-1974, when the impulsive successor to Papadopoulos, Brigadier General Dimitrios Ioannides, ordered the Cypriot National Guard on July 15, 1974, to overthrow Makarios and take control of the Government of Cyprus.[55]

During those six years of intermittent negotiation, Turkish Cypriots led a political life of their own, separate from that of the Greek Cypriots, partly in enclaves, partly in villages commingled with Greek Cypriots. They depended on their new leadership, established under the Provisional Turkish Cypriot Administration. It was a school for independence. Fazil Küçük, seeing Makarios re-elected in January 1968 without voter participation by Turkish Cypriots, held his own re-election by Turkish Cypriots, in retaliation. This was denounced as illegal by Makarios. Thus two parallel regimes functioned as states, one internationally recognized, the other not, while neither abandoned the thesis that its ultimate negotiating goal was a single government of Cyprus. In reality, Cyprus was already partitioned politically, although it was a patchwork territorially. The Turkish and Greek national contingents remained in place, as did UNFICYP. The London-Zürich Treaties were partially in force.

Relative peace prevailed between the communities until the surreptitious return of Grivas to Cyprus in 1971, backed by the junta in Athens. Tensions then rose as Grivas, in hiding, rebuilt EOKA into EOKA B and organized an overt political force against Makarios in the "Union of Fellow Combatants in the National Struggle."

Papadopoulos and his crew had apparently reached the conclusion that Makarios would never settle the Cyprus problem, whether by *enosis*, double *enosis*, or essential compromises with Turkish Cypriots. It alarmed them that by tolerating AKEL and flirting with the Soviet bloc and Beijing, the archbishop had become a danger to their regime in Greece. Papadopoulos decided to use a ready-made fifth column.

Prepared for that role was the Cypriot National Guard. It continued to have Greek officers seconded to it at the command level, most of whom were pro-*enosis* and sympathetic to the junta. They were inclined to accept the instructions of Athens, where their careers were established, rather than those of their local commander-in-chief, Makarios.[56]

The fault in the junta's policy lay in its want of political judgment and lack of restraint. The return of Grivas and the rebuilding of the extreme pro-*enosis* faction in Cyprus constituted a strategic miscalculation. Together these forces were loose cannons on the deck of island politics. They had a single narrow objective, *enosis* by force, and they left few if any options open to the Turks. The junta also underestimated Makarios, who was more than equal to their political challenge. He was immensely popular among Greek Cypriots and extremely resourceful in defending his ethnarchy against pro-*enosis* attack.

The death of Grivas from a heart attack on January 27, 1974, did not alleviate this intra-Greek Cypriot struggle for power, which was suddenly thrown into high gear by the change of regime in Greece. General Dimitrios Ioannides had led the coup against Papadopoulos in November 1973 from within the military junta. The reasons apparently included opposition to Papadopoulos's overcentralization of powers in himself, but also impatience over his ineffectiveness against Makarios. As successor to Makarios, Ioannides selected Nicos Sampson, a trigger-happy EOKA gunman dedicated to *enosis*, with a record of violence against Turkish Cypriots.[57] The National Guard seized Nicosia Radio on July 15, 1974, bombarded the presidential palace and the Archbishopric, but failed to kill Makarios, who escaped to London with British help.

Turkish Prime Minister Bülent Ecevit at once contacted Ioannides and sought Greek cooperation with Turkey under the Treaty of Guarantee. He also demanded the removal of Sampson, the withdrawal of all Greek officers from the National Guard, and a binding Greek guarantee of Cypriot independence. This was refused, on the ground that what was happening in Cyprus was a purely internal matter. Sampson was proclaimed president by the National Guard, once it had crushed resistance by Makarios's police.

Makarios himself proceeded to New York, addressing an electrified UN Security Council where he denounced the usurpation of his authority by Athens and won overwhelming Council endorsement.

Ecevit, rebuffed by Athens, now flew to London to seek British participation in joint military action under the Treaty of Guarantee; but Britain declined a combined military operation. Ecevit then fell back on Article 3 of the Treaty of Guarantee and prepared Turkish forces to act alone. On July 20, 1974, a sea and air operation of six thousand men (later augmented to forty thousand with heavy equipment) landed on Cyprus's northern coast, west of Kyrenia. After overcoming stiff resistance by the National Guard, the Turkish troops formed a triangle of occupation connecting the coast with northern Nicosia. The long isolation of Turkish Cypriot leadership from strategic supply and reinforcement was now ended.

These events brought about an untenable situation for Ioannides, whose loss of support among his own military colleagues is detailed in *The Rise and Fall of the Greek Colonels* by C. M. Woodhouse.[58] The option of war with Turkey was rejected by the junta, which unconditionally withdrew from power in favor of a return to a civilian regime headed by former Prime Minister Constantine Karamanlis. U.S. diplomatic efforts during and after this period deserve separate first-hand treatment.[59] In essence, U.S. efforts began too late and too feebly to forestall the coup against Makarios; and the United States had no leverage to prevent the inevitable Turkish military reaction to an imminent third threat of *enosis*.

So great was Greek-American detestation of the military regime in Athens that the initial Turkish landing on Cyprus was almost overlooked amid general approval of the return of Greek democracy. However, the subsequent expansion of the area of occupation by Turkish forces aroused intense Greek-American resentment. The expansion, justified by Ankara at the time by the failure of negotiations at Geneva between foreign ministers of Greece, the United Kingdom, and Turkey, evolved during August 14–16, 1974, to the present boundary ("Attila Line") of the Turkish Cypriot super-enclave, now established as the Turkish Republic of Northern Cyprus. There is no doubt that this boundary was pre-planned. The occupation covered (and still covers) roughly 37 percent of the land area of Cyprus and appeared permanent.

From the occupied zone, about 180,000 Greek Cypriots fled to the Greek Cypriot south, and to it at least 47,000 Turkish Cypriots from the south migrated by air and every possible land conveyance.[60] Territorial partition was now a fact. Mainland Turkish settlers also moved in and were given property.[61] The Cypriot power equation was now reversed.

Sampson resigned in Nicosia shortly after the Turkish landings as the junta backing him dissolved itself in Athens. He was replaced by the president of the House of Representatives, Glafcos Clerides, as acting president of the Republic.

The total casualty figures from these hostilities are not really known, but some estimates are six thousand Greek Cypriot dead, and over two thousand missing; fifteen hundred Turkish and Turkish Cypriot dead and two thousand wounded.[62] As of this writing, Greek Cypriot and Turkish Cypriot missing persons are still being discussed between the communal leaders. The Turkish losses included those in less well-defended enclaves and in many villages across the island, most of which were at the mercy of the National Guard or Greek Cypriot irregulars.

For both sides in this country of modest numbers, it was a costly and bitter experience, one which the UNFICYP, the United States, the United Kingdom, Canada, and many Greeks and Turks had worked hard for a decade to avoid. The event bore curious parallels to classic Greek tragedy, especially its inevitable ending. Distrust had triumphed over statesmanship. The final blow to a commingling of the two communities under any guise, such as cantonization, had been delivered by Greek Cypriot extremists, turned loose by a misguided military regime in Athens. EOKA's overconfident gamble foreshadowed its eclipse.

The current tendency of both Cyprus and Greece is to ignore *enosis* as an aspiration, but emphasize Hellenism as a common heritage and bond. Above all, the inclination has been to blame the United States for the island's misfortunes and to organize congressional pressure to punish the Turks by denial of military aid.

The United States should recognize this as a flight from reality. Group self-criticism, especially by small political entities, is a rare commodity. It is infinitely easier to target a larger outside force. To substantiate this allegation of U.S. "guilt," Greek Cypriot and mainland Greek political circles have periodically urged an opening of "the Cyprus file." Finally, in October 1988, a committee of the Greek governing party, PASOK,[63] issued a "report" on the "file," seeking to put primary blame on former Prime Minister Karamanlis and his Defense Minister Averoff for not sending a force to defend Cyprus. This met with considerable derision in the Greek press, which labeled it a partisan pre-election gambit by PASOK.[64]

On August 19, 1974, Rodger P. Davies, an exemplary Foreign Service officer newly appointed as U.S. ambassador to Cyprus, was assassinated inside his embassy along with a Cypriot female employee, Antoinetta Varnava, whose skull was blown apart as she tried to save him. The act was carried out by Greek Cypriot snipers in military uniform who took a visible firing position on a rise of land next to a nearby unfinished building. They used mounted heavy rifles and high-velocity, armor-piercing ammunition, which penetrated drawn shutters and hit the victims at a place to which they had withdrawn for safety.[65] The assailants' identity appeared to be established beyond reasonable doubt by close-range observers and by photographs. Although apprehended, they were never convicted of the killing, due to alleged lack of evidence.[66] One thing is sure: it would have been dangerously unpopular for any Cypriot authority to execute the killers at that time, as there was widespread suspicion, reflected in the Cypriot press, that the United States was in some way behind the Greek Cypriot disaster.

The administration in Washington gave Davies a national tribute on his body's arrival at Andrews Air Force Base, but it applied no sanctions on Cyprus. Instead, Congress saw fit in February 1975, despite presidential objections, to slap an arms embargo on Turkey, thereby seriously weakening the military strength of the second largest ground force in NATO. This caused the Turkish government to retaliate by suspending the use of our base facilities. U.S. security interests were obviously imperiled. The embargo was lifted in 1978 following great efforts by President Carter, and the bases returned to shared use.

Greek and Greek Cypriot pressures within the U.S. body politic still seek to develop in the American public an anti-Turkish bias, as well as a sense of primary American responsibility for the Cyprus tragedy, and thereby to direct the American public into the service of Greek Cypriot objectives. These include "internationalizing" the Cyprus question by convening an international conference of principal interested powers, as urged by the Soviet Union; by fostering resolutions in the United Nations calling for unconditional and immediate withdrawal of Turkish occupation forces and mainland settlers from Cyprus; by seeking to have the European Community (EC) condition full Turkish membership on the withdrawal of Turkish forces and settlers from Cyprus; by calling for the lifting of all restrictions on the return of Greek Cypriots to their homes in the north; and, naturally enough, nonrecognition of any legal status of the Turkish Federated State of Cyprus and its successor, the Turkish Republic of Northern Cyprus.

The Federated State had been proclaimed by Denktaş on February 13, 1975. There followed a referendum in the north approving the action. On November 15, 1983—using the hiatus between military rule in Turkey and an elected government—this state was converted by Denktaş into today's Republic, against Ankara's advice. International recognition, particularly among Muslim nations, has been sought by Denktaş, but so far without success. Only Turkey recognizes its statehood as of this writing.

All of these progressions, from the Provisional Administration of 1967 to the Turkish Republic of today, have been accompanied by offers from the Turkish Cypriot leadership to negotiate a bizonal, bicommunal federation with the south. They have been justified in placing the leadership in a position to meet Greek Cypriot negotiators on equal terms or to opt for final severance and permanent independence if the negotiations fail.

Disregarding the rhetoric which has characterized both the Turkish and Greek Cypriot statements over the years, the facts as of this writing appear as follows:

1. The balance of power on the island has been decisively shifted away from Greek Cypriot military preponderance. EOKA's foolhardiness in seeking a violent road to *enosis* has largely discredited it with the Greek Cypriot south. Turkish Cypriots now feel secure, under the cover of Turkish forces and within a single defensible region, against superior Greek numerical strength. Their new sense of security is the most precious result won by Turkish Cypriots. No future negotiation by them is likely to include a provision for the *total* evacuation of Turkish troops. As of this writing these may number from twenty to thirty thousand, and their drastic reduction becomes a bargaining chip in negotiations over a proposed demilitarization of Cyprus.

2. Makarios, who returned to the island in December 1974 after the Turkish landings, recognized that a bicommunal, federal system on Cyprus was the only feasible approach. In the last meeting of Makarios with Denktaş in February 1977, a few months before Makarios's death, the two leaders agreed on guidelines which, while very general, give implicit recognition to the principle of bizonality in paragraph 2 (see appendix 10). In 1979 at the meeting of Denktaş and Kyprianou, who had succeeded to the presidency following the death of Makarios, these guidelines were confirmed (see appendix 12). It must be stressed that neither statement of principles provides other than very broad generalities, and these have left room for many definitions and abundant charges of bad faith. Nonetheless, they are not disavowed by either side and provide a direction sign for the parties and for the UN secretary-general.

3. UN Secretaries-General Waldheim and Pérez de Cuéllar both expended great personal energy and made use of superb negotiators to identify common ground in a continuing effort now covering twenty-four years. There has been a mountain of proposals and counterproposals. The level of human talent devoted to the problem is only suggested by the *dramatis personae* at the start of this book. Pérez de Cuéllar, in particular, using the 1977 and 1979 communiqués, has brought his long experience in Cyprus as special representative of his predecessor, Waldheim, into the search for a procedure to begin talks toward a framework of shared understandings. His unparalleled expertise and dedication produced the "proximity talks" of 1984, during which he met separately with each communal leadership. These brought about a sufficient spectrum of agree-

ment to warrant his "framework" proposal of January 1985. This was to be signed in New York that month by Kyprianou and Denktaş, as a first step toward further negotiation on several fundamentals, such as territory, constitutional sharing of power, and external guarantees.

Preparatory to that meeting, Denktaş had offered to reduce the Turkish Cypriot zone from approximately 37 percent to 29 percent of the island's surface, to make concessions on Varosha, a Greek Cypriot suburb of Famagusta, and to open the Nicosia Airport. At the meeting, however, Kyprianou seems to have developed cold feet. He retreated from what had been understood by the UN Secretariat to be his willingness to sign a way-station accord, whereas Denktaş was ready to sign at once.

Further efforts by Pérez de Cuéllar throughout 1985 and into early 1986 seeking to amend the framework and clear the way for a partial agreement ran up against Kyprianou's unwillingness to proceed along the lines he was understood to have accepted in 1984. Backed by Greek Prime Minister Andreas Papandreou of Greece, Kyprianou insisted on an *initial* agreement by the Turkish Cypriots on: (1) a timetable for the total withdrawal of Turkish troops; (2) full freedom of movement on the island and the return to the north of such Greek Cypriots as desire to resettle; (3) the exit from Cyprus of mainland Turkish settlers; and (4) international guarantees (preferably by an international conference to include the Soviet Union) ensuring the Republic of Cyprus against any future foreign interventions. This would end the London-Zürich Treaty of Guarantee.

The March 29, 1986, revision of Pérez de Cuéllar's framework (appendix 13) was also accepted by Denktaş and rejected by Kyprianou, who was sharply criticized by Clerides, by AKEL, and by sectors of the Cypriot press for letting an historic opportunity go by.

Conclusions

What is apparent from over twenty years of intermittent negotiations between the communal leaders is that the current de facto division is less objectionable to the parties than the concessions that would be needed to achieve agreement. Separation has become institutionalized, and each side has an investment in its respective institutions of government. Kyprianou could never bring himself to legitimize a Turkish Cypriot constitution, with its own parliament and control over land and movement within and over its borders in what would be a very loose confederation. In addition, economic advantages to Greek Cyprus of such a confederation are quite unclear. The south, despite or because of the population displaced from the north, is more prosperous than is today's socialist Greece.

It remains to be seen whether the new president of Cyprus, Yeoryios Vassiliou, will or can adopt a significantly different approach. Intercommunal talks at the highest level, without preconditions, were reinitiated by Pérez de Cuéllar in 1988 and proceeded on schedule through the year, in Nicosia and New York. Emphasis was given to building confidence, and a settlement date by June 1989 was agreed upon publicly by the two sides. Although the target date passed, the conversations continued.

The issues, however, remain as formidable as ever. Denktaş is unlikely to abandon all Turkish military presence or to sign away a Turkish right of military intervention. Nor does Ankara appear likely to abandon this right. Denktaş is also unlikely to permit the return of tens of thousands of Greek Cypriots, even if they were willing to resettle under Turkish Cypriot rule, thereby upsetting the demographic preponderance of Turks. Furthermore, few Turkish Cypriots would be likely to elect to return to live under Greek Cypriot rule in the south. A revival of commingling is highly improbable. An international tribunal of property claims will probably be needed, which might well award higher value to the Greek Cypriot property abandoned in the north than to that left by the Turkish Cypriots in the south, given the discrepancy in population displacements and land values.

The best one could expect (and current chances look dim) would be for the formation of a loose confederation of the two states, each sovereign in its internal governance, but sharing limited delegated powers and allowing for island-wide freedom of trade and for freedom of movement short of resettlement.

A positive development with a possible bearing on the Cyprus problem is the partial thaw in Greek-Turkish relations. After making what political capital he could from anti-Turkish statements over a period of years, Greek Prime Minister Andreas Papandreou finally reacted to a series of conciliatory public statements by Turkish Prime Minister Turgut Özal and invited a personal meeting with Özal, which took place at Davos, Switzerland, on January 30 and 31, 1988.[67] Follow-up conversations between the two occurred in March 1988 at the NATO ministerial meetings in Brussels and during Özal's June 1988 state visit to Athens, the first such visit by a Turkish prime minister since 1952.[68] Public statements after each of these discussions indicated that the tone had been cordial.

At the Davos meeting, mechanisms were agreed upon to pursue bilateral issues through special mixed commissions and to resume top-level talks at regular intervals. A communiqué between the parties announced agreement that matters between them must never come to the point of war. Serious bilateral issues, such as the Aegean seabed boundaries, flight information and air boundary questions, and the treatment of nationals of either in the territory of the other were to be tackled by mixed task forces.

The unexpected warmth of these meetings evoked nervousness at first in both Turkish Cypriot and Greek Cypriot government circles,[69] who obviously feared some possible loss of leverage on the attention and support of their "motherlands." The meetings between Athens and Ankara seem to have generated pressures on the two Cypriot communities to resume serious talks under Pérez de Cuéllar's auspices. A parallel influence in this direction may be traceable to the atmosphere of 1988 U.S.–Soviet summitry and a certain convergence of Soviet and American views on the direction of a Cyprus settlement. In fact, the Greek Cypriot press on February 9, 1989, carried statements by the U.S. and Soviet embassy spokesmen showing a close approximation of views strongly supporting the intercommunal dialogue.[70]

The general condition on Cyprus has been peaceful, with no serious armed clashes in over fourteen years. The basic problem grinds on, but at a lower level of tension. Separation of the communities into two zones, together with the buffer zone and UNFICYP presence along the frontier, have served to assist the peace, unacceptable though the frontier is to Greek Cypriots. It will be the task of leaders of the two communities to take such small steps as they can to restore a measure of confidence, rather than provoke such border incidents as the one on November 15, 1988. Then, a barrier in the buffer zone in Nicosia, established by UNFICYP after the 1974 Turkish landings, was breached by several hundred Greek Cypriot demonstrators, using rocks, iron bars, and cans of gasoline. They were stopped at the line of Turkish forces. Nine UN soldiers were injured in the incident, and a few Greek Cypriots were injured by rocks thrown from the other side of the Green Line.[71]

Little by little, the communal leaders need to invite economic cooperation and increased freedom of movement to enable the island's population as a whole to realize the possibilities, however limited, that the area offers for a decent way of life. Only then, I suspect, will a sharing of political power develop over decades, as new generations turn against the intransigeance of the old.

For the United States and for NATO, any formula devised for a settlement is quite secondary to the liquidation of hostility between Greece and Turkey.[72] Front-end U.S. mediation today is not sought and would only hamper the efforts of the UN secretary-general. In fact, the only option open to the United States and its allies appears to be constant encouragement and the fullest backing of Pérez de Cuéllar in his patient labors. The Soviet Union continues to seek a role in the negotiation process and to propose an international conference at which it would sit. However, it does not oppose the current talks conducted by the UN Secretariat, and it clearly holds to a policy of preserving a nonaligned single state of Cyprus, though not ruling out a bizonal federation.

It is quite clear that even with active and constructive prodding by Greece, Turkey, the United Kingdom, the United States, and other interested UN member states, a reconciliation of the aspirations and claims of the two communities must be met by the leadership of those communities in direct negotiations. This is a process in which the United States Congress, above all, should not take sides. It is too prone to give way to pressures by ethnic constituencies favoring only one side. Such intervention invariably encourages one or both parties to seek to escape from the similar pressures of their own constituencies and take refuge in the mirage of external help. This stops the momentum, sidetracks the progress already made, and cannot serve U.S. security objectives. It is vital to insist that the parties understand that a true solution depends on them, and on them alone.

For Greece and Turkey to hold the two Cypriot communities to the position that intercommunal dialogue is the court of last resort, where painful compromises must be made—and that neither Greece nor Turkey will accept shifting the issue to the bilateral Greek-Turkish arena—will require a degree of steadfastness of purpose that may be hard to find in Athens and Ankara. What are the prospects?

Both have been through a severe testing of their stability and their democratic traditions during the past two decades. At different intervals both have experienced military rule, although different in motivation, philosophy, execution, and quality of leadership.

Greece saw its democracy vanish for seven years, beginning on April 21, 1967, to a cabal of senior, but not top-grade, officers who sought to exercise power indefinitely. They regarded the democracy they overthrew as corrupt and ineffective, endangering Greece's security by left-wing policies. Because they had no traditional or institutional mandate to occupy the seat of power even provisionally, they sought public support in various economic measures, in nationalistic programs such as *enosis*, and in U.S. support of their strong anti-communist orientation.

In the end, their rule was so patently arbitrary, inept, brutal, and dangerously reckless that, in July 1974, the armed forces collapsed from within, refusing to act against the Turkish intervention in Cyprus. It was the discredited junta itself that finally called for a return to democracy under Karamanlis.[73] Under Andreas Papandreou and his Pan-Hellenic Socialism, elected to power in 1981, there was little to inspire hope in terms of long-term constancy and statesmanship as regards Cyprus, until, perhaps, the year 1988. The future remained cloudy as Papandreou's electoral popularity declined.

Republican Turkey has gone through three military interventions to set democracy, as seen by the armed forces, on its feet. The total of outright military rule has been four years. Turkey has a tradition that the forces should stay out of politics, but may intervene to defend the Kemalist republic and its principles against threats from within, as well as from without. Kemalist principles are immutable. Upon them constitutions may be built and amended.

Republican Turkey has had three constitutions, those of 1924, 1961, and 1983. Together they represent a search for effectiveness and stability in the exercise of democracy. The latest constitution appears to offer Turkey the best chance for stability thus far, if economic problems can be solved. It is oriented toward encouragement of a presidential two-party system and away from splinter parties or excessive checks and balances, which taken together made the second constitution unworkable. Looking at Greece and Turkey, therefore, there are grounds for hope, but not for blindness to history, as we ponder the chances for the kind of statesmanship and constancy which could bring the two communities on Cyprus to an acceptance of some formula for peaceful co-existence.

It is also vital that the American public be well informed of what is currently happening. Misinformation works mischief on Capitol Hill. It may be too early to expect harmony between Greece and Turkey, but it should be realized that a fourth confrontation between them could irreparably damage both their own security interests and those of NATO, and thus of the United States.

It is grotesque that Cyprus should have twice threatened Free World security. It is today a question of federating two working democracies with fifteen years of separate experience. It is no longer a live question of double *enosis*, nor of annexation by either Greece or Turkey. Federation is difficult, but still possible, and would have economic advantages to both sides. If Turkish and Greek Cypriots together are mature enough to put behind them the hatred that has cost so many lives and to look upon each other with a new tolerance and understanding, we Americans can conclude that Rodger Davies lost his life in a good cause.

Cyprus has an ancient heritage, apart from that of either Greece or Turkey, of which all Cypriots could be proud. It has assets which, if intelligently used, can make it prosperous and serene. There are already strong signs that a self-awareness in both sectors of Cyprus is replacing, gradually, the older feeling of unwilling separation from a "motherland." If continued, this could be the first step toward partnership in a land of unparalleled beauty and exceptional human resources.

Appendix 1
London-Zürich Treaties of February 1959

(Constitution and treaties entered into force August 16, 1960)

Conference on Cyprus: Documents Signed and Initialed at Lancaster House on February 19, 1959

I. Memorandum Setting Out the Agreed Foundation for the Final Settlement of the Problem of Cyprus

The Prime Minister of the United Kingdom of Great Britain and Northern Ireland, the Prime Minister of the Kingdom of Greece and the Prime Minister of the Turkish Republic,

Taking note of the Declaration by the Representative of the Greek-Cypriot Community and the Representative of the Turkish-Cypriot Community that they accept the documents annexed to this Memorandum as the agreed foundation for the final settlement of the problem of Cyprus,

Hereby adopt, on behalf of their respective Governments, the documents annexed to this Memorandum and listed below, as the agreed foundation for the final settlement of the problem of Cyprus.

On behalf of the Government of the United Kingdom of Great Britain and Northern Ireland	On behalf of the Government of the Kingdom of Greece	On behalf of the Government of the Turkish Republic
Harold MacMillan	C. Karamanlis	A. Menderes

London, February 19, 1959.

Source: Great Britain, Colonial Office, *Conference on Cyprus: Documents Signed and Initialed at Lancaster House on February 19, 1959*, Command Paper No. 679, Misc. No. 4, 1959 (London: Her Majesty's Stationery Office, 1959). For the text of the Constitution of the Republic of Cyprus, see *Constitutional and Parliamentary Information*, cited in Bibliography. See also *United Nations Treaty Series*, vol. 382 (1960), 5475-86, pp. 3–253.

List of Documents Annexed

A.—Basic Structure of the Republic of Cyprus.

B.—Treaty of Guarantee between the Republic of Cyprus and Greece, the United Kingdom and Turkey.

C.—Treaty of Alliance between the Republic of Cyprus, Greece and Turkey.

D.—Declaration made by the Government of the United Kingdom on February 17, 1959.

E.—Additional Article to be inserted in the Treaty of Guarantee.

F.—Declaration made by the Greek and Turkish Foreign Ministers on February 17, 1959.

G.—Declaration made by the Representative of the Greek Cypriot Community on February 19, 1959.

H.—Declaration made by the Representative of the Turkish Cypriot Community on February 19, 1959.

I.—Agreed Measures to prepare for the new arrangements in Cyprus.

II. English Translation of the Documents Agreed in the French Texts and Initialled by the Greek and Turkish Prime Ministers at Zürich on February 11, 1959

(a) Basic Structure of the Republic of Cyprus

1. The State of Cyprus shall be a Republic with a presidential régime, the President being Greek and the Vice-President Turkish elected by universal suffrage by the Greek and Turkish communities of the Island respectively.

2. The official languages of the Republic of Cyprus shall be Greek and Turkish. Legislative and administrative instruments and documents shall be drawn up and promulgated in the two official languages.

3. The Republic of Cyprus shall have its own flag of neutral design and colour, chosen jointly by the President and the Vice-President of the Republic.

Authorities and communities shall have the right to fly the Greek and Turkish flags on holidays at the same time as the flag of Cyprus.

The Greek and Turkish communities shall have the right to celebrate Greek and Turkish national holidays.

4. The President and the Vice-President shall be elected for a period of five years.

In the event of absence, impediment or vacancy of their posts, the President and the Vice-President shall be replaced by the President and the Vice-President of the House of Representatives respectively.

In the event of a vacancy in either post, the election of new incumbents shall take place within a period of not more than 45 days.

The President and the Vice-President shall be invested by the House of Representatives, before which they shall take an oath of loyalty and respect for the Constitution. For this purpose, the House of Representatives shall meet within 24 hours after its constitution.

5. Executive authority shall be vested in the President and the Vice-President. For this purpose they shall have a Council of Ministers composed of seven Greek Ministers and three Turkish Ministers. The Ministers shall be designated respectively by the President and the Vice-President who shall appoint them by an instrument signed by them both.

The Ministers may be chosen from outside the House of Representatives.

Decisions of the Council of Ministers shall be taken by an absolute majority.

Decisions so taken shall be promulgated immediately by the President and the Vice-President by publication in the official gazette.

However, the President and the Vice-President shall have the right of final veto and the right to return the decisions of the Council of Ministers under the same conditions as those laid down for laws and decisions of the House of Representatives.

6. Legislative authority shall be vested in a House of Representatives elected for a period of five years by universal suffrage of each community separately in the proportion of 70 per cent, for the Greek community and 30 per cent, for the Turkish community, this proportion being fixed independently of statistical data. (*N.B.*—The number of Representatives shall be fixed by mutual agreement between the communities.)

The House of Representatives shall exercise authority in all matters other than those expressly reserved to the Communal Chambers. In the event of a conflict of authority, such conflict shall be decided by the Supreme Constitutional Court which shall be composed of one Greek, one Turk and one neutral, appointed jointly by the President and the Vice-President. The neutral judge shall be president of the Court.

7. Laws and decisions of the House of Representatives shall be adopted

by a simple majority of the members present. They shall be promulgated within 15 days if neither the President nor the Vice-President returns them for reconsideration as provided in Point 9 below.

The Constitutional Law, with the exception of its basic articles, may be modified by a majority comprising two-thirds of the Greek members and two-thirds of the Turkish members of the House of Representatives.

Any modification of the electoral law and the adoption of any law relating to the municipalities and of any law imposing duties or taxes shall require a simple majority of the Greek and Turkish members of the House of Representatives taking part in the vote and considered separately.

On the adoption of the budget, the President and the Vice-President may exercise their right to return it to the House of Representatives, if in their judgment any question of discrimination arises. If the House maintains its decisions, the President and the Vice-President shall have the right to appeal to the Supreme Constitutional Court.

8. The President and the Vice-President, separately and conjointly, shall have the right of final veto on any law or decision concerning foreign affairs, except the participation of the Republic of Cyprus in international organisations and pacts of alliance in which Greece and Turkey both participate, or concerning defence and security as defined in Annex I.

9. The President and the Vice-President of the Republic shall have, separately and conjointly, the right to return all laws and decisions, which may be returned to the House of Representatives within a period of not more than 15 days for reconsideration.

The House of Representatives shall pronounce within 15 days on any matter so returned. If the House of Representatives maintains its decisions, the President and the Vice-President shall promulgate the law or decision in question within the time-limits fixed for the promulgation of laws and decisions.

Laws and decisions, which are considered by the President or the Vice-President to discriminate against either of the two communities, shall be submitted to the Supreme Constitutional Court which may annul or confirm the law or decision, or return it to the House of Representatives for reconsideration, in whole or in part. The law or decision shall not become effective until the Supreme Constitutional Court or, where it has been returned, the House of Representatives has taken a decision on it.

10. Each community shall have its Communal Chamber composed of a number of representatives which it shall itself determine.

The Communal Chambers shall have the right to impose taxes and levies on members of their community to provide for their needs and for the needs of bodies and institutions under their supervision.

The Communal Chambers shall exercise authority in all religious, educational, cultural and teaching questions and questions of personal status. They shall exercise authority in questions where the interests and institutions are of a purely communal nature, such as sporting and charitable foundations, bodies and associations, producers' and consumers' co-operatives and credit establishments, created for the purpose of promoting the welfare of one of the communities. (*N.B.*—It is understood that the provisions of the present paragraph cannot be interpreted in such a way as to prevent the creation of mixed and communal institutions where the inhabitants desire them.)

These producers' and consumers' co-operatives and credit establishments, which shall be administered under the laws of the Republic, shall be subject to the supervision of the Communal Chambers. The Communal Chambers shall also exercise authority in matters initiated by municipalities which are composed of one community only. These municipalities, to which the laws of the Republic shall apply, shall be supervised in their functions by the Communal Chambers.

Where the central administration is obliged to take over the supervision of the institutions, establishments, or municipalities mentioned in the two preceding paragraphs by virtue of legislation in force, this supervision shall be exercised by officials belonging to the same community as the institution, establishment or municipality in question.

11. The Civil Service shall be composed as to 70 per cent. of Greeks and as to 30 per cent. of Turks.

It is understood that this quantitative division will be applied as far as practicable in all grades of the Civil Service.

In regions or localities where one of the two communities is in a majority approaching 100 per cent., the organs of the local administration responsible to the central administration shall be composed solely of officials belonging to that community.

12. The deputies of the Attorney-General of the Republic, the Inspector-General, the Treasurer and the Governor of the Issuing Bank

may not belong to the same community as their principals. The holders of these posts shall be appointed by the President and the Vice-President of the Republic acting in agreement.

13. The heads and deputy heads of the Armed Forces, the Gendarmerie and the Police shall be appointed by the President and the Vice-President of the Republic acting in agreement. One of these heads shall be Turkish and where the head belongs to one of the communities, the deputy head shall belong to the other.

14. Compulsory military service may only be instituted with the agreement of the President and the Vice-President of the Republic of Cyprus.

Cyprus shall have an army of 2,000 men, of whom 60 per cent. shall be Greek and 40 per cent. Turkish.

The security forces (gendarmerie and police) shall have a complement of 2,000 men, which may be reduced or increased with the agreement of both the President and the Vice-President. The security forces shall be composed as to 70 per cent. of Greeks and as to 30 per cent. of Turks. However, for an initial period this percentage may be raised to a maximum of 40 per cent. of Turks (and consequently reduced to 60 per cent. of Greeks) in order not to discharge those Turks now serving in the police, apart from the auxiliary police.

15. Forces, which are stationed in parts of the territory of the Republic inhabited, in a proportion approaching 100 per cent., by members of a single community, shall belong to that community.

16. A High Court of Justice shall be established, which shall consist of two Greeks, one Turk and one neutral, nominated jointly by the President and the Vice-President of the Republic.

The President of the Court shall be the neutral judge, who shall have two votes.

This Court shall constitute the highest organ of the judicature (appointments, promotions of judges &c.).

17. Civil disputes, where the plaintiff and the defendant belong to the same community, shall be tried by a tribunal composed of judges belonging to that community. If the plaintiff and defendant belong to different communities, the composition of the tribunal shall be mixed and shall be determined by the High Court of Justice.

Tribunals dealing with civil disputes relating to questions of personal status and to religious matters, which are reserved to the competence of the Communal Chambers under Point 10, shall be composed solely of judges belonging to the community concerned. The composition and status of these tribunals shall be determined according to the law drawn up by the Communal Chamber and they shall apply the law drawn up by the Communal Chamber.

In criminal cases, the tribunal shall consist of judges belonging to the same community as the accused. If the injured party belongs to another community, the composition of the tribunal shall be mixed and shall be determined by the High Court of Justice.

18. The President and the Vice-President of the Republic shall each have the right to exercise the prerogative of mercy to persons from their respective communities who are condemned to death. In cases where the plaintiffs and the convicted persons are members of different communities the prerogative of mercy shall be exercised by agreement between the President and the Vice-President. In the event of disagreement the vote for clemency shall prevail. When mercy is accorded the death penalty shall be commuted to life imprisonment.

19. In the event of agricultural reform, lands shall be redistributed only to persons who are members of the same community as the expropriated owners.

Expropriations by the State or the Municipalities shall only be carried out on payment of a just and equitable indemnity fixed, in disputed cases, by the tribunals. An appeal to the tribunals shall have the effect of suspending action.

Expropriated property shall only be used for the purpose for which the expropriation was made. Otherwise the property shall be restored to the owners.

20. Separate municipalities shall be created in the five largest towns of Cyprus by the Turkish inhabitants of these towns. However:—

(a) In each of the towns a co-ordinating body shall be set up which shall supervise work which needs to be carried out jointly and shall concern itself with matters which require a degree of co-operation. These bodies shall each be composed of two members chosen by the Greek municipalities, two members chosen by the Turkish municipalities and a President chosen by agreement between the two municipalities.

(*b*) The President and the Vice-President shall examine within four years the question of whether or not this separation of municipalities in the five largest towns shall continue.

With regard to other localities, special arrangements shall be made for the constitution of municipal bodies, following, as far as possible, the rule of proportional representation for the two communities.

21. A Treaty guaranteeing the independence, territorial integrity and constitution of the new State of Cyprus shall be concluded between the Republic of Cyprus, Greece, the United Kingdom and Turkey. A Treaty of military alliance shall also be concluded between the Republic of Cyprus, Greece and Turkey.

These two instruments shall have constitutional force. (This last paragraph shall be inserted in the Constitution as a basic article.)

22. It shall be recognized that the total or partial union of Cyprus with any other State, or a separatist independence for Cyprus (*i.e.*, the partition of Cyprus into two independent States), shall be excluded.

23. The Republic of Cyprus shall accord most-favoured-nation treatment to Great Britain, Greece and Turkey for all agreements whatever their nature.

This provision shall not apply to the Treaties between the Republic of Cyprus and the United Kingdom concerning the bases and military facilities accorded to the United Kingdom.

24. The Greek and Turkish Governments shall have the right to subsidise institutions for education, culture, athletics and charity belonging to their respective communities.

Equally, where either community considers that it has not the necessary number of schoolmasters, professors or priests for the working of its institutions, the Greek and Turkish Governments may provide them to the extent strictly necessary to meet their needs.

25. One of the following Ministries—the Ministry of Foreign Affairs, the Ministry of Defence or the Ministry of Finance—shall be entrusted to a Turk. If the President and the Vice-President agree they may replace this system by a system of rotation.

26. The new State which is to come into being with the signature of the Treaties shall be established as quickly as possible and within a period of not more than three months from the signature of the Treaties.

27. All the above Points shall be considered to be basic articles of the Constitution of Cyprus.

E. A.-T. S. L. F. R. Z. †A. M. F. K.

Annex I

A

The defence questions subject to veto under Point 8 of the Basic Structure are as follows:—

(a) Composition and size of the armed forces and credits for them.

(b) Appointments and promotions.

(c) Imports of warlike stores and of all kinds of explosives.

(d) Granting of bases and other facilities to allied countries.

B

The security questions subject to veto are as follows:—

(a) Appointments and promotions.

(b) Allocation and stationing of forces.

(c) Emergency measures and martial law.

(d) Police laws.

(It is provided that the right of veto shall cover all emergency measures or decisions, but not those which concern the normal functioning of the police and gendarmerie.)

(b) Treaty of Guarantee

The Republic of Cyprus of the one part, and Greece, the United Kingdom and Turkey of the other part:—

I. Considering that the recognition and maintenance of the independence, territorial integrity and security of the Republic of Cyprus, as established and regulated by the basic articles of its Constitution, are in their common interest;

II. Desiring to co-operate to ensure that the provisions of the aforesaid Constitution shall be respected;

Have Agreed as Follows:—

Article 1

The Republic of Cyprus undertakes to ensure the maintenance of its independence, territorial integrity and security, as well as respect for its Constitution.

It undertakes not to participate, in whole or in part, in any political or economic union with any State whatsoever. With this intent it prohibits all activity tending to promote directly or indirectly either union or partition of the Island.

Article 2

Greece, the United Kingdom and Turkey, taking note of the undertakings by the Republic of Cyprus embodied in Article 1, recognise and guarantee the independence, territorial integrity and security of the Republic of Cyprus, and also the provisions of the basic articles of its Constitution.

They likewise undertake to prohibit, as far as lies within their power, all activity having the object of promoting directly or indirectly either the union of the Republic of Cyprus with any other State, or the partition of the Island.

Article 3

In the event of any breach of the provisions of the present Treaty, Greece, the United Kingdom, and Turkey undertake to consult together, with a view to making representations, or taking the necessary steps to ensure observance of those provisions.

In so far as common or concerted action may prove impossible, each of the three guaranteeing Powers reserves the right to take action with the sole aim of re-establishing the state of affairs established by the present Treaty.

Article 4

The present Treaty shall enter into force on signature.

The High Contracting Parties undertake to register the present Treaty at the earliest possible date with the Secretariat of the United Nations, in accordance with the provisions of Article 102 of the Charter.'

E. A.-T. S. L. F. R. Z. †A. M. F. K.

(c) Treaty of Alliance between the Republic of Cyprus, Greece and Turkey

1. The Republic of Cyprus, Greece and Turkey shall co-operate for their common defence and undertake by this Treaty to consult together on the problems raised by this defence.

2. The High Contracting Parties undertake to resist any attack or aggression, direct or indirect, directed against the independence and territorial integrity of the Republic of Cyprus.

3. In the spirit of this alliance and in order to fulfil the above purpose a tripartite Headquarters shall be established on the territory of the Republic of Cyprus.

4. Greece shall take part in the Headquarters mentioned in the preced-

ing article with a contingent of 950 officers, non-commissioned officers and soldiers and Turkey with a contingent of 650 officers, non-commissioned officers and soldiers. The President and the Vice-President of the Republic of Cyprus, acting in agreement, may ask the Greek and Turkish Governments to increase or reduce the Greek and Turkish contingents.

5. The Greek and Turkish officers mentioned above shall be responsible for the training of the Army of the Republic of Cyprus.

6. The command of the tripartite Headquarters shall be assumed in rotation and for a period of one year each by a Cypriot, Greek and Turkish General Officer, who shall be nominated by the Governments of Greece and Turkey and by the President and the Vice-President of the Republic of Cyprus.

E. A.-T. S. L. F. R. Z. †A. M. F. K.

III. Declaration by the Government of the United Kingdom

The Government of the United Kingdom of Great Britain and Northern Ireland, having examined the documents concerning the establishment of the Republic of Cyprus, comprising the Basic Structure for the Republic of Cyprus, the Treaty of Guarantee and the Treaty of Alliance, drawn up and approved by the Heads of the Governments of Greece and Turkey in Zürich on February 11, 1959, and taking into account the consultations in London from February 11 to 16, 1959, between the Foreign Ministers of Greece, Turkey and the United Kingdom

Declare:—

A. That, subject to the acceptance of their requirements as set out in Section B below, they accept the documents approved by the Heads of the Governments of Greece and Turkey as the agreed foundation for the final settlement of the problem of Cyprus.

B. That, with the exception of two areas at

(a) Akrotiri—Episkopi—Paramali, and

(b) Dhekelia—Pergamos—Ayios Nikolaos—Xylophagou, which will be retained under full British sovereignty, they are willing to transfer sovereignty over the Island of Cyprus to the Republic of Cyprus subject to the following conditions:—

(1) that such rights are secured to the United Kingdom Government as are necessary to enable the two areas as aforesaid to be

used effectively as military bases, including among others those rights indicated in the Annex attached, and that satisfactory guarantees are given by Greece, Turkey and the Republic of Cyprus for the integrity of the areas retained under British sovereignty and the use and enjoyment by the United Kingdom of the rights referred to above;

(2) that provision shall be made by agreement for:—

(i) the protection of the fundamental human rights of the various communities in Cyprus;

(ii) the protection of the interests of the members of the public services in Cyprus;

(iii) determining the nationality of persons affected by the settlement;

(iv) the assumption by the Republic of Cyprus of the appropriate obligations of the present Government of Cyprus, including the settlement of claims.

C. That the Government of the United Kingdom welcome the draft Treaty of Alliance between the Republic of Cyprus, the Kingdom of Greece and the Republic of Turkey and will co-operate with the Parties thereto in the common defence of Cyprus.

D. That the Constitution of the Republic of Cyprus shall come into force and the formal signature of the necessary instruments by the parties concerned shall take place at the earliest practicable date and on that date sovereignty will be transferred to the Republic of Cyprus.

Selwyn Lloyd.
Alan Lennox-Boyd.

E. A.-T. F. R. Z. †A. M. F. K.

Annex

The following rights will be necessary in connexion with the areas to be retained under British sovereignty:—

(a) to continue to use, without restriction or interference, the existing small sites containing military and other installations and to exercise complete control within these sites, including the right to guard and defend them and to exclude from them all persons not authorised by the United Kingdom Government;

(b) to use roads, ports and other facilities freely for the movement

of personnel and stores of all kinds to and from and between the abovementioned areas and sites;
(c) to continue to have the use of specified port facilities at Famagusta;
(d) to use public services (such as water, telephone, telegraph, electric power, &c.);
(e) to use from time to time certain localities, which would be specified, for troop training;
(f) to use the airfield at Nicosia, together with any necessary buildings and facilities on or connected with the airfield to whatever extent is considered necessary by the British authorities for the operation of British military aircraft in peace and war, including the exercise of any necessary operational control of air traffic;
(g) to overfly the territory of the Republic of Cyprus without restriction;
(h) to exercise jurisdiction over British forces to an extent comparable with that provided in Article VII of the Agreement regarding the Status of Forces of Parties to the North Atlantic Treaty,[2] in respect of certain offences committed within the territory of the Republic of Cyprus;
(i) to employ freely in the areas and sites labour from other parts of Cyprus;
(j) to obtain, after consultation with the Government of the Republic of Cyprus, the use of such additional small sites and such additional rights as the United Kingdom may, from time to time, consider technically necessary for the efficient use of its base areas and installations in Cyprus.

IV. Additional Article to be Inserted in the Treaty of Guarantee

The Kingdom of Greece, the Republic of Turkey and the Republic of Cyprus undertake to respect the integrity of the areas to be retained under the sovereignty of the United Kingdom upon the establishment of the Republic of Cyprus, and guarantee the use and enjoyment by the United Kingdom of the rights to be secured to the United Kingdom by the Republic of Cyprus in accordance with the declaration by the Government of the United Kingdom.

S. L. E. A.-T. F. R. Z. †A. M. F. K.

V. Declaration Made by the Greek and Turkish Foreign Ministers on February 17, 1959

The Foreign Ministers of Greece and Turkey, having considered the declaration made by the Government of the United Kingdom on February 17, 1959, accept that declaration, together with the document approved by the Heads of the Greek and Turkish Governments in Zürich on February 11, 1959, as providing the agreed foundation for the final settlement of the problem of Cyprus.

E. Averoff-Tossizza †A. M. S. L. F. K. Fatin R. Zorlu

VI. Declaration Made by the Representative of the Greek-Cypriot Community on February 19, 1959

Archbishop Makarios, representing the Greek Cypriot Community, having examined the documents concerning the establishment of the Republic of Cyprus drawn up and approved by the Heads of the Governments of Greece and Turkey in Zürich on February 11, 1959, and the declarations made by the Government of the United Kingdom, and by the Foreign Ministers of Greece and Turkey on February 17, 1959, declares that he accepts the documents and declarations as the agreed foundation for the final settlement of the problem of Cyprus.

†Archbishop Makarios S. L. E. A.-T. F. R. Z. F. K.

VII. Declaration Made by the Representative of the Turkish-Cypriot Community on February 19, 1959

Dr. Kutchuk, representing the Turkish Cypriot Community, having examined the documents concerning the establishment of the Republic of Cyprus drawn up and approved by the Heads of the Governments of Greece and Turkey in Zürich on February 11, 1959, and the declarations made by the Government of the United Kingdom, and by the Foreign Ministers of Greece and Turkey on February 17, 1959, declares that he accepts the documents and declarations as the agreed foundation for the final settlement of the problem of Cyprus.

F. Kutchuk S. L. E. A.-T. F. R. Z. †A. M.

VIII. Agreed Measures to Prepare for the New Arrangements in Cyprus

1. All parties to the Conference firmly endorse the aim of bringing the constitution (including the elections of President, Vice-President, and the three Assemblies) and the Treaties into full effect as soon as practicable and in any case not later than twelve months from to-day's date (the 19th of February, 1959). Measures leading to the transfer of sovereignty in Cyprus will begin at once.

2. The first of these measures will be the immediate establishment of:—

(a) a Joint Commission in Cyprus with the duty of completing a draft constitution for the independent Republic of Cyprus, incorporating the basic structure agreed at the Zürich Conference. This Commission shall be composed of one representative each of the Greek-Cypriot and the Turkish-Cypriot community and one representative nominated by the Government of Greece and one representative nominated by the Government of Turkey, together with a legal adviser nominated by the Foreign Ministers of Greece and Turkey, and shall in its work have regard to and shall scrupulously observe the points contained in the documents of the Zürich Conference and shall fulfil its task in accordance with the principles there laid down:

(b) a Transitional Committee in Cyprus, with responsibility for drawing up plans for adapting and reorganising the Governmental machinery in Cyprus in preparation for the transfer of authority to the independent Republic of Cyprus. This Committee shall be composed of the Governor of Cyprus, the leading representative of the Greek community and the leading representative of the Turkish community and other Greek and Turkish Cypriots nominated by the Governor after consultation with the two leading representatives in such a way as not to conflict with paragraph 5 of the Basic Structure:

(c) a Joint Committee in London composed of a representative of each of the Governments of Greece, Turkey and the United Kingdom, and one representative each of the Greek Cypriot and Turkish Cypriot communities, with the duty of preparing the final treaties giving effect to the conclusions of the London Conference. This Committee will prepare drafts for submission to Governments covering *inter alia* matters arising from the retention of areas in Cyprus under British sovereignty, the provision to the United Kingdom Government of certain ancillary rights and facilities in the independent Republic of Cyprus, questions of nationality, the treatment of the liabilities of the present Government of Cyprus, and the financial and economic problems arising from the creation of an independent Republic of Cyprus.

3. The Governor will, after consultation with the two leading representatives, invite individual members of the Transitional Committee to assume special responsibilities for particular departments and functions of Government. This process will be started as soon as possible and will be progressively extended.

4. The headquarters mentioned in Article 4 of the Treaty of Alliance between the Republic of Cyprus, the Kingdom of Greece and the Republic of Turkey will be established three months after the completion of the work of the Commission referred to in paragraph 2*(a)* above and will be composed of a restricted number of officers who will immediately undertake the training of the armed forces of the Republic of Cyprus. The Greek and Turkish contingents will enter the territory of the Republic of Cyprus on the date when the sovereignty will be transferred to the Republic.

S. L. E. A.-T. F. R. Z.

Appendix 2
Makarios's "13 Points"

Amendments to the 1960 Cyprus Constitution proposed by Archbishop Makarios on 30 November 1963

1. The right of veto of the President and Vice-President to be abandoned.

2. The Vice-President of the Republic to deputise for the President in case of his temporary absence or incapacity to perform his duties.

3. The Greek President of the House of Representatives and its Turkish Vice-President to be elected by the House as a whole and not, as at present, the President by the Greek Members of the House and the Vice-President by the Turkish Members of the House.

4. The Vice-President of the House of Representatives to deputise for the President of the House in case of his temporary absence or incapacity to perform his duties.

5. The constitutional provisions regarding separate majorities for enactment of certain laws by the House of Representatives to be abolished.

6. Unified municipalities to be established.

7. The administration of justice to be unified.

8. The division of the Security Forces into Police and Gendarmerie to be abolished.

9. The numerical strength of the Security Forces and of the Defence Forces to be determined by a Law.

10. The proportion of the participation of Greek and Turkish Cypriots in the composition of the Public Service and the Forces of the Republic to be modified in proportion to the ratio of the population of Greek and Turkish Cypriots.

Source: Greek Communal Chamber (Cyprus), *Cyprus Today* (Nicosia, November–December 1963), pp. 1–8; as reprinted in Stanley Kyriakides, *Cyprus: Constitutionalism and Crisis Government* (Philadelphia: University of Pennsylvania Press, 1968), pp. 105–6; also in Necati Ertekün, *The Cyprus Dispute* (Nicosia: K. Rustem & Brother, 1980), p. 182.

11. The number of members of the Public Service Commission to be reduced from ten to five.

12. All decisions of the Public Service Commission to be taken by simple majority.

13. The Greek Communal Chamber to be abolished.

Appendix 3
UN Security Council Resolution 186 of 4 March 1964 Setting Up UNFICYP
(Document S/5575)

The Security Council,

Noting that the present situation with regard to Cyprus is likely to threaten international peace and security and may further deteriorate unless measures are promptly taken to maintain peace and to seek out a durable solution;

Considering the positions taken by the parties in relation to the treaties signed at Nicosia on 16 August 1960;[33]

Having in mind the relevant provisions of the Charter and its Article 2, Paragraph 4 which reads: "All members shall refrain in their international relations from the threat or use of force against the territorial integrity or political independence of any state, or in any other manner inconsistent with the purposes of the United Nations,"

1. *Calls upon* all Member States, in conformity with their obligations under the Charter of the United Nations, to refrain from any action or threat of action likely to worsen the situation in the sovereign Republic of Cyprus or to endanger international peace;

2. *Asks* the Government of Cyprus, which has the responsibility for the maintenance and restoration of law and order, to take all additional measures necessary to stop violence and bloodshed in Cyprus;

3. *Calls upon* the communities in Cyprus and their leaders to act with the utmost restraint;

4. *Recommends* the creation with the consent of the Government of Cyprus of a United Nations Peace Force in Cyprus. The composition

---

Source: United Nations, Security Council, *Official Records*, Nineteenth Year, Resolutions and Decisions (S.INF/19/Rev.1).

[33] Treaty of Guarantee (United Nations, *Treaty Series*, Vol. 382 (1960), No. 5475); Treaty concerning the Establishment of Republic of Cyprus (Ibid., No. 5476); and Treaty of Alliance between the Kingdom of Greece, the Republic of Turkey and the Republic of Cyprus (Ibid., Vol. 397 (1961), No. 5712).

and size of the force shall be established by the Secretary-General in consultation with the Governments of Cyprus, Greece, Turkey, and the United Kingdom of Great Britain and Northern Ireland. The commander of the Force shall be appointed by the Secretary-General and report to him. The Secretary-General shall keep the Governments providing the Force fully informed, shall report periodically to the Security Council on its operation;

5. *Recommends* that the function of the Force should be, in the interest of preserving international peace and security, to use its best efforts to prevent a recurrence of fighting and, as necessary to contribute to the maintenance and restoration of law and order and a return to normal conditions;

6. *Recommends* that the stationing of the Force shall be for a period of three months, all costs pertaining to it being met, in a manner to be agreed upon by them, by the governments providing the contingents and by the Government of Cyprus. The Secretary-General may accept voluntary contributions for that purpose;

7. *Recommends further* that the Secretary-General designate, in agreement with the Government of Cyprus and the Governments of Greece, Turkey, and the United Kingdom, a mediator, who shall use his best endeavours with the representatives of the communities and also with the aforesaid four Governments, for the purpose of promoting a peaceful solution and an agreed settlement of the problem confronting Cyprus, in accordance with the Charter of the United Nations, having in mind the well-being of the people of Cyprus as a whole and the preservation of international peace and security. The mediator shall report periodically to the Secretary-General on his efforts;

8. *Requests* the Secretary-General to provide, from funds of the United Nations, as appropriate, for the remuneration and expenses of the mediator and his staff.

Appendix 4
Letter of President Johnson to Prime Minister İnönü and İnönü's reply

Correspondence between President Johnson and Prime Minister İnönü, June 1964, as released by the White House, January 15, 1966.

White House Statement

At the request of the Government of Turkey, the White House is today releasing the texts of letters exchanged on June 5, 1964, between President Johnson and the then Prime Minister of Turkey İsmet İnönü on the Cyprus crisis. Steps subsequent to this exchange of letters led to the visit of Prime Minister İnönü to Washington later in that month and constructive discussions by the President and the Prime Minister of the issues involved.

A joint communiqué released at the conclusion of those discussions welcomed the opportunity for a full exchange of views by the two leaders and the occasion to consider ways in which the two countries could strengthen the efforts of the United Nations with respect to the safety and security of Cyprus. The communiqué noted that "the cordial and candid conversations of the two leaders strengthened the broad understanding already existing between Turkey and the United States."

The United States continues to value highly the close and friendly relations we maintain with Turkey.

President Johnson's Letter to Prime Minister İnönü, June 5, 1964

Dear Mr. Prime Minister:

I am gravely concerned by the information which I have had through Ambassador Hare from you and your Foreign Minister that the Turkish Government is contemplating a decision to intervene by military force to occupy a portion of Cyprus. I wish to emphasize, in the fullest friendship

Source: *Middle East Journal*, Summer 1966, pp. 386–93.

and frankness, that I do not consider that such a course of action by Turkey, fraught with such far-reaching consequences, is consistent with the commitment of your Government to consult fully in advance with us. Ambassador Hare has indicated that you have postponed your decision for a few hours in order to obtain my views. I put to you personally whether you really believe that it is appropriate for your Government, in effect, to present a unilateral decision of such consequence to an ally who has demonstrated such staunch support over the years as has the United States for Turkey. I must, therefore, first urge you to accept the responsibility for complete consultation with the United States before any such action is taken.

It is my impression that you believe that such intervention by Turkey is permissible under the provisions of the Treaty of Guarantee of 1960. I must call your attention, however, to our understanding that the proposed intervention by Turkey would be for the purpose of effecting a form of partition of the Island, a solution which is specifically excluded by the Treaty of Guarantee. Further, that Treaty requires consultation among the Guarantor Powers. It is the view of the United States that the possibilities of such consultation have by no means been exhausted in this situation and that, therefore, the reservation of the right to take unilateral action is not yet applicable.

I must call to your attention, also, Mr. Prime Minister, the obligations of NATO. There can be no question in your mind that a Turkish intervention in Cyprus would lead to a military engagement between Turkish and Greek forces. Secretary of State Rusk declared at the recent meeting of the Ministerial Council of NATO in The Hague that war between Turkey and Greece must be considered as "literally unthinkable." Adhesion to NATO, in its very essence, means that NATO countries will not wage war on each other. Germany and France have buried centuries of animosity and hostility in becoming NATO allies; nothing less can be expected from Greece and Turkey. Furthermore, a military intervention in Cyprus by Turkey could lead to a direct involvement by the Soviet Union. I hope you will understand that your NATO allies have not had a chance to consider whether they have an obligation to protect Turkey against the Soviet Union if Turkey takes a step which results in Soviet intervention without the full consent and understanding of its NATO Allies.

Further, Mr. Prime Minister, I am concerned about the obligations of Turkey as a member of the United Nations. The United Nations has provided forces on the Island to keep the peace. Their task has been difficult but, during the past several weeks, they have been progressively successful in reducing the incidents of violence on that Island. The United Nations Mediator has not yet completed his work. I have no doubt that the general membership of the United Nations would react in the strongest terms to unilateral action by Turkey which would defy the efforts of the United Nations and destroy any prospect that the United Nations could assist in obtaining a reasonable and peaceful settlement of this difficult problem.

I wish also, Mr. Prime Minister, to call your attention to the bilateral agreement between the United States and Turkey in the field of military assistance. Under Article IV of the Agreement with Turkey of July 1947, your Government is required to obtain United States consent for the use of military assistance for purposes other than those for which such assistance was furnished. Your Government has on several occasions acknowledged to the United States that you fully understand this condition. I must tell you in all candor that the United States cannot agree to the use of any United States supplied military equipment for a Turkish intervention in Cyprus under present circumstances.

Moving to the practical results of the contemplated Turkish move, I feel obligated to call to your attention in the most friendly fashion the fact that such a Turkish move could lead to the slaughter of tens of thousands of Turkish Cypriots on the Island of Cyprus. Such an action on your part would unleash the furies and there is no way by which military action on your part could be sufficiently effective to prevent wholesale destruction of many of those whom you are trying to protect. The presence of United Nations forces could not prevent such a catastrophe.

You may consider that what I have said is much too severe and that we are disregardful of Turkish interests in the Cyprus situation. I should like to assure you that this is not the case. We have exerted ourselves both publicly and privately to assure the safety of Turkish Cypriots and to insist that a final solution of the Cyprus problem should rest upon the consent of the parties most directly concerned. It is possible that you feel in Ankara that the United States has not been sufficiently active in your behalf. But surely you know that our policy has caused the liveliest resentments in Athens (where demonstrations have been aimed against us) and has led to a basic alienation between the United States and Archbishop Makarios. As I said to your Foreign Minister in our conversation just a few weeks ago, we value very highly our relations with Turkey. We have considered you as a great ally with fundamental common interests. Your security and prosperity have been a deep concern of the American people and we have expressed that concern in the most practical terms. You and we have fought together to resist the ambitions of the Communist world revolution. This solidarity has meant a great deal to us and I would hope that it means a great deal to your Government and to your people. We have no intention of lending any support to any solution of Cyprus which endangers the Turkish Cypriot community. We have not been able to find a final solution because this is, admittedly, one of the most complex problems on earth. But I wish to assure you that we have been deeply concerned about the interests of Turkey and of the Turkish Cypriots and will remain so.

Finally, Mr. Prime Minister I must tell you that you have posed the gravest of issues of war and peace. These are issues which go far beyond the bilateral relations between Turkey and the United States. They not only will certainly involve war between Turkey and Greece but could involve wider hostilities because of the unpredictable consequences which a unilateral intervention in Cyprus could produce. You have your responsibilities as Chief of the Government of Turkey; I also have mine as President of the United States. I must, therefore, inform you in the deepest friendship that unless I can have your assurance that you will not take such action without further and fullest consultation I cannot accept your injunction to Ambassador Hare of secrecy and must immediately ask for emergency meetings of the NATO Council and of the United Nations Security Council.

I wish it were possible for us to have a personal discussion of this situation. Unfortunately, because of the special circumstances of our present Constitutional position, I am not able to leave the United States. If you could come here for a full discussion I would welcome it. I do feel that you and I carry a very heavy responsibility for the general peace and for the possibilities of a sane and peaceful resolution of the Cyprus problem. I ask you, therefore, to delay any decisions which you and your colleagues might have in mind until you and I have had the fullest and frankest consultation.

Sincerely,
Lyndon B. Johnson

Prime Minister İnönü's Response to the President, June 13, 1964

Dear Mr. President,

I have received your message of June 5, 1964 through Ambassador Hare. We have, upon your request, postponed our decision to exercise our right of unilateral action in Cyprus conferred to us by the Treaty of Guarantee. With due regard to the spirit of candour and friendship in which your message is meant to be written, I will, in my reply, try also to explain to you in full frankness my views about the situation.

Mr. President,

Your message, both in wording and content, has been disappointing for an ally like Turkey who has always been giving the most serious attention to its relations of alliance with the United States and has brought to the fore substantial divergences of opinion in various fundamental matters pertaining to these relations.

It is my sincere hope that both these divergences and the general tone of your message are due to the haste in which a representation made in good-will was, under pressure of time, based on data hurriedly collected.

In the first place, it is being emphasized in your message that we have failed to consult with the United States when a military intervention in Cyprus was deemed indispensable by virtue of the Treaty of Guarantee. The necessity of a military intervention in Cyprus has been felt four times since the closing days of 1963. From the outset we have taken a special care to consult the United States on this matter. Soon after the outbreak of the crisis, on December 25, 1963, we have immediately informed the United States of our contacts with the other guaranteeing powers only to be answered that the United States was not a party to this issue. We then negotiated with the United Kingdom and Greece for intervention and, as you know, a tri-partite military administration under British command was set-up on December 26, 1963. Upon the failure of the London conference and of the joint Anglo-American proposals, due to the attitude of Makarios and in the face of continuing assaults in the island against the Turkish Cypriots, we lived through very critical days in February and taking advantage of the visit of Mr. George Ball to Ankara, we informed again the United States of the gravity of the situation. We tried to explain to you that the necessity of intervention to restore order in the island might arise in view of the vacuum caused by the rejection of the Anglo-American proposals and we informed you that we might have to intervene at any time. We even requested guarantees from you on specific issues and your answers were in the affirmative. However, you asked us not to intervene and assured us that Makarios would get at the United Nations a severe lesson while all the Turkish rights and interests would be preserved.

We complied with your request without any satisfactory result being secured at the United Nations. Moreover the creation of the United Nations force, decided upon by the Security Council, became a problem. The necessity for intervention was felt for the third time to protect the Turkish community against the assaults of the terrorists in Cyprus who were encouraged by the doubts as to whether the United Nations forces would be set up immediately after the adoption of the Security Council resolution of March 4, 1964. But assuring us that the force would be set up very shortly, you insisted again that we refrain from intervening. Thereupon we postponed our intervention once again, awaiting the United Nations forces to assume their duty.

Dear Mr. President,

The era of terror in Cyprus has a particular character which rendered ineffective all measures taken so far. From the very outset, the negotiations held to restore security and the temporary set-ups have all helped only to increase the aggressiveness and the destructiveness of the Makarios administration. The Greek Cypriots have lately started to arm themselves overtly and considered the United Nations as an additional instrument to back up their ruthless and unconstitutional rule. It has become quite obvious that the United Nations have neither the authority nor the intent to intervene for the restoration of constitutional order and to put an end to aggression. You are well aware of the instigative attitude of the Greek Government towards the Greek Cypriots. During the talks held in your office, in the United States, we informed you that under the circumstances we would eventually be compelled to intervene in order to put an end to the atrocities in Cyprus. We also asked your Secretary of State at The Hague whether the United States would support us in such an eventuality and we received no answer. I think, I have thus reminded you how many times and under what circumstances we informed you of the necessity for intervention in Cyprus. I do remember having emphasized to your high level officials our due appreciation of the special responsibilities incumbent upon the United States within the alliance and of the necessity to be particularly careful and helpful to enable her to maintain solidarity within the alliance. As you see, we never had the intention to confront you with a unilateral decision on our part. Our grievance stems from our inability to explain to you a problem which caused us for months utmost distress and from your refusal to take a frank and firm stand on the issue as to which party is on the right side in the dispute between two allies, namely, Turkey and Greece.

Mr. President,

In your message you further emphasize the obligation of Turkey, under the provisions of the Treaty, to consult with the other two guaranteeing powers, before taking any unilateral action. Turkey is fully aware of this obligation. For the past six months we have indeed complied with the requirements of this obligation. But Greece has not only thwarted all the attempts made by Turkey to seek jointly the ways and means to stop Greek Cypriots from repudiating international treaties, but has also supported their unlawful and inhuman acts and has even encouraged them.

The Greek Government itself has not hesitated to declare publicly that the international agreements it signed with us were no longer in force. Various examples to that effect were, in due course, communicated in detail, orally and in writing, to your State Department.

We have likewise fulfilled our obligation of constant consultation with the Government of the United Kingdom, the other guaranteeing power.

In several instances we have, jointly with the Government of the United Kingdom, made representations to the Greek Cypriots with a view to restoring constitutional order. But unfortunately, these representations were of no avail due to the negative attitude of the Greek Cypriot authorities.

As you see, Turkey has earnestly explored every avenue of consulting continuously and acting jointly with the other two guaranteeing powers. This being the fact, it can not be asserted that Turkey has failed to abide by her obligation of consulting with the other two guaranteeing powers before taking unilateral action.

I put it to you, Mr. President, whether the United States Government which has felt the need to draw the attention of Turkey to her obligation of consultation, yet earnestly and faithfully fulfilled by the latter, should not have reminded Greece, who repudiates treaties signed by herself, of the necessity to abide by the precept "pacta sunt servanda" which is the fundamental rule of international law. This precept which, only a fortnight ago, was most eloquently characterized as "the basis of survival" by your Secretary of State himself in his speech at the "American Law Institute," is now being completely and contemptuously ignored by Greece, our NATO ally and by the Greek Cypriots.

Dear Mr. President,

As implied in your message, by virtue of the provisions of Article 4 of the Treaty of Guarantee, the three guaranteeing powers have, in the event of a breach of the provisions of that Treaty, the right to take concerted action and, if that proves impossible, unilateral action with the sole aim of re-establishing the state of affairs created by the said Treaty. The Treaty of Guarantee was signed with this understanding being shared by all parties thereto. The "Gentleman's Agreement" signed on February 19, 1959 by the Foreign Ministers of Turkey and Greece, is an evidence of that common understanding.

On the other hand, at the time of the admission of the Republic of Cyprus to the United Nations, the members of the organization were fully acquainted with all the international commitments and obligations of the said Republic and no objections were raised in this respect.

Furthermore, in the course of the discussions on Cyprus leading to the resolution adopted on March 4, 1964 by the Security Council, the United States Delegate, among others, explicitly declared that the United Nations had no power to annul or amend international treaties.

The understanding expressed in your message that the intervention by Turkey in Cyprus would be for the purposes of effecting the partition of the island has caused me great surprise and profound sorrow. My surprise stems from the fact that the data furnished to you about the intentions of Turkey could be so remote from the realities repeatedly proclaimed by us. The reason of my sorrow is that our ally, the Government of the United States, could think that Turkey might lay aside the principle constituting the foundation of her foreign policy, i.e., absolute loyalty to international law, commitments and obligations, as factually evidenced in many circumstances well known to the United States.

I would like to assure you most categorically and most sincerely that if ever Turkey finds herself forced to intervene militarily in Cyprus this will be done in full conformity with the provisions and aims of international agreements.

In this connection, allow me to stress, Mr. President, that the postponement of our decision does naturally, in no way affect the rights conferred to Turkey by Article 4 of the Treaty of Guarantee.

Mr. President,

Referring to NATO obligations, you state in your message that the very essence of NATO requires that allies should not wage war on each other and that a Turkish intervention in Cyprus would lead to a military engagement between Turkish and Greek forces.

I am in full agreement with the first part of your statement, but the obligation for the NATO allies to respect international agreements concluded among themselves as well as their mutual treaty rights and commitments is an equally vital requisite of the alliance. An alliance among states which ignore their mutual contractual obligations and commitments is unthinkable.

As to the concern you expressed over the outbreak of a Turco-Greek war in case of Turkey's intervention in Cyprus in conformity with her rights and obligations stipulated in international agreements, I would like to stress that Turkey would undertake a "military operation" in Cyprus exclusively under the conditions and for the purpose set forth in the agreements. Therefore, a Turco-Greek war so properly described as "literally unthinkable" by the Honorable Dean Rusk could only occur in case of Greece's aggression against Turkey. Our view, in case of such an intervention, is to invite to an effective collaboration, with the aim of restoring the constitutional order in Cyprus, both Greece and the United Kingdom in their capacity as guaranteeing powers. If despite this invitation and its contractual obligations Greece were to attack Turkey, we could in no way be held responsible of the consequences of such an action. I would like to hope that you have already seriously drawn the Greek Government's attention on these matters.

The part of your message expressing doubts as to the obligation of the NATO allies to protect Turkey in case she becomes directly involved with the USSR as a result of an action initiated in Cyprus, gives me the impression that there are as between us wide divergence of views as to the nature and basic principles of the North Atlantic Alliance. I must confess that this has been to us the source of great sorrow and grave concern. Any aggression against a member of NATO will naturally call from the aggressor an effort of justification. If NATO's structure is so weak as to give credit to the aggressor's allegations, then it means that this defect of NATO needs really to be remedied. Our understanding is that the North Atlantic Treaty imposes upon all member states the obligation to come forthwith to the assistance of any member victim of an aggression. The only point left to the discretion of the member states is the nature and the scale of this assistance. If NATO members should start discussing the right and wrong of the situation of their fellow-member victim of a Soviet aggression, whether this aggression was provoked or not and if the decision on whether they have an obligation to assist the member should be made to depend on the issue of such a discussion, the very foundations of the Alliance would be shaken and it would lose its meaning. An obligation of assistance, if it is to carry any weight, should come into being immediately upon the observance of aggression. That is why Article 5 of the North Atlantic Treaty considers an attack against one of the member states as an attack against them all and makes it imperative for them to assist the party so attacked by taking forthwith such action as they deem necessary. In this connection I would like to further point out that the agreements on Cyprus have met with the approval of the North Atlantic Council, as early as the stage of the United Nations debate on the problem, i.e., even prior to the establishment of the Republic of Cyprus, hence long before the occurrence of the events of December 1963.

As you will recall, at the meeting of the NATO Ministerial Council held three weeks ago at The Hague, it was acknowledged that the treaties continued to be the basis for legality as regards the situation in the island and the status of Cyprus. The fact that these agreements have been violated as a result of the flagrantly unlawful acts of one of the parties on the island should in no way mean that the said agreements are no longer in force and that the rights and obligations of Turkey by virtue of those agreements should be ignored. Such an understanding would mean that as long as no difficulties arise, the agreements are considered as valid and they are no longer in force when difficulties occur. I am sure you will agree with me that such an understanding of law cannot be accepted. I am equally convinced that there could be no shadow of doubt about the obligation to protect Turkey within the NATO Alliance in a situation that can, by no means, be attributed to an arbitrary act of Turkey. An opposite way of thinking would lead to the repudiation and denial of the concept of law and of Article 51 of the United Nations Charter.

In your message, concern has been expressed about the commitments of Turkey as a member of the United Nations. I am sure, Mr. President, you will agree with me if I say that such a concern, which I do not share, is groundless especially for the following reasons: Turkey has distinguished herself as one of the most loyal members of the United Nations ever since its foundation. The Turkish people has spared no effort to safeguard the principles of the United Nations Charter, and has even sacrificed her sons for this cause. Turkey has never failed in supporting this organization and, in order to secure its proper functioning, has borne great moral and material sacrifices even when she had most pressing financial difficulties. Despite the explicit rights conferred to Turkey by the Treaty of Guarantee, my Government's respect for and adherence to the United Nations have recently been demonstrated once more by its acceptance of the Security Council resolution of March 4, 1964 as well as by the priority it has given to the said resolution.

Should the United Nations have been progressively successful in carrying out their task as pointed out in your message, a situation which is of such grave concern for both you and I, would never have arisen. It is a fact that the United Nations operations in the island have proved unable to put an end to the oppression.

The relative calm which has apparently prevailed in the island for the past few weeks marks the beginning of preparations of the Greek Cypriots for further tyranny. Villages are still under siege. The United Nations forces, assuaging Turkish Cypriots, enable the Greeks to gather their crops; but they do not try to stop the Greeks when the crops of Turks are at stake and they act as mere spectators to Greek assaults. These vitally important details may not well reach you, whereas we live in the atmosphere created by the daily reports of such tragic events.

The report of the Secretary-General will be submitted to the United Nations on June 15, 1964. I am seriously concerned that we may face yet another defeat similar to the one we all suffered on March 4, 1964. The session of March 4th had further convinced Makarios that the Treaty of

Guarantee did not exist for him and thereupon he took the liberty of actually placing the United Nations forces under his control and direction. From then on the assassination of hostages and the besieging of villages have considerably increased.

Dear Mr. President,

Our allies who are in a position to arbiter in the Cyprus issue and to orient it in the right direction have so far been unable to disentangle the problem from a substantial error. The Cyprus tragedy has been engendered by the deliberate policy of the Republic of Cyprus aimed at annulling the treaties and abrogating the constitution. Security can be established in the island only through the proper functioning of an authority above the Government of Cyprus. Yet only the measures acceptable to the Cypriot Government are being sought to restore security in Cyprus. The British administration set up following the December events, the Anglo-American proposals and finally the United Nations command have all been founded on this unsound basis and consequently every measure acceptable to Makarios has proved futile and has, in general, encouraged oppression and aggression.

Dear Mr. President,

You put forward in your message the resentment caused in Greece by the policy pursued by your Government. Within the content of the Cyprus issues, the nature of the Greek policy and the course of action undertaken by Greece indicate that she is apt to resort to every means within her power to secure the complete annulment of the existing treaties. We are at pains to make our allies understand the sufferings we bear in our rightful cause and the irretrievable plight in which the Turkish Cypriots are living. On the other hand, it is not the character of our nation to exploit demonstrations of resentment. I assure you that our distress is deeply rooted since we can not make you understand our rightful position and convince you of the necessity of spending every effort and making use of all your authority to avert the perils inherent in the Cyprus problem by attaching to it the importance it well deserves.

That France and Germany have buried their animosity is indeed a good example. However, our nation had already given such an example forty years ago by establishing friendly relations with Greece, right after the ruthless devastation of the whole Anatolia by the armies of that country.

Dear Mr. President,

As a member of the Alliance our nation is fully conscious of her duties and rights. We do not pursue any aim other than the settlement of the Cyprus problem in compliance with the provisions of the existing treaties. Such a settlement is likely to be reached if you lend your support and give effect with your supreme authority to the sense of justice inherent in the character of the American nation.

Mr. President,

I thank you for your statement emphasizing the value attached by the United States to the relations of alliance with Turkey and for your kind words about the Turkish nation. I shall be happy to come to the United States to talk the Cyprus problem with you. The United Nations Security Council will meet on June the 17th. In the meantime, Mr. Dirk Stikker, Secretary General of NATO, will have paid a visit to Turkey. Furthermore, the United Nations mediator Mr. Tuomioja will have submitted his report to the Secretary-General. These developments may lead to the emergence of a new situation. It will be possible for me to go abroad to join you, at a date convenient for you, immediately after June 20th.

It will be most helpful for me if you would let me know of any defined views and designs you may have on the Cyprus question so that I may be able to study them thoroughly before my departure for Washington.

Finally, I would like to express my satisfaction for the frank, fruitful and promising talks we had with Mr. G. Ball in Ankara just before forwarding this message to you.

Sincerely,
İsmet İnönü,
Prime Minister of Turkey

Appendix 5
UN General Assembly Resolution 2077 of 18 December 1965

"Question of Cyprus"

As proposed by First Committee, A/6166, adopted by Assembly on 18 December 1965, meeting 1402, by roll-call vote of 47 to 5.

The General Assembly,

Having considered the question of Cyprus,

Recalling Security Council resolutions 186 (1964) of 4 March 1964, 187 (1964) of 13 March 1964, 192 (1964) of 20 June 1964, 193 (1964) of 9 August 1964, 194 (1964) of 25 September 1964, 198 (1964) of 18 December 1964, 201 (1965) of 19 March 1965, 206 (1965) of 15 June 1965 and 207 (1965) of 10 August 1965, and the Council's consensus of 11 August 1964 with regard to Cyprus,[12]

Recalling the parts of the Declaration adopted on 10 October 1964 by the Second Conference of Heads of State or Government of Non-Aligned Countries, held at Cairo, regarding the question of Cyprus,[13]

Noting the report of the United Nations Mediator on Cyprus, submitted to the Secretary-General on 26 March 1965,[14]

Noting further that the Government of Cyprus is committed, through its Declaration of Intention and the accompanying Memorandum,[15] to:

(*a*) The full application of human rights to all citizens of Cyprus, irrespective of race or religion,

(*b*) The ensuring of minority rights,

Source: United Nations, General Assembly, Twentieth Session Resolutions adopted on the reports of the First Committee, pp. 9–10; also in Erketün, op. cit., pp. 231–32.

[12] *Official Records of the Security Council, Nineteenth Year*, 1143rd meeting, para. 358.

[13] See A/5763.

[14] *Official Records of the Security Council, Twentieth Year, Supplement for January, February and March 1965*, document S/6253.

[15] *Official Records of the General Assembly, Twentieth Session, Annexes*, agenda item 93, document A/6039.

(*c*) The safeguarding of the above rights as contained in the said Declaration and Memorandum,

1. *Takes cognizance* of the fact that the Republic of Cyprus, as an equal Member of the United Nations, is, in accordance with the Charter of the United Nations, entitled to enjoy, and should enjoy, full sovereignty and complete independence without any foreign intervention or interference;

2. *Calls upon* all States, in conformity with their obligations under the Charter, and in particular Article 2, paragraphs 1 and 4, to respect the sovereignty, unity, independence and territorial integrity of the Republic of Cyprus and to refrain from any intervention directed against it;

3. *Recommends* to the Security Council the continuation of the United States mediation work in conformity with Council resolution 186 (1964).

1402nd plenary meeting,
18 December 1965.

Appendix 6
Evros Communiqué of 10 September 1967

Communiqué Issued after Greek-Turkish Summit

Athens Domestic Service in Greek 2200 10 Sep 67
(Joint Greek-Turkish Communiqué)

[Text] The talks between the prime ministers of Greece and Turkey and their associates ended at Alexandroupolis at 2200 tonight. The second phase of the talks held today lasted eight hours. Immediately after the termination of the talks the two prime ministers and their associates received journalists and released the joint official communiqué, which is as follows:

1—The prime ministers of Turkey and Greece, Their Excellencies Süleyman Demirel and Konstandinos Kollias, held their first meeting in Keşan, Turkey, on 9 September 1967 and continued their talks the following day at Alexandroupolis, Greece. Foreign Minister Çağlayangil represented Turkey and Deputy Premier Grigorios Spandidhakis, Foreign Minister Oikonomou-Gouras, and Minister to the Premier Yeoryios Papadhopoulos represented Greece at the two meetings.

2—The two prime ministers reviewed the bilateral relations at their present stage by taking into consideration the main elements of the Greek-Turkish differences. They expressed their belief that the long-term interests of both countries require the strengthening of the ties of friendship, good neighborliness, and cooperation between the two countries, within the spirit of cordiality created by the two great statesmen Ataturk and Venizelos, and by taking into consideration the fact that they belong to the same alliance.

3—Within the same spirit the prime ministers expressed in detail their views on the question of Cyprus and underlined the very great importance which the peoples of both countries attach to this problem. They admitted

---

Source: Foreign Broadcast Information Service, *Daily Report*, "Greece," 11 September 1967, pp. J1–2.

that the restoration of good relations and cordiality between the two countries primarily depends on a just solution of this problem. Consequently, they agreed to continue through the proper channels the exploration of possibilities of achieving closer views on the question. They also recognized the need to adopt the necessary measures to avert an increase in tension in Cyprus and safeguard and ease efforts being exerted for a peaceful and agreed solution.

4—The prime ministers also admitted that the mutual interests of the two countries necessitate close cooperation in all fields of common interest, especially the economic field. They expressed the belief that the economic development of both countries requires an atmosphere of peace and security.

5—The prime ministers noted with satisfaction the coincidence of their views regarding respect for all agreements between their countries.

6—The talks have allowed the heads of the two governments to examine the major problems of the international situation, insofar as this situation affects the area in which the two countries are located.

Turkish Premier Demirel and the Turkish officials who attended the talks left by air from Alexandroupolis this evening. Prior to their departure they posed for pictures at the Garden of the Astir Hotel with Premier Kollias and the other members of the Greek delegation. The Turkish premier and the members of his delegation were seen off at the Alexandroupolis Airport by Premier Kollias, Deputy Premier Spandidhakis, Minister to the Premier Papadhopoulos, Foreign Minister Oikonomou-Gouras, Permanent Foreign Under Secretary Khristopoulos, and the other members of the Greek delegation.

Appendix 7
Appeal by UN Secretary-General to Cyprus, Greece, and Turkey on 24 November 1967

Document S/8248/Add.5
[*Original text: English*]
[*24 November 1967*]

The Secretary-General addressed the following new appeal to the President of Cyprus and the Prime Ministers of Greece and Turkey on 24 November 1967:

"The portents regarding Cyprus are increasingly ominous. Indications at this moment are that Greece and Turkey are at the brink of war over Cyprus. It is thus all too obvious that the United Nations through its appropriate organs must do all that it can to avert this catastrophe.

"As you know, because of my growing alarm over the situation, I asked Mr. José Rolz-Bennett, Under-Secretary for Special Political Affairs, to visit the capitals of the three Governments as my Personal Representative and to convey to those Governments my very deep concern about the deteriorating situation and to give whatever assistance he could to reverse the trend toward war. Mr. Rolz-Bennett left New York on 22 November, has been to Ankara and at this moment is in Athens. He has reported to me that the situation is very dangerous.

"As Secretary-General of the United Nations, therefore, I again appeal to the three States most directly involved—Cyprus, Greece and Turkey—in the strongest possible terms, to exercise utmost restraint particularly at this critical juncture, to avoid all acts of force or the threats of recourse to force, to be temperate in their public utterances relating to the Cyprus problem and to relations among them. It will be unavoidable that those who act otherwise, not only act in overt violation of their obligations under the United Nations Charter and the relevant resolutions of the Security Council, but will also bear responsibility for the ensuing war.

Source: United Nations, Security Council, Official Records, Doc. S/8248/Add.5, 24 November 1967.

"The problems of Cyprus are numerous and complicated and demand urgent solution if peace is to be preserved. Certainly one of the most critical, if not the most critical, at this time is the presence of non-Cypriot armed forces, other than the United Nations Force which is a peace force, on the island of Cyprus. This is more particularly so since such forces at present deployed there apparently exceed the previously agreed allowable numbers. I believe that the prevailing tension could be eased and the imminent threat of war removed by a reasoned and earnest effort by the three parties directly concerned to agree upon and arrange for a substantial reduction of the non-Cypriot armed forces now in hostile confrontation on the troubled island of Cyprus. In a practical sense, such reductions would need to be in stages and should envisage the ultimate withdrawal from the island of all non-Cypriot armed forces other than those of the United Nations. This would make possible the positive demilitarization of Cyprus and would be a decisive step toward securing peace on the island.

"I therefore appeal most urgently to your Government, as I am appealing to the other two, to agree to the reduction suggested and to undertake to work out a programme for the phased reduction looking toward ultimate complete withdrawal. I offer my assistance toward this end to the fullest extent and particularly may I assure you that UNFICYP would be available for all appropriate assistance in carrying out such a programme and in continuing to help maintain quiet.

"I call upon all Governments concerned to act in accordance with their obligations under the Charter. In this regard they should desist from the use of force or the threat of the use of force to achieve their ends; they should respect the sovereignty, independence and territorial integrity of the Republic of Cyprus; and they should refrain from any military intervention in the affairs of that Republic.

"I hope for your most serious and urgent attention to this appeal."

Appendix 8
Excerpts from the Archives of the National Security Council, 1964 and 1967

(Lyndon B. Johnson Library)

Summary Record on National Security Meeting No. 536
July 28, 1964—Ninth Foreign Ministers Meeting,
Cyprus, Mainland China[1]

Cyprus

At the request of the President, Under Secretary Ball summarized the current situation on Cyprus:

1. We put money in the bank with passing of every week without serious fighting on the Island.

2. Progress is being made in the Geneva negotiations being conducted by Dean Acheson. These talks are in their second round. Acheson has managed to establish close relations with both the Greek and the Turkish representatives. The talks will have to enter the third round before we know exactly how they will come out. . . .

3. . . . .

4. We are making a serious effort to build up the UN forces in Cyprus and. . . .

5. Every effort is being made to play down the Geneva talks. Acheson is working quietly and without press attention. . . .

. . . We have a moderately hopeful attitude toward the possibility of a solution of the problem.

McGeorge Bundy pointed out the importance of not letting the press know of our current optimism. It was agreed that no optimistic noises should be made to the press.

Source: Lyndon Baines Johnson Library, Austin, Texas, declassified and sanitized documents, as cited on each *infra*.

[1]National Security File, NSC Meetings, Box 1.

Sensitive
For the President Only

Summary Notes of 537th NSC Meeting
August 4, 1964, 12:35 PM[2]

Attack in Gulf of Tonkin—Cyprus

Under Secretary Ball: The situation in Cyprus has reached the crisis stage. Even though someone leaked to the press the "Acheson Plan," negotiations can probably continue in Geneva. The Greeks may be ready to get Makarios out of the picture by "instant Enosis," which would be agreed upon secretly by Greece and Turkey.

The situation on the island itself is not good. U Thant will be here Thursday and we will discuss with him contingencies if there is a blow-up. We are thinking of a UN Security Council meeting and a NATO Foreign Ministers meeting. The chances are better that we may get by without serious trouble, but it is a day-to-day problem. The Greek Cypriots are trying to delay progress in order to throw the entire problem into the General Assembly. Turkish military intervention becomes more difficult with the passage of time.

Secretary Rusk: Dean Acheson has done an extraordinary job keeping the door open during the long and difficult discussions in Geneva.

Bromley Smith

August 18, 1964
Memorandum for The President
Subject: Cyprus[3]

This is the main topic for the NSC meeting tomorrow; it is moving rapidly toward the point of decision. The Turk air attacks and now Soviet threats have brought the issue to a boil.

Whether or not the Soviets are serious, the Cypriots, Greeks, and Turks all seem to think so. The mood on the island has become violently anti-U.S. and pro-Soviet, which makes the Acheson plan all the harder to

---

[2]Ibid.

[3]Ibid.

achieve by agreement. Makarios may be playing with fire, but once again he has moved faster than Athens—or ourselves.

The one saving grace may be that Moscow's move is scaring Greece and Turkey into seeing reason. They may at last find a common interest in preventing Makarios and Moscow from coming out on top. But speed seems imperative if we are to push through a settlement by fiat before the Makarios-Moscow axis is firmed up.

I. *State seems to favor one more try at Geneva*, in hopes that Athens and Ankara may at last stop haggling and strike a bargain. In fact, their positions are not too far apart. The gut issue is how large a base the Turks get and whether it should be sovereign or on a long term lease. It's not clear that we have yet said everything we should to press Greeks and Turks once more, and we'll push this with Ball tomorrow.

II. *Should this fail, Acheson and Ball are thinking of a NATO pressure play to force a solution.* In essence Acheson himself would split the remaining difference between Greeks and Turks. We would then ask all the NATO powers to join us in: (a) telling Greeks and Turks to buy; (b) calling on Greece on behalf of Guarantor Powers to restrain Makarios; and (c) if this fails to maintain order, declaring that whatever violence may occur must be confined to the island.

To latter end, NATO would declare that: (a) No NATO-supplied arms could be used by Greece and Turkey against each other—if so, NATO will take measures to take back the arms and penalize the offender by denying him any more military aid; (b) the NATO powers would act under Article V to prevent Turk action against Greece or vice versa; and (c) if the Soviets intervened, NATO would move. This complex and ingenious plan raises several key questions:

A. *Granted that a NATO umbrella is desirable, can we get enough members to play?* Only a majority is technically needed, but if the Scandinavians or Low Countries balked, it would look thin. Would de Gaulle cause trouble? Would many insist on full explanation of the "Acheson award" or offer amendments?

B. *What are the consequences of taking the play away from the UN and giving it to NATO?* U Thant might be privately relieved, but can he publicly acquiesce? What about the SC resolutions?

C. *Do we want in effect to put the Sixth Fleet between Greeks and Turks if they seem to be going for each other?* This is what is called for, since we have the only power in the Eastern Mediterranean.

D. *Could Greece really enforce the terms on the Cypriots?* If Makarios smells a rat he'll appeal to the UN and to Moscow.

III. An alternative to bringing in NATO is Papandreou's scheme for *instant enosis*. He pleads that the only way to short-circuit the burgeoning Nicosia/Moscow axis is to impose *enosis* now. Then the Greeks would make a deal with the Turks. We feel the Turks would never buy unless the terms are worked out beforehand. But if they can be, Papandreou's plan may be simpler and more direct than the NATO scheme—or perhaps the two can be combined so as to reinforce each other. If Greeks and Turks turned to NATO (knowing already what they'd get) we'd be home.

IV. The ultimate question is whether a Greek-Turk deal, assuming we could get one, can be imposed on the island. The evidence is quite inconclusive. Makarios has outmaneuvered the Greeks every time so far, and now he thinks he has Soviet backing. I think you will want to press George on this; the rest of us have not made much progress.

Finally, whatever road we take, we have all the ingredients of major crisis shortly. Makarios will try every trick he has, and the Soviets are now committed to make at least some trouble. Ball and Acheson must still carry the main load, but I think you'll want at least a daily report.

This is a brief summary, and I think it gives you what you need for tomorrow, but if you have time, the relevant cables are attached.

R. W. Komer
McG. B.

Summary Notes of 541st NSC Meeting
August 25, 1964, 12:35 PM[4]

Congo—Cyprus—South Vietnam

Under Secretary Ball: As to Cyprus, the efforts of Dean Acheson to get the Turks and the Greeks to agree in Geneva on a plan to solve the problem has run into difficulty. The situation is serious. The Greeks might even try to force Enosis and then negotiate with the Turks. The Greeks may have decided not to do so because they are aware that the Turks would not tolerate such a solution. The present Greek government is so weak

---

[4]Ibid.

that they cannot handle the Cypriot leader Makarios and thus get Cyprus under their control. You can't hang a custard pie on a hook.

September 16 is an important day because a Greek-Turkish treaty expires on that date. The presence of 10,000 Greeks in Istanbul is covered by this treaty. Re-negotiation would call for Greek concessions. If the treaty lapses, the 10,000 Greeks in Turkey lose their rights.

Any deal by Makarios and the Cypriots with the USSR will move slowly. Makarios apparently hopes to delay any action until November when the UN General Assembly returns. He hopes to get a UN resolution granting full independence—without a treaty.

Our only policy is to live from day to day. At least the situation on the island is quiet for the moment and the UN forces there are stronger.

September 8, 1964
Memorandum For The Record[5]

The principal subject for discussion at the President's luncheon today was Cyprus. Those present with the President were: Secretary Rusk, Secretary McNamara, Under Secretary Ball, Mr. Dean Acheson, and myself [McGeorge Bundy].

Acheson and Ball revealed their agreement on the conviction that the only solution now would be a *fait accompli* in which the Turks would move to occupy the Karpass peninsula, triggering an instant *enosis* under Greek leadership, with the consequent supercession of Makarios. Acheson in particular emphasized that no negotiated solution was possible because of the weakness of Papandreou and the strength and intractability of Makarios. On the other hand, a program of indefinite delay could only strengthen the hand of Makarios and increase the danger that an eventual Turkish explosion would be both violent and undirected.

A number of questions were raised by the President. What would happen to the Turks on the island? Mr. Ball answered that he would expect most of them to stay and that, with luck, bloodshed would be limited. The President asked whether the Greeks would follow this scenario and whether they could control the Greek Cypriots. Ball and Acheson pointed

[5]Memos to the President. McGeorge Bundy. Vol. 6.

out that there already exists between Athens and Nicosia agreement to move to instant *enosis* if the Turks move against the island. They expected that this agreement would probably be carried out.

The Secretary of State asked whether Makarios would appeal to Moscow instead of to Athens. Mr. Ball thought he would not, and he said the appeal would not be answered in any serious way. I asked what would trigger the Turkish action, and Acheson answered that nearly anything would serve. The most immediate possibility was the refusal of troop rotation.

The President summarized by saying that Mr. Acheson's argument appeared to be that we must expect a resort to action in one way or another, and that the choice was whether it should be messy and destructive or controlled and eventually productive, in accordance with a plan. Mr. Acheson agreed with this definition of the problem. He indicated that in his discussions with a Turkish military leader the Turks had shown that there was great Turkish interest in such a plan and that the Turks would do their best to execute it with a minimum use of American weapons and a minimum report to these kinds of force—like air bombing—which were internationally unpopular.

Mr. Ball pointed out that it would be impossible to warn the Greeks of any planned Turkish action because of the danger of leaks to Nicosia. He also noted that the British would be troubled about this plan because of the status of Cyprus as a Commonwealth state. Mr. Acheson remarked that this might be true for Butler, but that Mountbatten would be friendly and that the British bases would be protected under this plan.

The President indicated his own doubt that the plan as put forward could in fact be neatly and tightly controlled, without risk of escalation. He thought that in particular the Greeks would be very likely to move with all their strength on the island against a Turkish lodgment, and he asked McNamara for a careful Joint Staff study of the problem. The President also noted that the next two months were not a good season for another war, and the question was raised whether it was essential to press along this road before November. No definite answer was given, and it was agreed that Mr. Ball would prepare a more detailed staff study of the entire plan, to include both its military and political elements.

McG. B.

November 23, 1967
Memorandum For The Record[6]

1. At approximately 10:30 on 22 November, it was concluded by Messrs. Katzenbach, Kohler, Battle, Read and Walsh that, unless dramatic action was quickly taken, the Turks would go to war.

2. Two courses of action were contemplated: (1) the extension of a Presidential invitation to King Constantine, President Sunay and their senior advisors to meet urgently with President Johnson to discuss the crisis. . . . (2) the urgent despatch of a Presidential emissary to the area. Names contemplated were Cyrus Vance, McGeorge Bundy, Douglas Dillon, John McCloy, Walt Rostow, Nicholas Katzenbach, and Lucius Battle.

3. The issue was discussed with the Secretary who promptly telephoned the President. The President accepted the Secretary's recommendation that an emissary be sent and requested that Cyrus Vance undertake this task.

4. Vance, who was in New York, was contacted at about 1130 by Under Secretary Katzenbach.

5. Arrangements were made with the DOD to provide a K-135 with an ETA from Andrews of 1515.

6. A message was promptly sent to Ankara and Athens notifying the respective Governments of the President's intent and requesting that the Mission be received.

7. Messrs. Walsh, Howison and Hollyfield were selected as Mission members and Miss Johnson as secretary.

Summary Notes of 579th NSC Meeting
November 29, 1967, 12:05 to 12:50 PM[7]

Cyprus

The President opened the meeting by requesting Secretary Rusk to give a summary of the current situation in Cyprus.

Secretary Rusk: Cyrus Vance, the President's special emissary, has done a superb job and has warded off war between Turkey and Greece.

---

[6]National Security File, NSC History of the Cyprus Crisis, December 1963–December 1967.
[7]National Security File, NSC Meetings, Box 2.

He did not want to embarrass Luke Battle but said that he was delighted to have had him as Assistant Secretary working on this problem on an hourly basis. He asked Mr. Battle to outline where we now are in our effort to end the Crisis over Cyprus.

Assistant Secretary Battle: Is optimistic that war between Greece and Turkey would be avoided. To Mr. Vance belongs the credit for the astonishing progress which has been made in keeping the Turkish-Greek crisis over Cyprus from turning into hostilities. Provisions of a statement which both Greece and Turkey have accepted (copy attached) were summarized. Mr. Vance is now in Cyprus trying to persuade Cyprus President Makarios to accept this agreement. Makarios could cause trouble in many ways, but the expectation is that he will not block the Vance effort.

The problem of Cyprus will be with us for some time to come, difficulties will rise in the future, for example, reaching an agreement to expand the role of the United Nations, but for the moment a Greek-Turkish war has been avoided.

Secretary Rusk: Turkey wants the United Nations Security Council to approve a new and expanded UN mandate covering Cyprus. We do not think Council action is necessary but the problem is in the hands of the Secretary General and the heat is off us. The Turks can more easily live with the failure of the Secretary General to obtain a new mandate from the UN Security Council than they could if we had agreed to get a new mandate and had been successful.

Everyone is appreciative that the President made Vance available for this assignment, adding that without his activity, Turkey would now be at war with Greece.

The President: Asked General Wheeler to summarize the military situation.

General Wheeler: Deleted.

CIA Director Helms: We have no reports of Soviet military activity in the area. However, the Russians are fishing in troubled waters by egging on the Turks and telling the Cypriots that Turkey was bluffing.

Appendix 9
Excerpt from President Ford's Report to the Congress October 4, 1976

To the Congress of the United States:

Pursuant to Public Law 94-104, I am submitting my sixth periodic report on the Cyprus negotiations and the actions which this Administration is taking to assist in the search of a lasting solution to the problems still facing the people of the Republic of Cyprus.

In my last report I reviewed recent steps taken by the Administration to bring about further progress in the Cyprus talks, and I emphasized the need for the parties to set aside procedural problems and move on to discussions of key substantive issues.

Our efforts during the past sixty days have been directed to encouraging the resumption of such negotiations. We have been in close contact with our major Western allies regarding new ideas which might contribute to progress in the Cyprus talks and have continued to work closely with United Nations Secretary General Waldheim. Secretary of State Kissinger met with Mr. Waldheim in New York in late August to discuss the Cyprus question. Following that meeting Secretary General Waldheim asked the chief Cypriot negotiators from both sides to come to New York for individual consultations with him on how the negotiations might best be resumed. These consultations developed into a series of joint meetings at which both sides discussed the issues which were blocking further progress. After these meetings, the two Cypriot negotiators agreed to continue their consultations in Nicosia, under the chairmanship of the Secretary General's Special Representative for Cyprus. It is my hope these talks will lead to resumption of meaningful discussion on the main issues.

In his meetings with the Foreign Ministers of Greece and Turkey at the United Nations last week, Secretary Kissinger urged their strong support once again for a new round of talks. We will continue to work as closely as possible with the Governments of Greece and Turkey, with the UN Secretary General, with our Western allies, and with the parties

---

Source: Press Release, Office of the White House, October 5, 1976.

themselves, to insure that every opportunity is seized in pursuing a just and lasting settlement on Cyprus.

To focus the world's attention on the need for rapid progress, Secretary Kissinger stated anew the position of my Administration in his speech before the UN General Assembly on September 30 when he emphasized that our overriding objectives remain the well-being of the Cypriot people and peace in the Eastern Mediterranean. Calling upon all concerned to undertake a new commitment to achieve these ends, he underlined once again the position I have repeatedly voiced:

> "A settlement must come from the Cypriot communities themselves. It is they who must decide how their island's economy and government shall be reconstructed. It is they who must decide the ultimate relationship of the two communities and the territorial extent of each area."

. . . .

My Administration will further intensify its efforts to bring both sides together again with the hope, based on their meetings in New York last month, that some further significant advances may occur.

The people of the United States remain keenly interested in promoting an equitable and lasting settlement on Cyprus. My Administration has been active at every opportunity in encouraging such a settlement. We believe the people of both the Greek Cypriot and Turkish Cypriot communities share equally a desire for peaceful, productive and secure lives. We will continue to use every opportunity further to encourage the leaders of both sides toward a common solution which will achieve these goals.

Gerald R. Ford
The White House
October 4, 1976

Appendix 10
Makarios-Denktaş Guidelines of 12 February 1977

1. Basic guidelines

(a) The constitutional proposals take into account the four guidelines which were agreed at the summit meeting of 12 February 1977, between President Denktaş and the late Archbishop Makarios, when the two leaders declared that they were "seeking an independent, non-aligned, bi-communal, Federal Republic." The following is the full text of the above-mentioned four guidelines:

> "1. We are seeking an independent, non-aligned, bi-communal, Federal Republic.
>
> "2. The territory under the administration of each community should be discussed in the light of economic viability or productivity and land ownership.
>
> "3. Questions of principles like freedom of movement, freedom of settlement, the right of property and other specific matters, are open for discussion taking into consideration the fundamental basis of a bi-communal federal system and certain practical difficulties which may arise for the Turkish Cypriot Community.
>
> "4. The powers and functions of the central Federal Government will be such as to safeguard the unity of the country, having regard to the bi-communal character of the State."

Source: United Nations, Security Council, "Report by the Secretary-General on the United Nations Operation in Cyprus (for the period 1 December 1977 to 31 May 1978), Doc. S/12723, 31 May 1978, Annex, p. 9.

Appendix 11
Excerpt of Letter from Rauf R. Denktaş to P. T. Hart, 1 June 1978

1 June 1978

Ambassador Parker Thompson Hart
4705 Berkeley Terrace, N.W.
Washington, D.C. 20007

The attached map indicates the areas which were under our control prior to 1974. The mixed villages indicate the ones in which Turks continued their resistance to the unconstitutional Greek Administration without abandoning their sector of village. The Turkish Cypriot inhabitants of 103 villages which had been vacated by nearly 30,000 Turks had moved to near-by Turkish stronghold for security where they lived for 11 years under extremely difficult conditions as refugees.

The agreement for exchange of population was culminated between myself and Mr. Clerides at the 3rd Vienna meeting in August 1975 in the presence of Dr. Kurt Waldheim, the Secretary-General of the United Nations, and it was fully implemented as agreed within one month in September of the same year. Thus, by the end of September all Turkish Cypriots who had continued their resistance in the South and had been treated as political hostages by the Greek Cypriots, namely, 65,000 Turks moved to the north and those Greek Cypriots who wanted to move south did so at their own pace again with the help of UNFICYP. Today, there is about 170 Turkish Cypriots in the South and about 1500 Greek Cypriots in the north. The Turkish Cypriots who moved north have been given the right of possession and use of appropriate Greek Cypriot property and the same procedure has been followed by the Greek Cypriots with regard to Turkish Cypriot property in the south pending a political settlement in

Source: Author's files.

which these aspects of the problem will be tackled and solved in an appropriate way.

. . . .

Sincerely,
Rauf R. Denktaş
President
Turkish Federated State of Cyprus

Appendix 12
Denktaş-Kyprianou Summit Agreement of 19 May 1979

1. It was agreed to resume the intercommunal talks on 15 June 1979.

2. The basis of the talks will be the Makarios-Denktaş guidelines of 12 February 1977 and pertinent UN resolutions on Cyprus.

3. There must be respect for human rights and the fundamental liberties of all the citizens of the republic.

4. The talks will cover all the territorial and constitutional aspects.

5. Priority will be given to agreement on the resettlement of Varosha under UN auspices, simultaneously with the commencement of the examination by the interlocutors of the constitutional and territorial aspects of a package solution. After agreement is reached on Varosha, this agreement will be implemented without waiting for the outcome of talks on other aspects of the Cyprus problem.

6. It was agreed to abstain from any action that would jeopardize the outcome of the talks. Special importance will be given to initial practical measures by both sides in order to promote good faith and mutual trust and to return to normal conditions.

7. Provision is made for the demilitarization of the Republic of Cyprus and matters connected with this will be discussed.

8. There will be sufficient guarantee for the independence, sovereignty, territorial integrity and nonalignment of the republic against total or partial union with any other country and against any form of partition or secession.

9. The intercommunal talks will be held continuously and continually and any delay is to be avoided.

10. The intercommunal talks will be held in Nicosia.

Source: Foreign Broadcast Information Service, *Daily Report*, Western Europe/Cyprus, 21 May 1979, pp. R2-3, monitored from Nicosia Domestic Service in Greek, 1350 GMT 19 May 1979. See also Erketün, op. cit., p. 360, for another English version of the agreement.

Appendix 13
Draft Framework Agreement on Cyprus Presented by the UN Secretary-General 29 March 1986

Recognizing with satisfaction that the initiative of the Secretary-General, which bore in mind the relevant United Nations resolutions and which began in August 1984 in Vienna and continued through the high-level proximity talks from September to December 1984 and the joint high-level meeting of January 1985 held in New York, has now resulted in an important step towards a just and lasting settlement of the Cyprus problem;

The parties agree on the following matters which are to be viewed as an integrated whole:

1.1 The Parties:

(a) Recommit themselves to the high-level agreements of 1977 and 1979;

(b) Indicate their determination to proceed, at the date referred to in paragraph 15.1 below, to the establishment of a Federal Republic that will be independent and non-aligned, bi-communal as regards the federal constitutional aspect and bi-zonal as regards the territorial aspect;

(c) Reaffirm their acceptance of those introductory constitutional provisions that were agreed upon at the intercommunal talks in 1981–1982:

(i) The Federal Republic of Cyprus shall have international personality. The Federal Government shall exercise sovereignty in respect of all of the territory. The attributes of international personality shall be exercised by the Federal Government in accordance with the federal constitution. The provinces or federated States may act in their areas of competence in accordance with the federal constitution and in a manner that would not duplicate the powers and functions of the Federal Government as defined in the federal constitution.

(ii) The people of the Federal Republic shall comprise the Greek Cypriot community and the Turkish Cypriot community. There shall be

Source: United Nations, Security Council, Document S/18102/Add.1, pp. 13–17.

a single citizenship of the Federal Republic of Cyprus regulated by federal law.

(iii) The territory of the Federal Republic shall comprise the two provinces or federated States.

(iv) The official languages of the Federal Republic shall be Greek and Turkish. The English language may also be used.

(v) The Federal Republic shall have a neutral flag and anthem to be agreed. Each province or federated State may have its own flag using mainly elements of the federal flag. The federal flag shall be flown on federal buildings and federal locations to the exclusion of any other flag.

(vi) The Federal Government shall observe the holidays of the Federal Republic. Each province or federated State shall observe the federal holidays as well as those established by it.

(vii) The parties reaffirm all other points that were agreed upon during the course of the intercommunal talks as contained in "revision" dated 18 May 1982 concerning general provisions, part I, fundamental rights and liberties, part II, as well as parts III and IV.

2.1 The powers and functions to be vested in the Federal Government of the Federal Republic shall comprise:

(a) Foreign affairs.

(b) Federal financial affairs (including federal budget, taxation, customs and excise duties).

(c) Monetary and banking affairs.

(d) Federal economic affairs (including trade and tourism).

(e) Posts and telecommunications.

(f) International transport.

(g) Natural resources (including water supply, environment).

(h) Federal health and veterinary affairs.

(i) Standard setting: weights and measures, patents, trademarks, copyrights.

(j) Federal judiciary.

(k) Appointment of federal officers.

(l) Defence (to be discussed also in connection with the treaties of guarantee and of alliance); security (as it pertains to federal responsibility).

2.2 Additional powers and functions may be vested in the Federal Government by common agreement of both sides. Accordingly, the residual powers shall rest with the provinces or federated States. Federal legislation may be executed either by authorities of the Federal Government or by way of co-ordination between the competent authorities of the Federal Government and of the two provinces of federated States.

3.1 The legislature of the Federal Republic will be composed of two chambers: a lower chamber with a 70-30 Greek Cypriot and Turkish Cypriot representation, and an upper chamber with a 50-50 representation. Federal legislation will be enacted with regard to the matters of federal competence as referred to in paragraph 2.1 above. The adoption of legislation on major matters, as for instance on ten of the twelve functions referred to in paragraph 2.1 above, will require separate majorities in both chambers. The adoption of legislation on other matters will require majorities of the membership in each chamber.

3.2 Appropriate constitutional safeguards and deadlock-resolving machinery including special provisions to facilitate action on matters necessary for the continued functioning of the Federal Government (e.g., on budgetary questions) will be incorporated in the federal constitution. In case of deadlock in the legislature, the proposed legislation may be submitted in the first instance to a conciliation committee of the legislature composed of three Greek Cypriots and two Turkish Cypriots, whose decision will be taken on the basis of majority vote including at least one Turkish Cypriot. If the deadlock persists, the President and Vice-President of the Federal Republic will, upon request, appoint on an *ad hoc* basis one person each, selected for their knowledge of the subject involved, who, with the assistance of experts as needed including from outside the Federal Republic of Cyprus, will advise the legislature on ways the deadlock could be resolved. The matter may also be submitted to a referendum among the population of the community which opposed the draft legislation. Legislation adopted by the legislature may be taken to the Constitutional Court for ruling as to whether it violates the constitution or is discriminatory against either community.

4.1 The Federal Republic will have a presidential system of government. The President and the Vice-President will symbolize the unity of the country and the equal political status of the two communities. In addition, the executive will reflect the functional requirements of an effective federal government.

4.2 The President will be a Greek Cypriot and the Vice-President will be a Turkish Cypriot. The President and the Vice-President will, separately or conjointly, have the right to veto any law or decision of the legislature and the Council of Ministers in areas to be agreed upon, it being understood that the scope will exceed that covered by the 1960 constitution. The President and the Vice-President will have the right, separately or conjointly, to return any law or decision of the legislature or any decision of the Council of Ministers for reconsideration.

4.3 The Council of Ministers will be composed of Greek Cypriot and Turkish Cypriot ministers on a 7 to 3 ratio. One major ministry will be headed by a Turkish Cypriot, it being understood that the parties agree to discuss that the Minister for Foreign Affairs will be a Turkish Cypriot. The Council of Ministers will take decisions by weighted voting, that is a simple majority including at least one Turkish Cypriot minister. It is understood that the parties agree to discuss that weighted voting will apply to all matters of special concern to the Turkish Cypriot community to be agreed upon.

4.4 Appropriate constitutional safeguards and deadlock-resolving machinery related to decisions by the Council of Ministers, including special provisions to facilitate action on matters necessary for the continued functioning of the Federal Government, will be incorporated in the federal constitution. In case of deadlock, the President and Vice-President of the Federal Republic will, upon request, appoint on an *ad hoc* basis one person each, selected for their knowledge of the subject involved, who, with the assistance of experts as needed including from outside the Federal Republic of Cyprus, will advise the Council of Ministers on ways the deadlock could be resolved. The matter may also be submitted to a referendum among the population of the community which opposed the draft decision. A decision by the Council of Ministers may be taken to the Constitutional Court for ruling as to whether it violates the constitution or is discriminatory against either community.

5.1 The Constitutional Court, when ruling on disputes relating to the distribution of powers and functions between the Federal Government and the provinces or federated States and on such other matters as may be assigned to it by the parties in accordance with the federal constitution, will be composed of one Greek Cypriot, one Turkish Cypriot and one non-Cypriot voting member.

6.1 As regards freedom of movement, freedom of settlement and right to property, a working group will discuss the exercise of these rights, including time-frames, practical regulations and possible compensation arrangements, taking into account guideline 3 of the 1977 agreement.

7.1 Territorial adjustments, in addition to the areas already referred to in the 5 August 1981 Turkish Cypriot proposals, will be agreed upon. These territorial adjustments will result in the Turkish Cypriot province or federated State comprising in the order of 29+ per cent of the territory of the Federal Republic. It is understood that when discussing the actual territorial adjustments the two sides will have in mind the 1977 high-level agreement including "certain practical difficulties which may arise for the Turkish Cypriot community" and the questions related to resettlement. Both sides agree to suggest special status areas adjacent to each other for the purpose of enhancing trust between the sides. These areas will remain under the respective civilian jurisdictions.

8.1 A timetable for the withdrawal of non-Cypriot military troops and elements, as well as adequate guarantees, will be agreed upon prior to the establishment of a transitional Federal Government. In the meantime, military deconfrontation measures will be pursued by both sides, using the good offices and assistance of UNFICYP.

8.2 The two sides undertake to discuss these issues in good faith and to consider each other's concerns on them.

9.1 A fund for development of the Turkish Cypriot province or federated State shall be established with a view to achieving an economic equilibrium between the two provinces or federated States. A fund will also be established to facilitate the resettlement of the Greek Cypriot displaced persons, and for the Turkish Cypriots displaced as a consequence of the implementation of paragraph 7.1. The Federal Government shall contribute to these funds. Foreign Governments and international organizations shall be invited to contribute to the funds.

10.1 The Varosha area and the six additional areas delineated in the Turkish Cypriot map of 5 August 1981 will be placed under United Nations interim administration as part of the UNFICYP buffer zone for resettlement by __________.

11.1 Both parties agree not to take any action tending to prejudice the process outlined in this agreement, both on the international scene and internally.

12.1 The Nicosia international airport will be reopened under interim United Nations administration with free access from both sides. The

United Nations will conclude the arrangements to that effect by __________.

13.1 Adequate machinery for considering allegations of non-implementation of confidence-building measures will be agreed upon. The Secretary-General will make appropriate recommendations to both sides in this regard.

14.1 The parties agree to establish working groups to work out the detailed agreements on the matters referred to in this Agreement, whose elements are interrelated and constitute an integrated whole. The working groups will carry out their work under the direction of joint high-level meetings. These joint high-level meetings will take place every three to four months, on the basis of an agenda prepared by the Secretary-General, to discuss the issues which remain to be negotiated under this agreement, to review the work and provide guidance to the working groups. The joint high-level meetings will be convened by the Secretary-General after adequate preparation.

14.2 Each working group will be composed of delegations from the two sides and will be chaired by a representative of the Secretary-General. The working groups will begin their meetings at the United Nations premises in Nicosia on __________. Each working group will prepare a programme of work and will submit it for approval and guidance to the joint high-level meeting which will take place at the United Nations premises in Nicosia on __________.

14.3 The representative of the Secretary-General chairing each working group will every three months prepare an assessment of the progress made by the working group, which will be presented to the next joint high-level meeting together with the view of the Secretary-General.

15.1 The parties agree that, the required working groups have completed their work and having obtained the approval of the two sides, the transitional Federal Government of the Federal Republic of Cyprus will be set up on __________.

16.1 The Secretary-General will remain at the disposal of the parties to assist in the elaboration of this agreement, and, if required, in its interpretation.

Notes

Foreword

1. International Seminar on the Cyprus Problem and Its Solution, sponsored by the Center for Mediterranean Studies, American Universities Field Staff, Rome, November 19–23, 1973. A confidential report of the meeting was produced by rapporteur Elie Kedourie of the London School of Economics.

1. Introduction

2. Education Advisory Committee, Parliamentary Group for World Government, *Cyprus School History Textbooks: A Study in Education for International Understanding—Extracts from Greek and Turkish School History Textbooks Used in Cyprus*, Barbara Hodge and G. L. Lewis, translators (London: World Security Trust, n.d. [but clearly 1966 or later]).
3. Frederica M. Bunge, ed., *Cyprus, a Country Study*, Foreign Area Studies (Washington, D.C.: American University, 1980), p. 23.
4. Of thousands of Greek islands and islets in the Aegean (2,383, according to A. Wilson in J. Alford, ed, *Greece and Turkey: Adversity in Alliance* [New York: St. Martin's Press, 1984], p. 94), for each of which Greece claims the maximum territorial waters, several large ones closely hug the Turkish coast, notably Lesbos, Khios, Samos, Kos, and Rhodes. This awkward fact of political geography has led to long-running disputes over territorial waters, airspace, and continental seabed claims.
5. Politico-religious leadership title, going back to Byzantine times.
6. Fraser Wilkins, first U.S. ambassador to Cyprus (1960–64), unpublished lecture to War Gaming Reserves, Naval War College, November 17, 1971, p. 16, and interview with author, January 7, 1989.
7. For complete texts of the elaborate agreements between the United Kingdom and the Republic of Cyprus concerning British sovereign base areas and many smaller sites (leased by Britain after 1960), as well as terms of British financial assistance to Cyprus, see UN Treaty Series No. 5476, starting at page 10.
8. See declassified *Summary Notes* of NSC Meetings, White House, August 4 and 25, 1964; Memorandum for the President, August 18, 1964; Memorandum for the Record, White House, September 8, 1964. (These notes and memoranda are reproduced in appendix 8.) See also volume I, ch. 4, part E, *Administrative History*, Department of State During the Administration of President Lyndon B. Johnson, November 1963–January 1969. All of the foregoing are in the Lyndon B. Johnson Library, Austin, Texas.
9. See map 1.

2. Antecedents of the 1967 Frontier Talks

10. Kenneth Torp, op. cit., p. 5.
11. Venizelos became the hero of Greece's expansion when the 1913 peace agreement to the Second Balkan War incorporated Crete into Greece.

12. Lucius D. Battle and Dennis P. Williams, *Cyprus: Two Decades of Crisis*, updated and revised by Taylor G. Belcher, Middle East Institute Problem Paper #16 (Washington, D.C.: Middle East Institute, July 1978), p. 4.
13. The late Galo Plaza Lasso, president of Ecuador, 1948–52, gave distinguished service to the United Nations in Lebanon (1958) and the Congo (1960). His Cyprus report resulted from visits to Nicosia, Ankara, Athens, and London between September 28, 1964 and March 2, 1965, and proposed intercommunal talks leading to a conference of the signatories of the London-Zürich Treaties, which he stated would have to be abrogated by agreement of the parties in favor of UN guarantees of Cypriot independence and of minority rights for Turk Cypriots, as well as agreed readjustments of the Constitution.
14. Belcher has informed me that when the Acheson Plan was prepared in Geneva he was deliberately left out of the process, since he was known to be opposed to it as infeasible. Belcher knew that without concurrence by Makarios, any such externally concocted arrangement would fail. Instead, his military attaché, Colonel Gussie, was called from Nicosia to the Geneva drafting sessions. What they wanted at Geneva, he said, was an embassy representative who was believed to be friendly to the concept, as Gussie was. (Letter to author, October 27, 1986.) Belcher was proved right in the course of time and in 1968 he was given the Department's Distinguished Service Award by Secretary Rusk.
15. Belcher has retained contact with Kyprianou, until February 1988 president of the Cyprus Republic, asking him (as he used to do when ambassador) what advantage he sees in garnering votes in the United Nations and at conferences of the nonaligned or East Bloc states in favor of the Greek Cypriot position, when these are pro forma, cheaply obtainable, and essentially meaningless. What would count would be a position that could be supported by the United Kingdom and Western Europe. Letter to author, op. cit.
16. Summary Notes of 579th NSC Meeting, November 29, 1967, p. 2, in Lyndon B. Johnson Library (see appendix 8).
17. Makarios introduced another shipment of Czech arms in 1966.

3. Final Greek Efforts to Negotiate *Enosis*

18. *Anorthotikon Komma Ergazomenou Laou*, Progressive Party of the Working People.
19. Concerning the right of the Republic of Cyprus to "sovereignty or control" over the Sovereign Base Areas in case the United Kingdom should at any time decide to divest themselves of these areas, see pp. 172 and 174, UN Treaty Series, vol. 382, no. 5476, Exchange of Notes between the United Kingdom and the Republic of Cyprus, August 16, 1960.
20. See oral history of Kenneth Torp, L. B. Johnson Library, AC80-59, p. 11.

4. Flash Point

21. Most of what follows is derived from UN Security Council documentation, from the firsthand account of Michael Harbottle in his book *The Impartial Soldier* (London: Oxford University Press, 1970), and from my recollections of the case.
22. See particularly UN Security Council Documents S/8246, 16 November 1967; S/8286, December 8, 1967; and Harbottle, *The Impartial Soldier*, pp. 146 et. seq.
23. The Turkish contingent remained in the North Nicosia enclave until superseded in 1974 by Turkish troops occupying northern Cyprus.

24. See Harbottle, op. cit., pp. 60–61. UNFICYP opposed such fortifications in principle but consented in this case.
25. Harbottle had succeeded Brigadier James Wilson in June 1966. The original problem had arisen in Wilson's time.
26. UN Security Council Documents S/7969, Supplement for April, May, and June 1967; also S/8248, 16 November 1967.
27. Harbottle, during an October 1986 visit to Washington from his home in England, told me that Denktaş's motives mystified UNFICYP but that on Cyprus the rumor circulated widely that the entire episode was planned to provide an opportunity for Denktaş to talk with his friend Glafcos Clerides, as it was known that Clerides visited Denktaş a number of times in prison. It is well known that their friendship goes back to boyhood days at the secondary-level English School in Cyprus. Both later studied law at Grey's Inn, London, although not at the same time.
28. UN Security Council Document S/8248, 16 November 1967, pp. 217, 218; paragraphs 7 and 8.
29. A disengagement was eventually engineered in that crisis by the late Ellsworth Bunker involving the establishment of a UN Observer Force in the Yemen.

5. Massacre and Reaction

30. UNSC S/8248, 16 November 1967.
31. Conversation with the author, October 1986.
32. UNSC S/8248, p. 221, paragraph 15.
33. Harbottle, October 1986.
34. UNSC S/8248, paragragh 24.
35. The Patriarchate in Istanbul has been, since Byzantine times, the seat of the "first among equals" (*primus inter pares*) of the Orthodox patriarchs. At the time of these events, the position was held by Athenagoras.

6. The Five Points

36. Harbottle wrote in 1976 that "Turkey in comparison only deployed a handful of its officers and noncommissioned officers to lead the various fighter groups around the island using the six monthly rotations of their national contingent as the means by which they could be infiltrated into Cyprus." Michael and Eirwin Harbottle, "The Greek and Turkish Confrontation," in *Case Studies on Human Rights and Fundamental Freedoms: A World Survey*, vol. 4 (The Hague: Martinus Nijhoff, 1976), p. 517.
37. This had not always been the case. My colleague in Athens, Phillips Talbot, tells me that in 1961, when he was assistant secretary of state, he tried to pass to Ambassador Hare, my predecessor in Ankara, urgent instructions from President Kennedy to try to stop the Turkish military government from hanging deposed Prime Minister Menderes and two of his cabinet, Zorlu and Polatkan. He could find no other way than to give the message to a U.S. communications sergeant in Germany who patched through a signal to the U.S. military in Ankara, which in turn gave Ambassador Hare a badly garbled text which nonetheless included the word "President" and was sufficient to afford the basis for a strong démarche. The military regime rejected the advice, and the three men were hanged, to the revulsion of a considerable element of Turkish public opinion, as I was to learn on arrival four years later.

38. See John G. Patsalides, "The Role of Canada in the Cyprus Crisis 1964–1968," doctoral dissertation, Department of Political Economy, University of Toronto, 1980.
39. Ibid.

7. Shuttle Diplomacy

40. For a vignette of President Johnson's decision to send Vance, see Lyndon Baines Johnson Library, NSC History of the Cyprus Crisis, "Vance Mission-i, Memorandum for the Record," November 23, 1967 (#18a). (See appendix 8.) Also at L. B. J. Library, Oral History Collection, Cyrus Vance, December 29, 1969, by Paige E. Mulhollan, pp. 1–12. Vance apparently recalls (mistakenly, I believe) that Turkish consent to his mission was received before his departure.
41. "Air Force One," as I understood it at the time, was a designation used for any aircraft under the direct orders of the president.
42. Walsh's complete record is classified and I have not seen it.
43. We felt sure that twenty thousand was a grossly exaggerated figure, and indeed it was, but there was no point in quibbling over figures at this juncture.

9. A Rose Garden in Cyprus

44. My understanding is that in this crisis it was usually Clerides who had the positive and imaginative approach, while Kyprianou was usually negative.
45. Kenneth Torp, op. cit., pp. 18–19, confirms my recollection that Ambassador Goldberg got UN Secretary-General U Thant out of bed at 8:00 A.M. that morning, insisting that he issue the appeal at once, given the six-hour time difference.
46. UN Security Council Document S/8248/Add.6, original text English, 3 December 1967, constituting U Thant's third appeal regarding this crisis.
47. UNSC, S/8248/Add 7. UNSC S/8248/Adds 1–9 carry all these exchanges.
48. See Oral History of Cyrus Vance, December 29, 1969, taken by Paige E. Mulhollan, pp. 9, 10, 12, Lyndon B. Johnson Library, Austin, Texas.
49. The contrast with Henry Kissinger's shuttle diplomacy between Egypt, Syria, and Israel following the October 1973 war is striking. A large press representation accompanied Kissinger on his flights and was afforded regular briefings.

10. Withdrawal, Standdown, and Détente

50. Letter dated November 28, 1986.
51. Later to become ambassador to the Soviet Union, then secretary-general of the Foreign Ministry, then ambassador to United Nations agencies in Geneva.
52. Letter to author dated November 28, 1986.
53. Ibid. In this connection, today's Turkish Republic of Northern Cyprus appears at this writing to have a solid political life of its own, despite its reliance on mainland Turkey's forces for its ultimate security. The Greek Cypriot-led Republic of Cyprus is quite independent of Athens, although it relies on it heavily for political support.
54. Clerides interrupted his studies for wartime service in the U.K. Royal Air Force. Denktaş studied after World War II.

11. Aftermath and Beyond

55. Bunge, ed., *Cyprus, a Country Study*, pp. 50–51 and 220–24.
56. Ibid., p.48.
57. William R. Crawford, Jr., U.S. ambassador to Cyprus, 1974–84, states that Sampson was a wild eccentric with negligible public following. His selection by the Greek junta to replace Makarios discredited the junta in Nicosia. (Interview with Crawford, February 15, 1989.)
58. (New York: Franklin Watts, 1985), pp. 156–163.
59. Theodore S. Couloumbis, *The United States, Greece and Turkey: The Troubled Triangle* (New York: Praeger, 1983), pp. 76–99, makes interesting reading, but should be tested by direct access to still-classified official files.
60. Denktaş uses the figure 65,000 Turkish Cypriots. See appendix 11.
61. Without title, as of this writing. American estimates of new settlers from the Turkish mainland run to approximately 30,000. Greek Cypriot figures on these Turkish settlers are twice this total.
62. Bunge, *Cyprus, a Country Study*, pp. 222–23.
63. PASOK (*Panhellinion Socialistiko Kinima*—Panhellenic Socialist Movement).
64. See Foreign Broadcast Information Service, *Daily Report: West Europe*, #235, 1988 (FBIS-WEU-88-235), pp. 62–65, monitoring the Athens paper *Kyriakatiki Elevterotypia*, 10 October 1988, p. 64, long article by Panos Loukakos.
65. From State Department oral sources at the time. See also lecture by the Hon. Fraser Wilkins, November 17, 1971, op. cit. (see note 6), p. 21.
66. For details of their trial in mid-May 1977, see FBIS, *Daily Report: West Europe*, on Cyprus, especially 16 May 1977, p. R-3, monitored from Greek Cypriot daily, *O Filelevtheros*, Nicosia, of 14 May 1977, p. 10. See also 1977 FBIS Reports of 19 April, 13 May, 17 May, 18 May, 19 May, 20 May, 23 May, 25 May, and 26 May. See also A. Borowiec, *The Mediterranean Feud* (New York: Praeger, 1983), p. 104, on the May 1977 trials, conducted, he writes, in a "festive" atmosphere very sympathetic to the accused, who served time for slightly over a year for illegal possession and use of automatic weapons and "malicious damage to the embassy building."
67. FBIS *Daily Report*, *West Europe*, 1 February 1988.
68. *The Economist*, 18 June 1988, pp. 49–50.
69. FBIS *Daily Report*, *West Europe*, Cyprus, 25 March 1988, p. 11.
70. FBIS, *Daily Report*, *West Europe*, Cyprus, 10 February 1989, p. 19, quoting *O Filelevtheros*, 9 February 1989.
71. FBIS-WEU-88-221, p. 26, 16 November 1988, monitoring broadcast of Nicosia Domestic Service in Greek of 15 November 1988.
72. See, for example, appendix 9 for a 1976 statement of principles by U.S. President Gerald R. Ford.
73. Rinn S. Shin, ed., *Greece, a Country Study*, Foreign Area Studies (Washington, D.C.: American University, 1985), p. 68.

Selected Bibliography

The following bibliography, far from exhaustive, is intended to assist students and other readers in obtaining useful perspectives on the ongoing Cyprus problem, its impact on Greece and Turkey and relations between the two, and the related dilemmas that Cyprus creates for the North Atlantic Treaty Organization and for the United States. This selection does not imply endorsement of the views of the authors.

Books

Adams, T. W. *AKEL: The Communist Party of Cyprus*. Stanford: Hoover Institution Press, 1972.

Adams, T. W., and Alvin J. Cottrell. *Cyprus between East and West*. Washington Center of Foreign Policy Research, School of Advanced International Studies, The Johns Hopkins University. Baltimore: Johns Hopkins University Press, 1968.

Alford, Jonathan, ed. *Greece and Turkey: Adversity in Alliance*. Adelphi Library Series. New York: published for International Institute for Strategic Studies by St. Martin's Press, 1984.

Ball, George W. *The Past Has Another Pattern: Memoirs*. New York: W. W. Norton, 1973.

Battle, Lucius D., and Dennis P. Williams. *Cyprus: Two Decades of Crisis*. Middle East Institute Problem Paper #11 (December 1974). Updated and revised by Taylor G. Belcher as Middle East Institute Problem Paper #16. Washington, D.C.: Middle East Institute, July 1978.

Borowiec, Andrew. *The Mediterranean Feud*. Praeger Special Studies. New York: Praeger, 1983.

Bunge, Frederica M., ed. *Cyprus, a Country Study*. 3rd ed. Foreign Area Studies, American University. Washington, D.C.: Superintendent of Documents, U.S. Government Printing Office, 1980.

Center for the Study of Foreign Affairs, Foreign Service Institute, U.S. Department of State. *Perspectives on Negotiation: Four Case Studies and Interpretations*. Washington, D.C.: U.S. Government Printing Office, 1986.

Clogg, Richard. *A Short History of Modern Greece*. Cambridge and New York: Cambridge University Press, 1979.

Couloumbis, Theodore S. *The United States, Greece, and Turkey: The Troubled Triangle*. Studies of Influence in International Relations. New York: Praeger, 1983.

Ertekün, Necati. *The Cyprus Dispute and the Birth of the Turkish Republic of Northern Cyprus*. Rev. ed. Nicosia, Northern Cyprus: K. Rüstem Brother, 1984. (Originally published as *In Search of a Negotiated Cyprus Settlement*, Rüstem, 1981.)

Grivas, George. *The Memoirs of General Grivas*. New York: Praeger, 1965.

Harbottle, Michael. *The Impartial Soldier*. London: Oxford University Press, 1970.

Harbottle, Michael and Eirwen. "Cyprus: The Greek and Turkish Confrontation." In *Case Studies on Human Rights and Fundamental Freedoms: A World Survey*. Vol. 4 (of 5). Published on behalf of the Foundation for the Study of Plural Societies. The Hague: Martinus Nijhoff, 1976.

Harris, George S. *Troubled Alliance: Turkish-American Problems in Historical Perspective, 1945–1971*. AEI-Hoover Policy Studies, 2; Hoover Institution Series, 33. Washington, D.C.: American Enterprise Institute for Public Policy Research, 1972.

Joseph, Joseph S. *Cyprus: Ethnic Conflict and International Concern*. American University Studies. New York: Peter Lang, 1985.

Karageorgis, Vassos. *The Ancient Civilization of Cyprus: An Archeological Adventure*. Cowles Education Corp. Geneva: Nagel, 1969.

———. *Cyprus: From the Stone Age to the Romans*. London: Thames and Hudson, 1982.

Kyriakides, Stanley. *Cyprus: Constitutionalism and Crisis Government*. Philadelphia: University of Pennsylvania Press, 1968. Bibliography includes very useful documentary sources.

Kuniholm, Bruce R. *The Origins of the Cold War in the Near East: Great Power Conflict and Diplomacy in Iran, Turkey, and Greece*. Princeton: Princeton University Press, 1980.

Meyer, A. J. *The Economy of Cyprus*. Cambridge: Harvard University Press, 1969.

Nyrop, Richard F., ed. *Turkey, a Country Study*. 3d ed. Washington, D.C.: Foreign Area Studies, American University, 1980.

Oberling, Pierre. *The Road to Bellapais: The Turkish Cypriot Exodus to Northern Cyprus*. Social Science Monograph, Boulder. Brooklyn College Studies in Change no. 25. Distributed by Columbia University Press, 1982.

Polyviou, Polyvios G. *Cyprus, Conflict and Negotiation, 1960–1980*. New York: Holmes and Meier, 1980.

Rikhye, Indar Jit, Michael Harbottle, and Bjorn Egge. *The Thin Blue Line*. A study sponsored by the International Peace Academy. New Haven and London: Yale University Press, 1974.

Shin, Rinn S., ed. *Greece, a Country Study*. Washington, D.C.: Foreign Area Studies, American University, 1985.

Stephens, Robert. *Cyprus, a Place of Arms*. London: Pall Mall Press, 1966.

United Nations Department of Public Information. *The Blue Helmets: A Review of United Nations Peacekeeping*. New York: United Nations, 1985.

Vance, Cyrus R. *Hard Choices: Four Critical Years in Managing America's Foreign Policy*. New York: Simon & Schuster, 1983.

Volkan, Vamik D., M.D. *Cyprus—War and Adaptation, A Psychoanalytic History of Two Ethnic Groups in Conflict*. Charlottesville: University Press of Virginia, 1979.

Weintal, Edward and Charles Bartlett. *Facing the Brink: An Intimate Study of Crisis Diplomacy*. New York: Charles Scribner's Sons, 1967.

Woodhouse, C. M. *The Rise and Fall of the Greek Colonels*. New York: Franklin Watts, 1985.

Documents, Articles, and Other Source Materials

Background Notes: Cyprus. Department of State, 1984.

"Communal Attitudes Toward the Cyprus Conflict: A Report to the Department of State." Washington, D.C.: Middle East Institute, October 23, 1984.

Constitutional and Parliamentary Information. Published quarterly. Geneva, Switzerland: Interparliamentary Bureau (6 rue Constantin). For the Constitution of the Republic of Cyprus, see no. 44 (October 1960), pp. 141ff (articles 1111); and no. 45 (January 1961), pp. 1ff (articles 112199, plus mention of Annex I, Treaty of Guarantee, and Annex II, Treaty of Military Alliance).

Cyprus. Constitutions of the World series. Dobbs Ferry, N.Y.: Oceana, July 1972.

Foreign Broadcast Information Service, *Daily Reports: Western Europe* (includes Turkey, Greece, and Cyprus). A U.S. Government publication. P.O. Box 2604, Washington, D.C. 20013.

Haass, Richard N. "Managing NATO's Weakest Flank: The United States, Greece, and Turkey." *Orbis*, Fall 1986.

Kuniholm, Bruce R. "Rhetoric and Reality in the Aegean: U.S. Policy Options toward Greece and Turkey." *SAIS Review* VI (Winter/Spring 1986).

Lyndon Baines Johnson Library. A presidential library administered by the National Archives and Records Administration. Austin, Texas 78705. Administrative History. State Department. Vol. 1, ch. 4, part E, "The Cyprus Crisis."

———. Memos to the President. McGeorge Bundy. Vol. 6. Bundy for President, 9/8/64.

———. National Security File. NSC History of the Cyprus Crisis, December 1963–December 1967. Memo for the Record, 11/23/67 (#18a).

———. National Security File. NSC Meetings, box 1. Summary Notes: 7/28/64, pp. 1–2; 8/4/64; Briefing Memo for 8/18/64 meeting (8/18/64); Summary Notes: 8/25/64, p. 1.

———. National Security File. NSC Meetings, box 2. Summary Notes: 11/29/67.

———. Oral History Collection. Cyrus R. Vance. Oral history of his mediation of 1967 Cyprus crisis. December 29, 1969.

———. Kenneth Torp. Oral history. June 23, 1970.

Patsalides, John G. "The Role of Canada in the Cyprus Crisis 1964–1967." Draft doctoral dissertation. University of Toronto, Department of Political Economy, 1980.

United Nations Documents. The UN "S" series of the Security Council from 1963 on carry the regular reports to the Council by the UN Secretary General; maps of deployment of the UNFICYP; correspondence on the subject of Cyprus from Greece, Turkey, the Republic of Cyprus, and the Turkish community leadership as it evolved into the Turkish Federated State of Cyprus and the Turkish Republic of Northern Cyprus. Extensive debate and associated documentation, including the Galo Plaza Report, and all resolutions adopted by the Council and the Assembly should be consulted. The file is too bulky to be listed here in detail.

United Nations Treaty Series. Vol. 382 (1960). Nos. 5475 to 5486, pp. 3–253 (contains the August 16, 1960 texts of the agreements between the United Kingdom, Turkey, Greece, and the Republic of Cyprus).

Index

About the Author

Parker T. Hart is a retired Career Minister of the U.S. Foreign Service and former assistant secretary of state for Near East and South Asian affairs (1968–69). He was U.S. ambassador to Kuwait (1962–63), Saudi Arabia (1961–65), and Turkey (1965–68), and director of the Foreign Service Institute. From 1969 to 1973 he was president of the Middle East Institute.